Coming of Age
Strides in African Publishing

Essays in Honour of Dr Henry Chakava at 70

Editors
Kiarie Kamau
Kirimi Mitambo

**East African
Educational Publishers Ltd.**

Nairobi • Kampala • Dar es Salaam • Kigali • Lilongwe • Lusaka

Published in Kenya by
East African Educational Publishers Ltd.
Kijabe Street, Nairobi
P.O. Box 45314, Nairobi – 00100, KENYA
Tel: +254 20 2324760
Mobile: +254 722 205661 / 722 207216 / 733 677716 / 734 652012
Email: eaep@eastafricanpublishers.com
Website: www.eastafricanpublishers.com

East African Educational Publishers also has offices or is represented in the following countries: Uganda, Tanzania, Rwanda, Malawi, Zambia, Botswana and South Sudan.

© EAEP, 2016

First published 2016

All rights reserved

ISBN: 978-9966-56-184-8

Printed in Kenya by
Ramco Printing Works Ltd.

Contents

Foreword v
A Note From the Publishers xiv
About the Contributors xv

1 The Guru of Publishing: Assessing Henry Chakava's Contribution in Africa
   by Kiarie Kamau 1

2 Henry Chakava: The Gory and Glory of African Language Publishing
   by Ngũgĩ wa Thiong'o 15

3 The Triangle that Defined AWS: Nairobi – Ibadan – London
   by James Currey 27

4 Publisher and Intellectual: The Work of Henry Chakava
   by Simon Gikandi 42

5 African Orature: Back to the Roots
   by Mĩcere Gĩthae Mũgo 57

6 The Dominance of the Textbook in African Publishing
   by Ayo Ojeniyi 70

7 Popular Fiction Publishing in Africa: Does it Have a Place?
   by David Mailu 95

8 East African Publishing and the Academia
   by Emilia Ilieva and Hillary Chakava 106

9 Publishing in East Africa: A Close Examination of Uganda (1985-2015)
   by James Tumusiime 129

10 Indigenous Publishing in Africa: The Need for Research, Documentation and Collaboration
   by Hans M. Zell 141

11 Shared Visions and Challenges in Publishing in Africa: Henry Chakava and CODESRIA
   by Francis B. Nyamnjoh 159

12 African Publishing in the Digital Age
   by Roger Stringer 187

13 Internationalising the African Book
   by Mary Jay 201

14 Lobby for the Book: The Politics of African Publishing and the Growth of Professional and Trade Organisations
   by Lily Nyariki 217

15 Training Opportunities for African Publishers
   by Richard A. B. Crabbe 236

16 Copyright and Copyright Infringement: The Legal and Institutional Framework in East Africa
   by Marisella Ouma 256

Appendix 270

Index 272

Foreword

I am delighted to write the Foreword to this book celebrating Henry Chakava at 70. The occasion affords me an opportunity to recall and reflect on aspects of Africa publishing over the many years we have known each other, and to indulge in memories of shared magic moments in various places in Africa, Europe, the US and India. Through these recollections a picture may emerge to give witness to the importance of this celebration for those interested in the development of African book publishing. The recollections are about Henry the man, a friend, and Henry the publisher, a colleague and 'brother in arms'. I ask readers of this Foreword to bear with its personal tone for two reasons: first because the Papers in this collection are by distinguished scholars and practitioners in the publishing industry and have covered widely and in depth, Henry's success as a publisher in Kenya; and secondly, because our friendship has been a source of strength and provided great and joyful times.

Henry and I came into publishing at just about the same time in 1972 (interestingly the year UNESCO designated as International Book Year). We came from different backgrounds and to very different companies. He joined Heinemann, a British multinational, famous for the African Writers Series in addition to its success in educational publishing in the UK and Kenya. He came from academia having been a lecturer for a brief period at the University of Nairobi from which he had graduated a year before.

I joined Tanzania Publishing House (TPH) after seven years as Foreign Service Officer with stints in Addis Ababa and Beijing (then Peking). TPH was until then a joint venture company between Macmillan Education and the National Development Corporation; a relationship that was proving untenable and that for practical purposes was more theory than the reality.

TPH was the first publishing company to be set up in Tanzania that was not part of a religious denomination. The Tanzania branches of East African Literature Bureau, East African Publishing House, Oxford University Press (OUP) and Longmans, operated in Tanzania as sales offices. The OUP office in Dar had an influential friend in State House who argued that OUP was a not-for-profit organisation and secured for them the most prominent and profitable author, Mwalimu Julius Nyerere and his 'Freedom' series as well as the lucrative dictionary *Kamusi ya Kiswahili Sanifu* of the Institute of Swahili Research.

Tanzania and Kenya were politically very different countries. While in Kenya there had been expressions of intent to build a society based on 'African socialism', as set out in the national document *Sessional Paper No. 10 of 1965 on African Socialism and its Application to Planning in Kenya*; its blueprint was a sophisticated liberal apologia for a capitalist system that was to be developed by the post-colonial Kenya state. In Tanzania, on the other hand, after the Arusha Declaration in 1967 (on Socialism and Self Reliance), nationalisation of businesses and buildings, establishment of *Ujamaa* villages and support of armed struggle being waged by Southern Africa liberation movements, were the guiding national policies: one could not find more different environments in which publishing companies would operate.

Henry is fond of telling a story about how I 'kicked' him out of my office the first time he visited, as he puts it, because he was a 'representative of a filthy multinational company.' We did not meet properly until 1981 when we found ourselves stranded at Dakar airport at past 2.00 a.m. going to attend the UNESCO Regional Meeting of Experts on National Book Strategies in Africa. For the first time we spent a lot of time together in and outside the conference and discovered how convergent our views were on the state of publishing in Africa, and in our imagination of what it could be in the hands of committed indigenous African publishers. Henry was elected Vice-Chairman of the conference, a position that we would take advantage of to influence the outcome of its proceedings.

In most international conferences organisers tend to prepare before, or privately during the conference, a draft report to submit to the participants for discussion and adoption at the end. In addition to being a more efficient way to produce such a document, it is also a strategy to micromanage the process so as to ensure that the conclusions serve the conference organisers' interests, by crafting documents supposedly reflecting consensus of ideas and positions expressed during the conference.

That was the case at the conference. Henry and I found the draft to be so different from discussions that had taken place, and new perspectives that had emerged, that we demanded a redrafting of it. Despite determined defence of the original document by the organisers of the conference, we were adamant that the draft document should reflect the views of the participants and not the preconceived positions of the conference organisers. The debate was heated and although this was the first time Henry and I ever worked together, it was a source of great satisfaction that we could put the experiences we were bringing from our two backgrounds, academia and diplomacy to play a key role in redrafting the document. Revisiting the document, (http://unesdoc.unesco.org/images/0004/000475/047510 EB.pdf) thirty-four years later, it's remarkable how its grounding ideas and ethos have motivated studies on the gamut of issues concerned with African publishing, provided frameworks for policy analyses and recommendations to African governments, donors and other funding agencies.

A series of conferences and meetings followed in which Henry was an active member of a collegiate of like-minded publishers, progressive partners among northern institutions and donors notably: 1984 (First Dag Hammarskjöld Foundation on Developing Autonomous Publishing Capacity in Africa, Arusha I, followed by Arusha II in 1996, and Arusha III in 2002), 1985 (African Books Collective founding meeting), 1991 (Bellagio Conference on Publishing and Development) leading to the foundation of the African Publishers Network at the Zimbabwe International Book Fair in 1992. The Bellagio conference was a landmark and important milestone in the evolution of African publishing studies and the progenitor of offshoot projects such as the Bellagio Publishing Network Newsletter and Bellagio Studies in Publishing. Equally worth mentioning were the financial and organisational support provided by Canadian Organisation for Development through Education (CODE) that led to the birth of the Children's Book Project (CBP) in Tanzania.

The success and influence of Bellagio stemmed from the high level and intellectual honesty of the representatives from the participating parties: senior officials of the donor and funding organisations on the one hand, and on the other, African active publishers and scholars who espoused and defended the right and imperative of Africa 'telling its own story' through books emanating from its indigenous publishers. It is to the credit of the Rockefeller Foundation, SIDA, NORAD, DANIDA, the Netherlands Ministry of Foreign Affairs, UNESCO, the Dag Hammarskjöld Foundation, the World Bank, ADEA, INASP and the CTA that the Bellagio conference and subsequent meetings in different places were freed from the fetters of 'officialdom' and 'donor mentality'; while on the African side, open, uninhibited, frank and critical arguments characterised written and spoken interventions. The concept of 'donors and recipients' was changed and replaced by the healthier 'donors and doers'.

Despite these encouraging international relations, relations between the Heinemann Company in Nairobi, and London became difficult. Finally, the only resolution was for Henry to initiate negotiations to buy out the shares of Heinemann UK, as he explains in detail in his book, *Publishing in Africa: One Man's Perspective*.

It was a privilege that Henry took me into confidence about the move; and every now and then, we discussed the best strategies for carrying the negotiations forward. When the day of announcing the conclusion of the negotiations and launch of EAEP arrived, Henry invited me and gave me the honour of speaking at the gala dinner celebrating the success of the first transformation of a multinational into an indigenous owned company.

Ironically, at that time relations between Kenya and Tanzania were frozen, borders were closed and no flights operated between the two countries. It was difficult to get to Nairobi from Dar es Salaam as the borders between the two countries were closed and there were no flights to or from Kenya. I had to fly to Kilimanjaro airport, take a shuttle bus to Arusha, find a Tanzania bus to take me to the Kenyan border, cross it on foot and then look for a Kenyan bus to take me to Nairobi. Luck was on my side and I was able to make it to the venue of the function no more than thirty minutes before it began.

The change from being a branch of a multinational company to an independent indigenous company was more than a corporate change. The London mother company, like all imperial, metropolitan based companies aimed to squeeze as much profit as possible from its Kenya branch. Often in similar situations in other companies, the head office sets near impossible profit targets for branch managers, who in turn must go all out to ensure they are met even if they have to work their employees to death.

The branch managers, as would be expected, have an interest in meeting the targets because their bonuses are pegged on the profits they make. So, even when branch managers are natives – and they usually would be for their knowledge of local conditions and government officials – they are no less ruthless and may even be more so than their principals in the European capitals. This is the comprador commercial culture, which in many ways humiliates the natives until conditions are ripe for their liberation.

By breaking away from London and becoming an independent indigenous company, Henry was ushering into the Kenya publishing industry a nationalist movement that would encourage other branches of UK publishers to follow suit, the most prominent being Longman which became Longhorn and Macmillan which became Moran. There were two important outcomes of the changes: greater commercial success than they had ever achieved, with profit remaining in Kenya, thereby breaking the myth of superiority of expatriate management; and a flowering of local content publishing across the board. Local language publishing, children's books and fiction were the most obvious products of the new publishing scene. From being 'a representative of a filthy multinational' Henry became a pioneer in the indigenisation of foreign publishing companies providing a how-to model.

Henry's other contributions to African publishing

It is difficult to think of any major initiative in African publishing in the last thirty-five years, in which Henry has not been a participant in one way or another. He was on the very first NOMA Award Managing Committee (the Jury) for three years 1980-1982. He was a founding member of the African Books Collective and remains a member of its

Council of Management. His role in APNET as head of training and the development of the training curriculum is recognised by all as being one of the most notable accomplishments of APNET. His involvement in the Kenya Publishers Association and National Book Development Council of Kenya, at various times as Chairman and in other capacities, may not have always endeared him to all publishers and other book related institutions. By the nature of Kenya society and politics, it probably could not be any different. He was one of the founding members and Chairman of the East African Book Development Association (EABDA) established in 2000 to bring together Book Development Councils in the region to promote reading. EABDA was responsible for the growth of Book Weeks (country book fairs) and the popular children reading tents amongst their activities. The Nairobi International Book Fair, which is by far the most important in the region, might not have been so successful without Henry's active participation in its early days.

Intellectual contribution to publishing

If Henry had only been a successful textbook publisher and kept his knowledge of publishing to himself, he would be imitating the multinationals whose principal aim is to make money and who prefer to operate in relative silent dark environment in which their skills are truly 'awesome' in the original pre-social media meaning. Henry has been an educator, writing extensively about publishing and giving useful tips about how to succeed in the business to those who are prepared to learn from him. He prepared a paper for the first Dag Hammarskjöld Foundation Seminar at Arusha in 1984 entitled, "An Autonomous African Publishing House: A Model" in which he presented everything that the prospective middle size publishing house had to think about, complete with estimates of necessary funding, editorial, marketing and distribution strategies; he has been crusading for African publishers to pay great attention to marketing and distribution, giving us the colourful phrase, 'the Achilles' heel of African publishing' and pointing out most graphically how most African publishers '....'light a lamp and hide it behind the bushel'; he popularised the idea of the publishing house being in between the cathedral and the stock exchange (*Kati ya Kanisa na Sokoni*); he has written extensively about copyright and the inherent injustice of the existing discriminatory order that does not take any interest in African realities of knowledge creation and dissemination. He has done so, untrammelled by the slavish behaviour of accommodating oneself to the hoo-ha of those that built their industries on pirating others' books for ages, but are now vociferous advocates of rigid application of copyright convention. He has summed up for all of us the objective of the publishing, reminding us that, "It is not so much the strength of your bottom line but the contribution that you make to the academic and cultural welfare of your society that will be remembered".

Courage, commitment and vision

At some point in our meetings and while socialising, I noticed that Henry was constantly trying to straighten one of his two little fingers, which was bent at about ninety degrees from the second joint. I controlled my curiosity for quite some time until I could no longer resist asking him what had happened to the little finger. His narration of what happened to him and how he narrowly escaped assassination was as chilling as any violent scene in an action film. Henry is also a master story-teller with a skill in understatement and sangfroid. I was stuck and humbled by the calm and self-composure as he explained the ordeal.

If the importance and threat of African publishing were ever in doubt, here was a living example. Agents of the state (they must have been) of a political party to which he had taken a life membership, felt sufficiently threatened by the books Henry published to want to eliminate him. Not least amongst these books were the critical works of Ngũgĩ wa Thiong'o, subsequently banned. This has to be the only reasonable assumption about the reason behind the crime as no investigation was ever carried out to find its perpetrators and to bring them to justice. Had he been cowed down by the threats before the attack and after, and stopped publishing Ngũgĩ altogether, there might have been questions about his motivation for publishing his works: whether the motivation was the profits that the books would bring or the accolades he would garner for publishing such a successful and pioneering author.

It had to be great courage, lofty principle and an indomitable spirit that kept him doing what he believed to be right. At Tanzania Publishing House in the seventies, we published a number of books that were critical of the state. I was often asked how we got the courage to publish these books and how we escaped censorship that was presumed to exist in a one party controlled society that claimed to be socialist.

There was no censorship in Tanzania although it was always suggested that as most of those books were in English, and the majority of the Tanzanians then, as now, do not read books in English, there was no reason for the state to intervene to stop us publishing the books we liked to publish and also since the small elite left was no threat to the state.

When we were working on Issa Shivji's book, *The Silent Class Struggle in Tanzania (1972)*, the chairman of the Board wanted to stop its publication. As the then General Manager who I was understudying before taking over emphatically stated that we would publish it and I strongly supported that position, the chairman went to inform Mwalimu Nyerere (behind our backs) and to seek his advice. In a note to the chairman, Mwalimu replied that his job was of President and the job of TPH's General Manager was to publish books; each should do his job. After that, it did not take courage to continue to publish progressive and critical books.

But that was because Mwalimu Nyerere knew that we, generally, shared the same ideology; indeed that we were further left of him. How many of us would stick our necks out to publish an author's novel, essay or poetry, in defence of his / her freedom of expression and our concomitant right to publish it? We know from experience how publishers (the majority) refuse to comment on any government policy regarding books and publishing, on the excuse that any comment that is not in full support of the policy might lead to government excluding them from book tenders. These publishers do not have even the most basic trade union solidarity in defence of their interests. They excel only in working behind their colleagues' backs, shamelessly cutting deals and hoping they will benefit from their silence on public interest issues, when by standing firmly together they might do better for the industry and for themselves as a whole.

When we, *Wazee* of publishing in Africa, call for commitment to secure a respectable place for African publishers in the international community of purveyors of knowledge, we are driven by a nationalist and Pan-Africanist dream. We expect the current and future generations to advance the industry forward towards that dream, out of respect for and advancement of our culture and identity as Africans albeit of different nationalities.

Regrettably, the preponderance of African enterprises do not survive after the generation of their founders. This is bad for all enterprises but more so for publishing, because successful publishing is rooted in traditions of excellence gained through painstaking labour for generations. Henry has retired from active involvement in the business, but remains influential as Chairman of the Board. We are reassured by the succession plan under way that it will ensure EAEP's growth from strength to strength, and following in his footsteps, it will keep it at the 'peak of publishing' where it has been for all the years Henry has been in charge.

Walter Bgoya
Dar es Salaam, 2016

A Note From the Publishers

Emerging with a double First Class Honours in Literature and Philosophy and subsequently receiving post-graduate scholarship offers from local and international universities, Dr Henry Chakava's star started to shine immediately after college.

His meteoric rise from an Editor at Heinemann to Managing Director in just four years, became the launching pad of this versatile publisher's journey towards redefining the African publishing scene. This journey has seen him causing positive ripples in the publishing pool in Africa and beyond. It is against this background that some of his friends in publishing and academia decided to come up with this *Festschrift*.

Coming of Age Strides in African Publishing is therefore a noteworthy *Festschrift* written in honour of Dr Henry Chakava; with essays written by great minds that have interacted with Dr Chakava at professional, scholarly and personal levels for decades.

As a never-relenting believer in the unity of purpose, Dr Chakava played pivotal roles in the formation of bodies that continue to shape African publishing to date. Beginning with the Kenya Publishers Association, African Publishing Network, African Books Collective, among others, he set to show the way on what belief and charisma can do to an otherwise neglected industry.

Although confronted by a myriad of publishing challenges and the unforgiving political climate of the late 70s and early 80s; his persistence in developing a level playing ground for publishing in Africa saw him become the first Kenyan-African to acquire a British-owned publishing house, Heinemann Kenya, rename it East African Educational Publishers and go ahead to publish the continent's most revered authors.

We would like to take this opportunity to express our appreciation to all the contributors for sparing time and resources to write such powerful and inspiring Papers. We are indebted to their accepting to share their pieces of knowledge as invaluable gifts to Dr Chakava during his 70th birthday celebrations. By so doing they have re-affirmed that his contribution to publishing in Africa shall continue to be echoed by all who believe in the place of knowledge in personal and national development.

About the Contributors

Walter Bgoya

Walter Bgoya is a publisher and former diplomat. He served in the Ministry of Foreign Affairs on the Africa desk working with liberation movements and leaders, and as a diplomat in Ethiopia and China. Because of this background he was a member of Mwalimu J.K. Nyerere's team during the Burundi Peace Process from 1996 to 1999.

Bgoya headed the state-owned Tanzania Publishing House from 1972 to 1990 and later left to form Mkuki na Nyota Publishers – a publishing house that publishes scholarly, literary and children's books in Swahili and English. He chaired the series of seminars about publishing development in Africa under the auspices of the Dag Hammarsjköld Foundation, and has been widely published on African social, cultural issues.

He has held various high public offices in the publishing and printing industries as well as in the Tanzania Port Authority where he was Vice Chairman of the Board (1995-2005). Until March 2016 he was Deputy Chair of the Content Committee of the Tanzania Communications Regulatory Authority. He is a founder publisher and Chair of African Books Collective (ABC); a founder publisher of the African Publishers Network, and was the longest serving Chair of the Jury of the NOMA Award for Publishing in Africa.

Kiarie Kamau

Kiarie Kamau is the Chief Executive Officer of East African Educational Publishers (EAEP). He has been in publishing for 15 years and holds both BA (Hons) and MA degrees from the University of

Nairobi. He has presented Papers on Publishing and Literature in local and international forums, some of which have been published in books and journals. Some of his published works include: *Notes on Chinua Achebe's A Man of the People*, EAEP (2002); 'Promoting Local Authorship in Kenya', published in *Contemporary Publishing and Book Trade in Kenya,* edited by D.C, Rotich and K.S. Buigutt Moi University Press (2009); 'The State of Publishing in East Africa', published in *Logos* 26/3 (2015). Kiarie is also an ardent commentator on literary issues in the dailies.

Ngũgĩ wa Thiong'o

Ngũgĩ wa Thiong'o is Distinguished Professor of English and Comparative Literature at the University of California, Irvine. He is the recipient of ten Honorary Doctorates, including: Honorary Doctor of Humane Letters, Albright College; Honorary PhD, Roskilde, Denmark; Doctor of Letters honoris causa, University of Leeds, 2004; Honorary Doctor of Literature and Philosophy, Walter Sisulu University, 2004; Honorary Doctor of Letters, University of Dar es Saalam, 2013; and Honorary Doctor of Letters, University of Bayreuth, 2014. He is also an Honorary Foreign Member of the American Academy of Arts and Letters, 2003 and a member of the American Academy of Arts and Sciences, 2014.

Renowned worldwide, as a novelist, playwright, essayist and academic, Ngũgĩ wa Thiong'o's contributions to the body of critical writing on African literature, politics and society have been highly significant, and have profoundly influenced other writers, critics, scholars and students. Among his famous publications include: *Decolonizing the Mind*; *In the House of the Interpreter*; *Globalectics*; *In the Name of the Mother*; *Writers in Politics*; *Remembering Africa*; *Dreams in a Time of War: A Childhood Memoir; A Grain of Wheat*; *Devil on the Cross*; *Petals of Blood*; *The River Between*; *Weep Not, Child*; and *I Will Marry When I Want*.

About the Authors

James Currey

James Currey started his publishing career with the Oxford University Press in Cape Town in 1959. The more frustrated he became by South Africa, the more excited he became by Africa itself in its independence decade. He was one of the founders of The New African, the radical review which introduced South African readers to new writers like Ngũgĩ, Kofi Awoonor, Masizi Kunene, Bessie Head, Dennis Brutus and Ayi Kwei Armah. James Currey enabled the Editor of The New African to escape from South Africa by jumping off a ship in Cape Town docks and had to flee South Africa to escape arrest and interrogation.

In OUP London he became the publisher of Three Crowns, the series which included plays by Wole Soyinka, Joe de Graft and J. P. Clark. In 1967 he went to work at Heinemann with Alan Hill and Keith Sambrook who gave their absolute support to all titles that Chinua Achebe wanted to publish. Aig Higo and Henry Chakava enabled James Currey to build up the rate of publishing in the African Writers Series, totalling 270 titles by 1984. In that year new owners of Heinemann demanded that James Currey stop publishing new work in the African Writers Series.

In 1985 he and his wife Clare founded James Currey Publishers to publish leading academic work in African Studies with co-publishers in Africa and the United States. Henry Chakava of EAEP and Walter Bgoya of Mkuki na Nyota helped James Currey Publishers to survive and thrive.

Simon Gikandi

Simon Gikandi is Robert Schirmer Professor of English at Princeton University and was editor of PMLA, the official journal of the Modern Languages Association (MLA) for five years (2011-2016). A Kenyan, he graduated with a B.A. [First Class Honours] in Literature from the University of Nairobi (1979). He was a British Council Scholar at the University of Edinburgh in Scotland from which he graduated with an M.Litt. in English Studies in 1982. He has a PhD in English from

Northwestern University (1986). He has authored and co-authored many books and articles including *Reading the African Novel, Reading Chinua Achebe, Writing in Limbo: Modernism and Caribbean Literature, Maps of Englishness: Writing Identity in the Culture of Colonialism*, and *Ngũgĩ wa Thiong'o*, which was a Choice Outstanding Academic Publication for 2004.

His latest book, *Slavery and the Culture of Taste* (2011), has won Prestigious Awards.

Mĩcere Gĩthae Mũgo

Mĩcere Gĩthae Mũgo, Emeritus Meredith Professor for Teaching Excellence Department of African American Studies Syracuse University – NY, USA; past Chair of the Department of African American Studies; past Director of the Africa Initiative and past Director of Graduate Studies in AAS at SU, is a poet, playwright and literary critic who has published six books, eight co-edited supplementary school readers, three monographs and edited the journal, *Third World in Perspective*. Her works include: *Writing and Speaking from the Heart of my Mind* (selected essays and speeches); *Art, Artists and the Flowering of Pan-Africana Liberated Zones* (monograph); *My Mother's Poem and Other Songs* (poetry); *The Long Illness of Ex-Chief Kiti* (play); *Daughter of My People, Sing!* (poetry); *Visions of Africa* (literary criticism), *African Orature and Human Rights* (monograph); *Gikũyũ, Shona and Ndebele Ethics and Aesthetics* (monograph); *Mũthoni wa Kĩrĩma – Mau Mau Woman Field Marshal: Interrogating Silencing, Erasure and Manipulation of Female Combatants' Texts* (monograph) and *The Trial of Dedan Kimathi* (play, co-authored with Ngũgĩ wa Thiong'o. Mĩcere is a recipient of numerous honors, including the following: the Flora Nwapa Award for excellence in writing; Distinguished Mwalimu Julius Nyerere Award from the University of Dar es Salaam; College of Arts and Sciences Award for Excellence in Master Level Teaching and Distinguished Africanist Award from the New York African Studies Association for her contribution to scholarship.

At the Kenya 50th jubilee in December 2013, she was awarded the Elder of the Burning Spear and in November 2002, *The East African Standard Century* listed her among 'The Top 100: They Influenced Kenya Most During the 20th Century.' Mĩcere is also a member of numerous organisations and serves on many committees, advisory/executive boards and directorships – locally as well as internationally. A committed community activist, Mĩcere is a passionate advocate for human rights especially as they have been historically denied to marginalised groups. She describes her daughters, Mũmbi and the late Njeri, as her best friends and indispensable comrades in the struggle for social justice.

Ayo Ojeniyi

Ayo Ojeniyi attended the Universities of Ife (now Obafemi Awolowo University) and Ibadan both in Nigeria, and graduated with B.Sc. (Biological Sciences) with honours and a Master of Business Administration (MBA) in 1974 and 1982 respectively. He also attended various courses in Publishing and Management locally and abroad.

He first worked at Heinemann Education Books (Nigeria) Ltd, now HEBN Publishers Plc, as a clerk, after leaving the grammar school in December 1969, and re-joined the company as Editor-in-Training in 1976. He rose through the ranks, and was elevated to the Board as Publishing Director in 1986, Managing Director/Chief Executive Officer in 1995, Vice-Chairman/Chief Executive Officer in 2010 and finally the Chairman/Chief Executive Officer in November 2012. He retired meritoriously from his executive position in 2014 after thirty-eight years, and has been retained as the Chairman of the company.

He was a former Board member of Obafemi Awolowo University Press Ltd, the Nigerian Educational Research and Development Council (NERDC), and Afro-Asian Book Council based in New Delhi, India. A former President of the Nigerian Publishers Association, he was also a former Vice-Chairman, African Publishers Network (APNET).

Ayo Ojeniyi is currently on the Council of Management of African Books Collective (ABC) based in Oxford, UK. He is a Fellow, Nigerian Institute of Publishers and Honorary Fellow, Science Teachers Association of Nigeria (STAN).

He is the author of a number of papers on publishing, education, science, religion, etc., and co-edited a book, *Issues in Book Publishing in Nigeria – Essays in Honour of Aigboje Higo at 70* (2005) and contributed to another book, *Education in the 21st Century – Legal, Cultural and Environmental Issues* (2009).

David Maillu

David G Maillu, is a renowned author of over 70 books and innumerable articles. One of his biggest literary contributions is in writing and publishing over 40 titles for children. As a scholar, Maillu has practically demonstrated the indisputable foundation of African aesthetics by publishing his research titled 'African Indigenous Political Philosophy'. He was the founder-member and leader in the writing and compiling the *Holy Text of African Religion the Ka, Holy Book of Neter*. Maillu holds a doctorate in African Literature and Political Philosophy.

Emilia Ilieva

Emilia Ilieva is a Professor of Literature at Egerton University, Kenya. Her publications in the areas of African literary history, sociology and aesthetics of African literature, and African women's writing have

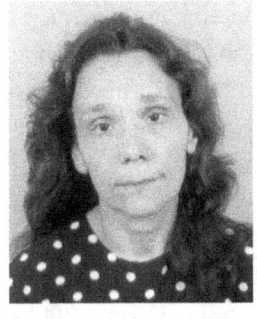

appeared in such journals as *Vostok, Research in African Literatures, World Literature in English, African Literature Today, Journal of Third World Studies*, and *Egerton Journal of Humanities, Social Sciences and Education*. Entries by her are included in the *Encyclopaedia of Post-Colonial Literatures in English* (London: Routledge), *The Encyclopaedia of World Literature in the 20th Century* (New York: St James Press), *The Companion to African Literature in English* (James Currey and Indiana University Press), *Encyclopaedia of Life Writing* (Fitzroy Dearborn Publishers), *Historical Companion to Postcolonial Literatures in English* (Edinburgh University Press), and *Encyclopaedia of Activism and Social Justice* (SAGE Publications). She has also translated Ngũgĩ wa Thiong'o's novel, *Petals of Blood*, into Bulgarian.

Masaya Hillary Chakava

Masaya Hillary Chakava is an Assistant Lecturer in Communication and Media at Egerton University, Kenya. He holds a Bachelor of Education (Arts) degree from Egerton University and a Master of Arts in Communication Studies from the University of Nairobi. He is currently pursing a doctorate degree in Communication Studies at the Jomo Kenyatta University of Agriculture and Technology.

James Tumusiime

Dr James Rwehabura Tumusiime was born in 1950 in Mbarara, Southwestern Uganda. He studied Agriculture and Economics at Makerere University, but became more widely known for the cartoon strips *Ekanya* and *Bogi Benda*, which he syndicated in a number of African daily newspapers. He spent five years in Kenya (1981-1986).

When he returned to Uganda after the NRA war, he spearheaded the founding of *The New Vision* newspaper in 1986 and Fountain Publishers in 1988. He set up the National Book Trust of Uganda (NABOTU) in 1997, and participated in the setting up of the East African Book Development Association (EABDA). He has served on several international boards, including the African Publishers Network (APNET) as its vice-chairman (1997-2002), the Afro-Asian Book Council (AABC) as its first African chairman (2008-2010) and The International Board of Books for Young People (IBBY) 2008-2012, as its first member from Sub-Saharan Africa.

He served as Chairman of Council of Mbarara University of Science and Technology (MUST) 2003-2011, and Chairman of I@MAK Publications Board of Makerere University (2003-2008) and chairman of the Uganda Tourism Board since 2012. He founded Radio West in 1998 and Igongo Cultural Centre in 2008.

He was awarded a PhD (Honoris causa) from United Graduate College and Seminary International in 2013.

Hans M. Zell

Hans Zell has been author, editor, and publisher on African topics for over four decades, and has written extensively on many aspects of publishing and book development in Africa. In addition to a substantial number of articles published in journals, he is also the author of several books, training manuals, and African studies reference resources.

He was the founder of the quarterly bibliographic and book trade journal *The African Book Publishing Record*, which started in 1975 and which he edited until 2002. In a part-time capacity, he was the Senior Consultant to African Books Collective from 1986 to 1995, and between

1979 and 1995 also acted as the Secretary to the Managing Committee of the Noma Award for Publishing in Africa.

Francis B. Nyamnjoh

Francis B. Nyamnjoh holds a BA (1984) and an MA (1985) from the University of Yaounde, Cameroon, and a PhD (1990), from the University of Leicester, UK. He joined the University of Cape Town in August 2009 as Professor of Social Anthropology from the Council for the Development of Social Science Research in Africa (CODESRIA), Dakar, Senegal, where he served as Head of Publications from July 2003 to July 2009. He has taught Sociology, Anthropology and Communication Studies at universities in Cameroon and Botswana, and has researched and written extensively on Cameroon and Botswana, where he was awarded the 'Senior Arts Researcher of the Year' prize for 2003. In October 2012 he received a University of Cape Town Excellence Award for 'Exceptional Contribution as a Professor in the Faculty of Humanities'. He is recipient of the 'ASU African Hero 2013' annual award by the African Students Union, Ohio University, USA.

He is a B2 rated Professor and Researcher by the South African National Research Foundation (NRF) since 2010; a Fellow of the Cameroon Academy of Science since August 2011; a fellow of the African Academy of Science since December 2014; and Chair of the Editorial Board of the South African Human Sciences Research Council (HSRC) Press since January 2011. His most recent scholarly books include *Negotiating an Anglophone Identity* (2003), *Rights and the Politics of Recognition in Africa* (2004), *Africa's Media, Democracy and the Politics of Belonging* (2005), *Insiders and Outsiders: Citizenship and Xenophobia in Contemporary Southern Africa* (2006), *Mobile Phones: The New Talking Drums of Everyday Africa* (2009), *The Postcolonial Turn: Re-Imagining Anthropology and Africa* (2011), *Side@Ways: Mobile Margins and the Dynamics of Communication in Africa* (2013).

Dr Nyamnjoh has published widely on globalisation, citizenship, media and the politics of identity in Africa. He has also published seven ethnographic novels, *Mind Searching* (1991), *The Disillusioned African* (1995), *A Nose for Money* (2006), *Souls Forgotten* (2008), *The Travail of Dieudonné* (2008), *Married but Available* (2009), *Intimate Strangers* (2010), and *Homeless Waters* (2011), a play *The Convert* (2003), a collection of short stories, *Stories from Abakwa* (2007), and a collection of poems, *Predicaments* (2011).

Roger Stringer

Originally from England, **Roger Stringer** emigrated to Zimbabwe in 1980 and became a Zimbabwe citizen in 1982. He holds a BA in Latin from the University of Leeds (1972) and an MBA from the University of Zimbabwe (1989). After obtaining a Post-graduate Diploma in Librarianship (1974)

Stringer was admitted as a Chartered Member of the Library Association (now the Chartered Institute of Library and Information Professionals) in 1976.

He worked as a librarian in public library services in the UK and in Zambia and, after moving to Zimbabwe, was appointed Librarian at Gweru Teachers' College. In 1985, he moved into academic publishing when he accepted the position of Editorial Assistant at the University of Zimbabwe in Harare. Stringer developed the University's publishing programme and the Publications Office into a fully-fledged university press until he left at the end of 1993. Since then, he has been providing freelance publishing, editorial and book-packaging services to publishers, organisations and individuals, trading as TextPertise.

Stringer has always maintained a strong professional interest in publishing and book-development in Zimbabwe, particularly as a trustee and Vice-Chairman of the Zimbabwe International Book Fair Trust, and as a Founder Member of the African Publishers Network (APNET).

Mary Jay

Mary Jay has worked for African Books Collective (ABC) since its foundation in 1989, and was CEO from 1995-2012. She is currently a Director, and serves as a strategic consultant to ABC. She has been published in journals, explaining and furthering the cause of ABC: African owned, comprising 155 publishers from 24 countries, seeking to strengthen indigenous African publishing through cultural activities and promotion, marketing and distribution of African-published books, and harnessing the digital age. She has published essays in ABC titles: *The African Writers' Handbook* and *African Scholarly Publishing*. She is co-editor of *Courage and Consequence: Women Publishing in Africa*. She was a co-organiser with the Dag Hammarskjöld Foundation of one of the series of seminars about publishing development in Africa. She is a Trustee of the International African Institute, and is on the General Council of the Caine Prize for African Writing. She was a Trustee, Jury member and Secretary to the Managing Committee of the Noma Award for Publishing in Africa, until it ceased. Prior to 1989, she was deputy publisher in Hans Zell Publishers, and Assistant Editor of *The African Book Publishing Record*.

Lily Nyariki

Lily Nyariki holds a Bachelors of Arts Degree in Literature and two postgraduate diplomas in Librarianship and Mass Communication from the University of Nairobi (Kenya) and the Leeds Metropolitan University (UK) respectively. She has worked for the public sector, NGOs and international

organisations for over 30 years. Currently, she is based at Moi University Eldoret – Kenya, where she works as a Librarian in charge of the University Bookshops.

Lily is a seasoned, well exposed professional with multiple skills. Since 1994, Lily has continued to offer her services as a consultant for various institutions including the Dag Hammarskjold Foundation, UNESCO, UNICEF and the Association for the Development in Africa as consultant in Monitoring and Evaluation, information management, publishing and the book trade.

She is a published author of a book titled *Publishing and Book Trade in Kenya,* and has several papers in peer reviewed publications. She has a special interest in developing and nurturing the habit of reading especially among children and has since 2011 worked with New Dawn Educational Centre to develop their school library.

Richard A. B. Crabbe

Richard Crabbe is a Senior Communications and Publishing Consultant at the World Bank, Washington, DC. From 2002 to 2012, he served as Head of Client Relations in the World Bank's Office of the Publisher. Prior to joining the World Bank in 2002, he was General Manager/CEO of Africa Christian Press in Accra, Ghana (1982-2002). In 2014, he was lead author for *Textbook Development in Low Income Countries: A Guide for Policy and Practice*, and led the team that prepared a 12-module e-course for the manual.

In his over 37 year career in publishing, he has also served as Chairman, African Publishers' Network (APNET); Member, Executive Committee of the International Publishers Association (IPA); Member, UNESCO Publications Board; and Steering Committee Member of the Working

Group on Books and Learning Materials, Association for the Development of Education in Africa (ADEA). Other involvement includes Director/Council member, CODE (Canada), Book Aid International, UK; Board member, Media Associates, International; International Book Bank, USA.

Educated in Ghana and the U.S., Richard holds a Master's degree in Communications (magna cum laude) and a Bachelor's in Biochemistry (Hons).

Marisella Ouma

Marisella Ouma is an Intellectual Property Law expert specialising in copyright and related rights. She was the Executive Director of the Kenya Copyright Board (KECOBO) from 2006 to 2015. She has served on various Boards such as the Anti Counterfeit Agency and the Kenya Industrial Property Institute in Kenya. She holds a PhD From Queen Mary, University of London, an LLM from Stockholm University and LLB from the University of Nairobi. She has also contributed to the development of various intellectual property policies and laws in Kenya and within the region including the recently published Traditional Knowledge Bill in Kenya. She has also participated in various discussions on protection of traditional knowledge at the international, regional and national level. She has taught at the University of Nairobi, and is also a visiting lecturer at the Africa University, Mutare, Zimbabwe. She has worked on various research projects such as ACA2K and Open A.I.R. She has published several papers and book chapters on Copyright and related rights.

1

The Guru of Publishing: Assessing Henry Chakava's Contribution in Africa

By Kiarie Kamau

Background information

> *(Dr Henry Chakava) is one of the most courageous publishers in Africa or anywhere else in the world ... He is a visionary whose feet are firmly planted in the real world. (2006: 113-115)*
>
> Prof. Ngũgĩ wa Thiong'o

Right from his formative years, Henry Chakava was, shall I say, cut for 'a love affair with books'. At the University of Nairobi, he devoured tomes of academic text and at the completion of his Bachelor's degree in 1972, he emerged with a double First Class Honours in Literature and Philosophy.

His sterling performance instantly earned him post-graduate scholarship offers from local and international universities. If the Department of Literature was eager to have him advance studies in the field, the Department of Philosophy was even more aggressive in the approach.

The government of Kenya extended to him a scholarship to pursue literature. Unfortunately, this suffered some delays and in the meantime, the Department of Philosophy and Religious Studies appointed him a Tutorial Fellow. A professor in this department, Bishop Stephen Neill, made arrangements for him to secure a foreign scholarship to study philosophy. The proposal he submitted for a Master's degree was so good that his professors recommended that he should enrol for PhD directly. However, his studies were derailed by lack of an appropriate supervisor for his thesis on African philosophy.

Meanwhile, lecturers at the Department of Literature, University of Nairobi, were urging him to return to the department and one of them, Professor Andrew Gurr arranged a temporary job for him at the Nairobi office of Heinemann Educational Books (HEB), as he organised a scholarship in either the United Kingdom or United States.

As fate would have it, Henry Chakava was to bid farewell to a life in the academia, and settle in publishing, a profession he embraced with much enthusiasm, and perfected over time. But to say that Henry abandoned the academic life would be a misnomer since, as we shall see, his career in publishing provided even a better pedestal on which to read widely, interact and share academic platforms with intellectuals from different fields of knowledge, prepare and present research papers in different forums, including in leading universities in the world, among other academic engagements. Little wonder then that Prof. Ngũgĩ wa Thiong'o has this to say about him:

> If he had chosen academic life, he would, in all likelihood, have turned out to be a leading professor in any academy ... In choosing publishing, he became a producer of knowledge in the broadest sense of the term by enabling and giving African intellectual production continental and global visibility. (2006: 113)

Heinemann Educational Books Ltd. (HEB)

As we have already hinted, Henry Chakava's entry into publishing was purely accidental. And Henry was not overly enthusiastic about getting into publishing. Having been rated by the highly respected Professor of Literature, Andrew Gurr as his best student in ten years, and having been subjected to a tug-of-war between the Literature and Philosophy departments, Henry must have set his mind to pursue a life in academics.

Alan Hill, the Group Chairman of Heinemann had this to say about Henry's first interview:

> At the interview, there was a complete failure of communication with the candidate. Henry didn't seem to care whether he got the job or not. Andy Gurr was disappointed, and suggested a second interview, but this time out of the office – a suggestion supported by Henry's friends Ngũgĩ and Taban lo Liyong. 'Did you give him a beer?' asked Taban. 'No', replied David. 'Well then, what do you expect! See him again and give him a beer.' The advice was followed. And Henry put up a stunning performance, and walked away with the job. (Chakava, 1988: 246-247)

That was in 1972, and Henry's stunning performance at the interview replicated itself when he ventured into publishing, thus rising through the ranks to the position of Managing Director in 1976, all packed within a period of only four years.

Publishing of creative works

The African Writers Series and Beyond

Heinemann is, without any doubt, synonymous with the African Writers Series (AWS). This is the Series that, thanks to the progressive publishing approach of Alan Hill, bequeathed unto us the iconic *Things Fall Apart*; the evergreen *A Grain of Wheat*; and the monumental *Mine Boy*, among many other great literary works. It is the Series that gave verve and voice to many literary luminaries across Africa: Chinua Achebe in West Africa; Ngũgĩ wa Thiong'o in East Africa; Nuruddin Farah in North Africa; Alex la Guma in South Africa; and Dambudzo Marechera in Central Africa, to mention but a few.

It is against the background of this rich backlist that Henry Chakava had the challenging, yet stimulating responsibility of expanding, while still maintaining, the quality of creative works that had already been published. Challenging because whereas a few months before, he had been a student of Ngũgĩ wa Thiong'o at the University of Nairobi, he now found himself on the other side of the 'classroom', with Ngũgĩ as his 'student'. At Heinemann, Henry would become Ngũgĩ's editor, and the author-editor relationship would blossom into a long-lasting friendship that is still intact to-date. Stimulating, therefore, because he found himself interacting on a one-on-one basis with most of the leading names, sharing and learning from each other, and extending the friendship to family levels.

One of Ngũgĩ's works that Henry published is *Petals of Blood*, an experience that he terms as pleasurable and enriching. He gives an interesting account of the experience in his *Publishing in Africa: One Man's Perspective*:

> Contrary to popular belief among academics and other creative writers who think we automatically accept Ngũgĩ's books for publication, the script of *Petals*, then under the working titles, 'Wrestling with God' or 'Wrestlers with God', was sent out for readers' reports ... I personally gave it an in-depth report. Although all the reports recommended publication, they raised serious issues about the timing, movement, and content of the story ... Ngũgĩ took all these criticisms seriously and with great humility. He retrieved the script and reworked it for a long time, constantly coming back to seek clarification about some of the readers' criticisms ... Quite frankly, I cannot tell you which edition of *Petals of Blood* is in print, having read several versions of that novel both in manuscript and proof! (Chakava, 1996: 58-59)

Ngũgĩ's is just but one of the many experiences he has had with iconic writers. He often regales stories with insightful accounts of working with Chinua Achebe, Meja Mwangi, David Rubadiri, Taban lo Liyong, Grace Ogot, Sam Kahiga, Okot p'Bitek and many others of the old generation.

When he led other like-minded local entrepreneurs to buy-off the British-owned Heinemann and set up East African Educational Publishers (EAEP) in 1992, he also presided over many other changes that included product realignment. To this end, works published under AWS found a new home, the Peak Library Series, which has recently given birth to the African Classics Series (ACS). Under the Peak Library Series, the same model of discovering, nurturing and publishing creative talent from many parts of Africa has continued. Some of the recent names include the young Nigerian Diekoye Oyeyinka with *Stillborn*; Yusuf Dawood from Kenya with *Eye of the Storm*; and the Cameroonian Francis Nyamnjoh's *A Nose for Money*.

But much more important is Henry's bold and experimental approach to publishing. He has published drama, poetry, and even created room for the genre of literature that had hitherto been dismissed as 'pulp fiction' – Popular Fiction. He came up with a special imprint for the same, 'Spear Books Series' in 1975.

The Spear Books Series

Ever since David Maillu stirred the hornet's nest in literary circles by publishing what was viewed by conservatives as pornographic literature, any work that did not conform to the 'serious' literary tradition set by the Achebes and Ngũgĩs of the time was dismissed as pulp fiction. Few publishers would venture into publication of works whose focus was romance, crime, adventure, and such other 'light themes'.

Until Henry Chakava discovered John Kiriamiti. A convict, Kiriamiti had taken to writing while away in the drab prison life. He would later send his unsolicited manuscript to Henry Chakava, who gave it the same attention that others from established authors got. After vigorous reworking by the author based on readers' reports, and upon professional editing and packaging, *My Life in Crime* was released in 1984 to wide acclaim. Within a period of 12 months, it had sold 10,000 copies, thus outnumbering the copies sold for works of what was viewed as 'serious literature'.

My Life in Crime became the pillar of Spear Books Series, and gave pride of place to other works that focused on the so-called light thematic concerns. John Kiriamiti became emboldened to write even more, and to-date he has four other works of fiction to his credit: *My Life with a Criminal: Milly Story, Son of Fate, The Sinister Trophy* and *My Life in*

Prison.

What is most gratifying is that through Spear Books, young and upcoming authors have had their works published, with some winning prestigious awards – Onduko Bw'Atebe's *The Verdict of Death* won the inaugural Wahome Mutahi Literary Award in 2006.

Children's literature

In his keynote address at the Zimbabwe International Book Fair in 1988, Chinua Achebe described children's imported literature as 'beautifully packaged poison', and called upon every African parent to write at least one book for his child.

Achebe was upset that African children in schools in Africa continued to read storybooks that were far removed from their social, environmental and cultural setting, and often, such works only served to alienate the children and at times, were a source of deviant behaviour. Achebe's was therefore a clarion call to all creative writers in Africa, and publishers too, to write and publish books that would resonate with the true African setting.

Fortunately, Henry Chakava was in attendance. He immediately took up this challenge and launched a Series of children's books at Heinemann. He started by reissuing some of the already published books, some by Achebe himself, and commissioning new ones. The storybooks received instant success, with demand for more such storybooks rising by the day. Henry published the storybooks under different series names depending on the level of the learner: Sunbird Readers for lower primary; Sparrow Readers for middle primary and Junior Readers catering for upper primary school pupils. To-date, the categories have expanded exponentially.

Other publishers – local and multinationals – also came onto the scene, resulting in a wide variety of children's storybooks being made available for all levels. A visit to any bookshop in Nairobi or any other part of Kenya is a good testimony that Achebe's challenge, and Henry's experimental approach to publishing, have been a boon to home-grown children's fiction.

Publishing in African languages

The Masomo ya Msingi experiment and other works in Kiswahili

As we have already seen, Heinemann's forte in the 1970s and 80s was in the arena of creative works, while the textbook market was largely dominated by Oxford University Press and Longman. Yet still, none of them had ventured into the publishing of Kiswahili textbooks for primary schools.

After defying the advice of his bosses in London, Henry captures his next experiment in publishing with a tinge of nostalgia:

> The breakthrough came with my adventure into primary school publishing. I decided to start with Kiswahili, a language to which the government was giving lip service, but which did not even have a detailed syllabus, let alone textbooks ... I embarked on this ambitious project in 1977 ... The first three textbooks came out in 1980 and were an instant success. The Ministry of Education's first order was for more than 100,000 copies of each and even included Books 4 and 5, which were not yet published! (Chakava, 1996: 52).

Thus, the famous Kiswahili course, 'Masomo ya Msingi', was born. The course was to later become the bread and butter of EAEP for many years, owing to the consistent sales over the years.

Yet, apart from earning generous revenue for the company, Henry's bold experiment also underscored his deep held philosophy in publishing – the need to give recognition to African languages. Whereas the government of the day had dillydallied in the release of a Kiswahili syllabus for primary schools, and whereas management position in London was against publishing for primary schools, least of all in Kiswahili, Henry saw the need to have textbooks that would help the young learn and appreciate their national language.

The success of Masomo ya Msingi became a good launching pad for publication of more works in Kiswahili, especially in the area of fiction. To-date, EAEP enjoys a rich list of creative works in Kiswahili, from children's storybooks to full length adult novels. Some of these works have been selected as set books in Kenya, Tanzania and Uganda, and are written by both seasoned as well as upcoming Kiswahili authors. Among the leading ones are: *Asali Chungu,* a novel by Said Ahmed Mohamed; *Chembe cha Moyo*, poetry by Alamin Mazrui; *Visiki*, a play by Khaemba Ongeti; and *Alidhani Kapata na Hadithi Nyingine*, an anthology of short stories compiled by P. Iribemwangi.

Publishing in other African languages

Ever since the famous essay by the Nigerian critic, Obi Wali, "The Dead End of African Literature" in 1963, the debate on what defines African literature is still a hot topic in literary circles. In his essay, Obi declared that the literature written in European languages did not qualify as African literature.

Achebe differed strongly with Obi's position, but Ngũgĩ wa Thiong'o was to embrace the position and actually shift to publishing creative works in his native tongue, Gĩkũyũ. Ngũgĩ found support in Henry Chakava. Although Henry's position in this matter is not radical in approach, he has given value to African languages, and experimented with the publication of Ngũgĩ's first novel in Gĩkũyũ, *Caitaani Mutharaba-ini* (Devil on the Cross) and his play, *Ngaahika Ndeenda* (I Will Marry When I Want), both published in 1980.

The reception of both works was really impressive. James Currey captures this succinctly:

> The demand for both books was almost equal. By the end of 1980 three impressions totalling 15,000 of the novel and 13,000 of the play had been printed (Currey, 2008: 137).

Those in the publishing world in Africa know very well that an annual sale of more than 5,000 copies of a creative work written in English (or in French for that matter) is quite impressive by any standards. Yet these were works, written in Gĩkũyũ, and outselling some of the best fiction written in European languages. It was a testimony that there was a gap that needed to be filled, and both Ngũgĩ and Henry were keen to take up the gauntlet.

To-date, apart from publishing Ngũgĩ's works in Gĩkũyũ, EAEP has published in five other local languages in Kenya: Dholuo, Kikamba, Ekegusii, Lugooli, and Kimeru. It has also published curriculum materials in seven Zambian local languages: Cibemba, Chitonga, Silozi, Chinyanja, Kiikaonde, Luvale and Lunda.

Trade publications

Most publishing companies in Africa focus on the school book market. The considerations of ready market, often buttressed by government and donor funding, make this kind of publishing much more attractive than trade publishing, which is considered a risky undertaking. Yet, the market for trade publications is there, and with a good product well promoted, returns on investment are generous.

Before the publication of Michael Blundell's autobiography, *A Love Affair with the Sun*, the Kenyan market and the larger East African market was starved of good biographical works. Apart from Oginga Odinga's *Not Yet Uhuru* – published in 1967; and David Goldsworthy's *Tom Mboya: The Man Kenya Wanted to Forget* – published in 1982, there was no other local biographical work worthy of mention.

The avant-garde Henry Chakava took note of this gap and acquired Kenway Publications, a small company that focused on trade publications, and made it a subsidiary of EAEP. Under Kenway, he created a vibrant line of publishing, targeting biographical works, safari guides, comic books, cookery books and other such trade publications. Some of the well-known titles published by Kenway Publications include: Njenga Karume's autobiography, *Beyond Expectations: From Charcoal to Gold*; *Akokhan*, a comic book by Frank Odoi; and *On Safari in Kenya* by Michael Gore.

Kenway has now metamorphosed into a versatile avenue through which the group company, EAEP issues non-conventional, innovative and experimental products, thus taking care of a wide variety of reading tastes.

Umbrella book bodies and book awards

Henry Chakava is a firm believer in unity of purpose. He appreciates the value that accrues from the synergy between and among players in the publishing industry. It is this belief that saw him initiate the idea of a publishers' association in Kenya, culminating in the formation of the Kenya Publishers Association (KPA) way back in 1972. It is instructive to note that he had just been employed by Heinemann, a British-owned company, had not fully understood the politics of publishing, and the temptation to rest on his laurels was real, given the prestigious position at Heinemann.

KPA has grown from strength to strength and helped influence education and publishing policies in Kenya over the years. One of the landmark achievements of KPA was the liberalisation of the book industry in the 1990s, which saw an end to government monopoly in the supply of school textbooks. Previously, primary and secondary schools would only use government published titles as main course books, while those published by commercial publishers were taken as reference materials. Needless to mention, revenues were rather low, resulting in many publishers being under-capitalised and hence unable to make mid-term to long-term investments.

KPA is now recognised by the Ministry of Education, and involved in many policy decisions especially those relating to the Kenya Institute of Curriculum Development (KICD). It is also highly respected in the region and beyond, particularly because of the success of the Nairobi International Book Fair, which it organises every September. With regard to book awards, KPA helped set up the Jomo Kenyatta Prize for Literature in 1974, with the inaugural winner being *Kill Me Quick* by Meja Mwangi. KPA still manages the Prize, in collaboration with the Text Book Centre. In 2006, KPA launched yet another book prize, the Wahome Mutahi Literary Award.

Other book related bodies that Henry has helped to found are: National Book Development Council of Kenya (NBDCK); East African Book Development Association (EABDA); Children's Literature Association of Kenya (CLAK); Council for Promotion of Science Publications for

Children in Africa (CHISCA); African Publishers Network (APNET); African Books Collective (ABC) and the Zimbabwe International Book Fair (ZIBF).

Some of these bodies are still active today. NBDCK is a non-governmental and non-profit organisation that has been active in a number of ways. It has been organising local writing competitions, hence encouraging creative writing, discovering new talent especially among the youth and generally growing the list of fine works of art. It has also partnered with the Canadian Organisation for Development through Education (CODE) to run the prestigious Burt Award for African Literature. The Award targets unpublished manuscripts written for young adults. The prize money is generous, with the 1st Prize winner getting close to Kshs. 1,000,000 (9,000 Canadian Dollars).

ABC has its headquarters in Oxford, and was set up in 1989 to provide an avenue through which the European reading audience could access books published in Africa, more so trade publications. Currently, ABC has embraced the Print-on-Demand (POD) service, whereby member publishers in Africa send electronic versions for printing in small quantities depending on the number of copies ordered.

Henry Chakava the academic

In the early paragraphs of this Paper, we quoted Ngũgĩ wa Thiong'o where he predicted that if Henry Chakava "had chosen academic life, he would, in all likelihood, have turned out to be a leading professor in any academy". Ngũgĩ went ahead and acknowledged that:

> Even now (Henry Chakava) writes with great clarity on
> a wide range of subjects, particularly on the philosophy
> and political economy of his chosen field. (wa Thiong'o,
> 2006: 113)

The above is an apt description of the academic in Chakava the publisher. He has presented well researched papers in local, regional and international forums; is published in leading global journals including in the revered *Logos*; has contributed papers and done introductory essays in major books on publishing such as in Hans Zell's *Publishing, Books & Reading in Sub-Saharan Africa: A Critical Bibliography*; as well as published the well-known authority in publishing, *Publishing in Africa: One Man's Perspective*.

To share his vast knowledge and experience in publishing over the years, Henry has served as a Visiting Lecturer in Publishing at the Department of Publishing & Book Trade, Faculty of Information Sciences, Moi University in Kenya.

National and international honours

Henry Chakava's contribution to the body of knowledge in publishing is therefore enormous. And it has rightfully earned him many local and international awards and honours. On the regional and international scene, he is the recipient of an Honorary Doctorate from Oxford Brookes University in the UK in 2005, and the Prince Clause Award, bestowed upon him by the Dutch Government in 2006. In 2004, he was declared Winner of the inaugural Zimbabwe International Book Fair (ZIBF) Award for life-long contribution to the African Publishing Sector.

On 12th December 1994, the Kenyan Head of State decorated him with a Head of State Commendation (HSC) medal on the country's National Day Celebrations, for service to the nation. Twelve years later, he was again honoured by the Head of State by being decorated with the medal of Moran of the Burning Spear (MBS) on 12th December 2006.

In addition, the Government of Kenya has recognised his leadership skills and appointed him to serve state corporations in various capacities over the years. To this end, he has served as Chairman of the Kenya Institute of Administration (KIA); Chairman of the Kenya Copyright Board (KECOBO); Director, Tea Research Foundation of Kenya (TRFK), and Director, National Bank of Kenya (NBK).

Little wonder that in 2013, the Standard Media Group listed him among the top 50 Kenyans who have made the greatest contribution in 50 years of Independence in Kenya.

Conclusion

In his autobiography *In Pursuit of Publishing*, the Group Chairman of Heinemann, Alan Hill gives a fitting description of Henry Chakava:

> I was later to appoint ... able and resolute men in East Africa (Henry Chakava) and the Caribbean (Ian Randle). These were not the poodles sought after by multinational companies, but high-minded local citizens who were strong enough to stand on their own feet. (Hill, 1988: 209)

Alan Hill goes further to observe that:

> Henry himself had been educated in the true sense of the word; he had intellectual depth, a warm personality and true modesty. (Hill, 1988: 247)

And he was not disappointed by his choice:

> When (Henry) became Managing Director, I only told him one thing: 'Get this business onto a profitable basis, and you can publish whatever you like.' Henry has proved to be one of the most successful and respected publishers in Africa...if he has any time left over, he is always in demand to address symposia in various parts of the world. (Hill, 1988: 247)

But Allan Hill was describing the Henry Chakava of 1970s and 1980s. Sadly, he did not have the privilege of giving a value judgement of Henry of the new millennium – the indefatigable publisher who has traversed the length and breadth of the publishing terrain in Africa like a colossus. The versatile lover of the book who combines intellectual depth with modern commercial considerations. The affable communicator who has discovered, nurtured and developed many budding authors and editors. The visionary who confronts change and challenge with admirable flexibility. The technologically savvy septuagenarian on the run to embrace electronic publishing.

Indeed, the guru of publishing in Africa.

References

Chakava, Henry. 1996. *Publishing in Africa: One Man's Perspective*. Oxford: Bellagio Publishing Network.

Currey, James. 2008. *Africa Writes Back: The African Writers Series and the Launch of African Literature*. Oxford: James Currey.

Hill, Alan. 1988. *In Pursuit of Publishing*. London: John Murray Publishers John Murray Publishers and Heinemann.

wa Thiong'o, Ngugi. 2006. "The Courage of a Practical Visionary". In *Prince Claus Awards (2006)*, edited by Fariba de Bruin-Derakhshani and Barbara Murray. The Hague: Prince Claus Fund, 2006.

Wali, Obiajunwa. 1963. "The Dead End of African Literature", *Transition*, No. 10 (September, 1963): 13-16.

2

Henry Chakava: The Gory and Glory of African Language Publishing

By Ngũgĩ wa Thiong'o

I

I had just left Kamĩtĩ Maximum Security Prison, a prison graduate, on December 12, 1978, with a novel manuscript, written on toilet paper and in Gĩkũyũ, under the title: *Caitaani Mũtharabainĩ*. In the novel, I had played with the idea that it was not Christ who should have been executed on the Cross but the Devil himself. Jesus was an opponent of the Roman Imperialism, a proponent of the kingdom of the least among us, a visionary who saw the poor, among whom he walked, as inheriting the earth; the Devil was an ally of the Roman Imperialism and its oppressive practices, a self-serving criminal whose followers, exploiters of the poor, have as much chance of entering heaven as a camel through the eye of the needle.

Writing it had made me better able to cope with life in the solitary, almost as if, through stolen pen and stolen toilet paper, I was in daily combat against the forces that had incarcerated me. But a manuscript, no matter the conditions of its coming into being, was just an incomplete project until it reached the reader through a publisher. The publisher is the most crucial link between the writer and the reader. Would my publisher want to publish a Gĩkũyũ language novel?

Henry Chakava was then the head of Heinemann Kenya, a branch of a UK-based firm by the same name. In 1962 Heinemann had come up with the brilliant idea of an African Writers Series. Beginning with Chinua Achebe's *Things Fall Apart*, the list had turned African writing in English and European languages into a global phenomenon. But despite the name and the phenomenal growth, the AWS had never published anything in an African language. At best, they had created Europhone African Literature. Their branches, in Nigeria and Kenya, had followed suit. Up to my arrest and imprisonment I had faithfully followed that model: I was an Anglophone. My novels, *The River Between, Weep Not, Child, A Grain of Wheat* and *Petals of Blood*, were in the Europhone tradition.

I was in a dilemma! The Moi regime had just taken over the reigns of power from Jomo Kenyatta, who had passed on, literally three months before. The new regime had kept us 'illegally' in prison for those three months, for, by their own laws, the new leader was supposed to let us free on the death of President under whom I had been imprisoned without trial. He could retain us a day longer only under new detention orders. I was also aware that although it was Jomo Kenyatta who had imprisoned me, it was Daniel arap Moi, then Home Affairs Minister, who had signed the order for my imprisonment, a punishment for my having co-written the play, *Ngaahika Ndeenda,* and having it performed by Kamĩrĩthũ. So I knew that the new Moi regime was not any less hostile to my writing in an African language, my own in particular. And now I had come out of prison with yet another major work in Gĩkũyũ and was going to ask Henry Chakava to do something that Heinemann had never done before: bring out a novel in Gĩkũyũ, moreover, a language that had never had a novel in it. For those reasons, I was hesitant in approaching Chakava.

I should not have been. He never even raised any of my concerns as a problem. He was going to publish the novel; and he was going to give it the same kind of editorial resources that he had given to my Anglophone works. Indeed he saw this as probably the opening chapter in publishing in African languages. He had already shown his commitment to that direction by having all the major African writers at the time, translated into Kiswahili, against the grain of the original Europhone African Writers Series. The word went out: he was going to publish a novel that I had written on toilet paper at Kamĩtĩ Maximum Security Prison.

And then came the real test to his commitment: Chakava started getting anonymous telephone threats. A joke? A kind of April Foolishness? They became more intensified and shrill as the date approached. Their frequency and intensity did not slow Chakava. The threats mongers struck!

A week before the publication, assassins waited for him at the gate of his house in Lavington. They tried to drag him into the boot of their car. An approaching motorist foiled the plot. One of the attackers thought of finishing the job on the spot, or make an irrevocable damage and aimed a machete at Chakava's head, just about managed to move it, simultaneously raising his hand as a shield. The assassin cut off Chakava's finger. Then they fled the scene. The finger had to be re-attached.

Alarmed about his safety, the parent company, Heinemann, London, asked him to abandon the project. Though I was keen that the novel come out, I did not want Chakava to risk his life over a book. I let him know that whatever he decided to do, I would understand. He did not say yes or no, he just pressed ahead with the plans to issue the novel.

Clearly the failed abduction, and the near-loss of his finger, did not deter him. *Caitaani Mũtharabainĩ* (later translated into English as *Devil on the Cross)*, came out as scheduled, in 1981, alongside the play, *Ngaahika Ndeenda*.

It is in keeping with Chakava's character, that he hardly ever talks about this defiance and the courage. When twenty four years later, I invited him to give a lecture at the International Center for Writing and Translation at the University of California, Irvine on publishing in Africa languages, I had to coax him to talk about it. His attitude was simply that, he was a publisher, he had accepted the novel on its own merit as literary text, and not pretext to make an ideological statement or heroic stand. The threats had challenged his integrity as a publisher, and he stood by that integrity.

But that was not the end of the saga of the challenges he faced in publishing my Gĩkũyũ language works. Following my return home from prison, the Kamĩrĩthũ Community Education and Cultural Centre, planned to put up *Maitũ Njugĩra,* another of my Gĩkũyũ language drama, not at

Limuru, but at the Kenya National Theatre, a kind of the rural folk going to the city to claim their share of the national space. Chakava helped us book the theatre by paying, in advance, for all the days and times of our intended performance. Well, the attempt ended with the doors of the national theatre locked up, armed police patrolling the area, and others, in full riot gear, in line formation at the Central Police Station, ready to attack. This time, Chakava received no threats or any attempts on his life but he never recovered the money he had paid.

As if to ensure that group would never again pose challenges, the regime sent three truckloads of armed police to Kamĩrĩthũ and razed the original open-air stage to the ground. Theatre in the area was banned. Later 1982, in London, for the launch of the of English translation of *Devil on the Cross*, I learnt, that following the Kenya Air Force coup attempt, a 'red carpet' awaited me at the Jomo Kenyatta International Airport, on my return. I was forced into exile.

The obvious parallel between prison and exile is the fact of being forced away from home, and I reacted to both in a similar fashion. In prison I had written a Gĩkũyũ language novel; in exile, I wrote another in Gĩkũyũ in a completely English language environment. In *Matigari ma Njirũngi*, I further experimented with the narrative structures of oral tales, in theme and form. The theme of quest served me well because I was really challenging the culture of silence and fear prevailing in Kenya under the Moi regime. So what about a character who breaks that silence by asking questions to members of the different social classes? As for the form, what about the repetition, so common in oral tales? *Matigari* was to my exile what *Devil on the Cross* was to my prison. Writing them, under trying conditions, was my way of fighting back, and, frankly, bolstering my spirits. But once again came the question of publishing it.

It was obvious that it had to be done in Kenya. No English publisher would undertake to bring out a book in an African language. Even if there had been such a publisher, he would have to face the fact that there were hardly any Gĩkũyũ language reading public in Europe. He would have to be committed enough to print it in London and then export it to Kenya.

But repression in Kenya had intensified. My effigies were being burnt in the streets under the orders of the regime. Rumour-mongering, in private or public spaces, had become a crime. Dreaming about the possible death of the President, had long been criminalised. Once again I turned to Henry Chakava.

He brought it in Kenya in 1986 to an incredible reception by the reading public who soon started talking about the man Matigari, who was going round the country asking questions about Truth and Justice. In a short time, the fearless Matigari became a legend.

The government reaction was completely unexpected. Horrified by intelligence reports that there was a man going about the country asking such questions and spreading rumours at a time where rumour-mongering had been criminalised, the Moi regime set out to arrest Matigari. But on realising that he was just a fictional character, they went for the book itself. A police squad raided all the bookshops in the country and the publisher's warehouse where they 'arrested' all the copies of the book. Fortunately Chakava was not harmed.

The next act in the saga involved *Mũrogi wa Kagogo*, translated into English as *Wizard of the Crow*. It was another novel written in exile. I started it sometimes in 1996, almost ten years after *Matigari*. I was then Eric Maria Remarque Professor of Languages and also Professor of Comparative Literature and Performance Studies at New York University, Manhattan, but I lived in New Jersey. It was quite a task. The story took control of me, and I literally followed it, as it wandered all over the imaginary territory of Aburĩria. But it went beyond Aburĩria to Asia, and America, and even meandered in space, and it was a relief when about six years later, I had contained it into a book.

I have always joked that *Mũrogi wa Kagogo* has the unique quality of being the only novel in history ever written between two oranges. This is because I began writing it in Orange, New Jersey, a professor at New York University, and completed it in Orange County, California, where I moved in 2002 as Distinguished Professor of English and Comparative Literature and Director of the International Center for Writing and Translation

(ICWT), at the University of California, Irvine. It was at the ICWT that Henry Chakava gave a seminar on Publishing in African Languages. The political climate in the country had changed dramatically. The Moi dictatorship had been replaced by a kind of multiparty democracy, and this had ushered a new leader, Mwai Kĩbaki, my once Professor of Economics in my undergraduate days at Makerere of the colonial 1960s.

It was during his visit in Irvine that Chakava and I started talking about my return to Kenya. I would go back home, as the guest of the East African Educational Publishers, but we agreed that my return, whenever it happened, should climax with the launching of the new novel: *Mũrogi wa Kagogo*. Such a launch would be a fitting crown to my return home after 22 years in forced exile. When the moment came in 2004, Henry Chakava sought to organize the activities around the theme, 'Reviving the Spirit'. This was meant as a tribute to the renaissance spirit of the 1970s around the Department of Literature. It was a period of dynamic public lectures; the period when artists and writers exiled from Uganda, Malawi and South Africa congregated in Nairobi and contributed to that indefinable spirit embodied in the changes of the English Department into that of Literature following the great Nairobi debate. Despite the creeping authoritarianism, it was a decade of optimism, before dictatorship and darkness descended on the land, the culture of silence and fear reigned, and the renaissance light became a distant memory of what we could have become.

At a personal level, I was returning to a Kenya where my mother Wanjikũ and my first wife, Nyambura, had died without my being able to bury them. My other mothers and members of the extended family who had been part of my youth, had similarly passed on. 'Reviving the Spirit' was what drove my return home, after 22 years of exile. Along with me, was my wife Njeeri and my youngest children, Mũmbi and Thiong'o. Like me, Njeeri and the children were all looking forward to the launch of the novel they had seen me struggle with from 1996 in Orange, New Jersey to 2003, Orange County, California. Mũmbi and Thiong'o went to stay with their Aunt in Mang'u, but they would be back in Nairobi on the night of the launch. Well, a week before the launch of *Mũrogi wa Kagogo,* four armed gunmen broke into our hotel room, and savagely attacked my wife and I. Like Chakava in 1982, we barely escaped with our lives. Was this the 'red carpet' that I had been warned about way back in 1982?

We debated whether we should not flee our country once again, and back to my country of exile. Despite the trauma, Njeeri and I agreed that we would not let them drive us out of Kenya; that we would not give them satisfaction of flight; the launch of *Mũrogi wa Kagogo* would go on as scheduled.

Chakava and the publishers would have completely understood, had we decided to abandon the launch. Once we said yes, he became even more determined to see it through and ensure that the terror did not kill the spirit.

On looking back, there seems to have been a pattern, a conscious dogged attempt to prevent an African language literary enterprise. In 1982, a week before the launch of *Caitaani Mũtharabainĩ,* Chakava is attacked, loses his finger. In 1986, a few weeks after the publication of the next novel in Gĩkũyũ, Police raid Chakava's warehouse and 'arrest' *Matigari,* the book; and now, 2004, and a week before the launch of *Mũrogi wa Kagogo,* the third novel in Gĩkũyũ, my wife and I, barely escape with our lives!

Despite that pattern of violence, a pattern in some way reminiscent of a similar violence against African language newspapers, poems and songs during the 1950's State of Emergency, the modern Gĩkũyũ language novel was born. More important, Chakava launched a programme of publishing in African languages, other than Kiswahili. Chakava was the publishing mind behind the re-emergence of the still struggling African language publishing in post-colonial Kenya.

II

I have known Chakava for many years now; and our relationship has gone through many transformations. He was my student before he became my publisher. This was at the University of Nairobi where I taught between 1968 to 1969 and then 1972 to 1977. In my time, the department had changed from that which centred English National Literature – from Spencer to Spender, to use Abiola Irele's formulation – as the world, and hence its name, Department of English, to one which centred Africa in World Literature, and hence its new name, The Department of Literature.

Chakava was one of the many brilliant products of the latter: I remember him as the student who clocked A's in all his papers in all the subjects with all the teachers, and his First Class Degree was not a surprise. Chakava would thus have gone to become an outstanding Academic, writing books for others to read, but he chose the path of a publisher, ensuring that what others wrote reached the reader. In so doing he came to shape the production of knowledge in Kenya and East Africa, becoming a pioneer in book production by Africans for Africa. In the process he nurtured and lured many young talent into the industry; discovered many talented writers such as John Kariamiti.

His role as a pioneer has been recognised by the many awards he has won, including an Honorary Doctorate from Oxford Brookes University, UK. Henry Chakava became the leading publisher in the continent, a visionary and a model of an Africa centred publishing enterprise.

The Heinemann that Chakava joined soon after college, was in every way a branch of London. The majority of shareholders were London-based. It published texts already approved from London, often a local reprint of what had been done in London. So technically he was fulfilling a vision centred in the London of the parent company. In a few years, he had started initiating Kenya-based publishing ideas. And in the end, the majority of shareholders became increasingly Kenyan, finally buying out the British shareholders, and turning the Company into a wholly Kenyan enterprise. This was reflected in the change of name: from Heinemann Kenya it became the East African Educational Publishers (EAEP). In some ways, this is his legacy for Kenya and Africa: for in doing so he also created a model of how an Africa emerging from years of colonial and imperialist economic domination can develop. He created a model of national development. To understand the implications of the Chakava model, we have to put what he did in the context of colonial history and the colonial mode of production.

III

The first act and indeed the signal victory of the colonial capitalism was the destruction of the African artisan class. These were the workers in iron, copper and gold. These artisans made things with the raw materials around them. They made jewellery: copper rings for body decorations: leg, arm, neck and earrings. They were the minds and hands behind defence industry: they made spears, arrowheads, swords. They made cooking utensils: they sustained a textile industry with clothes out of leather, and the bark of trees. All industrial growth in all countries in the world were a continues development of that tradition and that class, always learning from previous experiences or through contact with innovations from friendly or enemy encounters. You build on a tradition not destroy it, as did colonial capitalism to the African genius and self-belief.

In short, colonialism disabled the class that used to make things for use and exchange, from the raw materials around them. Colonial domination killed that tradition of invention and manufacture, from the materials around us. They, the newcomers, encouraged the export of raw materials to their home origins where their own artisan class made things out of the same raw materials. They took our gold, copper, diamond, by force or trickery, and fueled their own inventions and manufacture. The genius of imperialism or colonial capitalism, was how they stole our raw materials or got them very cheaply, sometimes for the price of fake beads, and then sold what they had made out of our raw materials back to us but at higher price. That was how Africa was turned into an exporter of raw materials and an importer of the finished goods. This was basically the system that Africa inherited and even nationalised at independence.

The publishing industry followed the same neo-colonial route. Africans wrote, they exported what they wrote to European publishers, who processed the literary raw material, bound them into books, which they then sent back to African schools and colleges. In so doing they also controlled the content that shaped our minds. It was a cultural reflection of what was happening at the economic level as a whole. That was the prevailing practice when Chakava took over, and changed the foreign owned Heinemann Kenya into the Kenyan owned and run, East African Educational Publishers, not by forcible nationalisation, but by buying out the foreign shareholders.

Today, East African Educational Publishers, fully owned and run by Africans, is one of the largest publishing houses in Africa. Their pride and self-confidence were in full display during their recent celebration of fifty years since the publication of *Weep Not, Child*. But they were also celebrating their own fifty years of existence in Kenya and East Africa. Although Chakava has left the day-to-day work of the Company to his Managing Director and his team, he must have been very pleased to see how the company he had shaped, was covered so widely in all the Kenyan media, as a Kenyan institution. It was also symbolic that the fifty years of *Weep Not, Child*, the first novel by a Kenyan African, coincided with fifty years of the Company, and both, with fifty years of Kenya's independence.

While the original London-based African Writers Series have collapsed, the EAEP has been able to keep many of them alive in English and in translation, while also generating new writers, new titles, and mapping new directions in education and general publishing. Trusting Kenya and Africa as his starting point, he has come up with things, MADE IN AFRICA, which he can sell within Africa and outside Africa. Made in Kenya; Made in Africa: that should be the song we should be hearing across Africa.

That's why I call Chakava's, an alternative model to that which has been followed by African governments and policy makers. These policy makers have continued with the colonial model, where Africa rents her resources to the West: raw materials in exchange of finished goods made out of those very resources. When they are able to charge a few more dollars for their raw materials, when they invite foreign corporation to occasionally make things with the same resources within the continent and then sell them to the same continent, when they depend on foreign expertise, on a foreign 'NGOship', they call it development. Walter Rodney called it underdevelopment, or the development of underdevelopment.

The result of this development of underdevelopment, often championed by African governments as some kind of vision twenty thirty, or fifty or a hundred, is there for all to see. Africa is the biggest continent in the world, it could contain, within it all America, all Europe, China and India. It follows that Africa has the largest quantity of raw materials. And yet Africa is the poorest continent. Go to any capital in the Western world, look at every street, and you will not find a single Africna owned bank, an African owned trading company, an African owned industry. Indeed you will not find an Africa made brand of any vehicle in their streets.

It is the very opposite is the streets of any African capital. Banks, insurance companies, manufacturing enterprises, big hotel chains, oil drilling companies, mining companies, these and more are owned by foreign corporations even where they carry African names or fronted by African directors. We bend over backwards to make local conditions conducive to foreign investors: what about bending over backwards to create conditions for local enterprise? Foreign NGOs, actually funded by foreign governments, run our social services, in the process strengthening the mind of dependency, instead of that independence and self-reliance.

The Chakava model is the only one that can make Africa not just catch up with West, but surpass it. Africa should aim at nothing less than surpassing the exhausted West in everything: manufacture, invention, good governance, in the humanity's march to a better and more humane tomorrow.

IV

He was once my student whose papers I graded. Then he became my publisher who graded my manuscripts; but most important he became a friend who has stood by me in times of happiness and sorrow, even in those times when being seen with me was a dangerous thing.

Time and again, I have found refuge in Chakava's house. He and his wife and family never seemed to mind the fact that, in giving us refuge, they could be putting themselves in danger. Chakava has never tried to distance himself from me, as my publisher. Even when my effigies were being burnt everywhere orchestrated by the Moi regime, and even some Kenyan academics and former colleagues were denouncing me, and certainly distancing themselves from me and my work, Chakava never wavered as my publisher. He was even questioned as to whether the royalties due to me were the ones financing Ngũgĩ and his dissident activities abroad – dissidence being the state's translation of the fact that throughout my days of Exile, I worked with the London based Committee for the Release of Political Prisoners in Kenya, and literally went from capital to capital to explain and expose Moi's reign of terror.

Henry Chakava was never directly or indirectly involved in my political activities, unless ensuring that my family got their dues from royalties as per my request. But he never wavered in his professional relationship with me as my publisher. And while he subjected all my manuscripts to the normal process, first sending them out for reader's reports, never treating them any differently than those of a beginner in terms of the steps he took before accepting them, but once he accepted to publish he never wavered.

But in a more fundamental sense, Chakava has proved a great friend to the Kenyan and the larger Africa family. Nothing shows that friendship better than his having steered East African Educational Publishers from an enterprise beholden to the foreign into one beholden to Kenya and Africa. What heights could Africa not reach, were Africa to control her natural resources, made things with them, and then traded with others accordingly?

This calls for a mental revolution which starts with a belief in the capacity of African people to take control of their destiny instead of leaving it to foreign NGOism and Foreign Corporationism. Though still struggling from ferocious competition from the better funded foreign corporations, East Africa Educational Publishers, under Henry Chakava, were able to do it, connecting with the world but from their base in Kenya and Africa. Others can do it. And hopefully African states will come up with policies and a mind-set that encourages and supports a national innovative entrepreneurship that accepts and works from its base in Africa.

At 70, Henry Chakava can proudly say that he has played his part and shown the way.

3

The Triangle that Defined AWS: Nairobi – Ibadan – London

By James Currey

Chinua Achebe said in his Foreword to Alan Hill's autobiography, *In Pursuit of Publishing*:

> This is the story of how one visionary with a small band of colleagues who shared his enthusiasms built in half a century and practically from scratch the biggest educational publishing company in the Commonwealth. (Hill,1988 : ix)

Eight years later, in the Foreword to Henry Chakava's *Publishing in Africa: One Man's Perspective*, Chinua Achebe had this to say:

> One of Alan Hill's star pupils was Henry Chakava whom he snatched away from a very promising academic career in literature and philosophy and who is today one of the most pivotal indigenous publishers in Africa. (Chakava, 1996 : xiv)

On his part, Alan Hill the Group Chairman of Heinemann:

> Aig Higo started as our Nigerian Manager on 1 January 1965. He was just the sort of overseas manager I liked to appoint: somebody first rate but new to the game, rather than a second rate with lots of experience ... I was later to appoint similarly able and resolute men in East Africa (Henry Chakava) and the Caribbean (Ian Randle). (Hill, 1988 : 209)

Keith Sambrook started at Heinemann Educational Books (HEB) on 1 January 1963 and found on his desk the manuscript of Ngũgĩ's *Weep Not, Child*. He shared Alan Hill's enthusiasms and he made them work in Asia and Africa. They rapidly decided that this first novel should also appear in hardback to get reviews and library sales and international distribution. The first thirty titles Keith Sambrook and Chinua Achebe selected for the African Writers Series (AWS) began to shape the development of African literature. Keith Sambrook had worked in Ghana at the time of independence and had a deep sympathy with African aspirations.

Fortunately, Ngũgĩ's promise had been recognised by Chinua Achebe in 1962 at the Mbari conference at Makerere. However, by the time of the tenth anniversary of the African Writers Series in 1972, there were only a few books by East African writers. This was in marked contrast to West Africa where the team of Aig Higo and Chinua Achebe had made Heinemann the publisher of first choice against competition from other publishers in London and Nigeria.

In the three East African countries of Uganda, Tanzania and Kenya the Series was being marketed effectively from the Heinemann-Cassell sales office by Bob Markham and he had been introducing writers who were mostly from western and southern Africa to bookshops, universities and schools. In its second decade the Series was to flower with bold experiments from all over Africa.

Publishing editor in East Africa

Bob Markham and Keith Sambrook decided in about 1971 to find a young editor from East Africa to develop school textbooks and to encourage East African authors to come to the African Writers Series. David Hill, second son of Alan and Enid Hill, was sent out to set up an editorial department in the Nairobi office and to help select an East African editor.

Ngũgĩ had recommended Henry Chakava who was one of his outstanding students and had gone on to postgraduate studies. Bob Markham and David had decided before his interview that he was the man for the job, but unfortunately he interviewed badly. Professor Andy Gurr, Ngũgĩ and Taban lo Liyong thought that it would be a good idea if he was interviewed again outside the office. According to David Hill, Taban lo Liyong asked him, 'Did you give him a beer.' 'No' replied David Hill. 'Well then, what do you expect? See him again and give him a beer?' He walked away with the job. His imaginative contribution to building up the African Writers Series made Heinemann the publisher of first choice in East Africa, as it already was in West Africa. He was to make a vital contribution to the flowering of the Series in its second decade.

Many of the initiatives were now to come from Nairobi where Henry Chakava, in collaboration with writers such as Ngũgĩ, Okot p'Bitek and Taban lo Liyong, revealed on the printed page the influence of the oral tradition. At the same time, Henry Chakava with the help of editors such as Laban Erapu and Simon Gikandi, gave chances to a new generation of exceptional writers such as Meja Mwangi, Mwangi Ruheni and Rebeka Njau, who used the imported form of the novel to reveal the social realities of life in East Africa and the deep scars of Mau Mau.

An international triangle of choice

Chinua Achebe was to say in 1989:

> As for the African Writers Series, in 1962 I was invited to be its founding editor and I was to spend a considerable part of my literary energy in the following ten years wading through a torrent of good, bad and indifferent writing that seemed in some miraculous way to have been waiting behind the sluice gates for the trap to be released.

In 1971 I went to visit Chinua Achebe in his war blackened home at the University of Nigeria at Nsukka where the Nigerian Federal soldiers had torn the campus and its library apart. He handed over the manuscript of *Girls at War* (1972 AWS 100). He told me that he felt the time had come to hand the job as Editorial Adviser over to another writer. He and I agreed Ngũgĩ would be his natural successor and that he would help to increase the number of East African writers. Ngũgĩ immediately accepted but after six weeks, understandably, said that he feared that it would affect his writing energy and that therefore he should not take up the position.

Our initial reaction was disappointment as I have recorded in *Africa Writes Back*. However, Aig Higo, Alan Hill, Keith Sambrook and I, after discussing other possible candidates, took a positive decision to widen the African publishing input into the Series. It suddenly seemed so obvious. With the appointment of Henry Chakava, Heinemann now had an active editorial office in Nairobi. So we decided that we would replace the Editorial Adviser to the Series with a triangular system of consultation between publishing editors in Ibadan, London and Nairobi. Aig Higo kept us in touch with the active Nigerian literary scene with the help of Akin Thomas, his editorial director. An important result was that the two companies found new readers and editors, often of outstanding excellence. In Nairobi Simon Gikandi and Laban Erapu stood out.

Henry Chakava's own reports were incisive. I sent him the manuscript of the Zimbabwean Dambudzo Marechera's *The House of Hunger* (1978 AWS 207) with a plea for swift report. A university lecturer reacted against it saying that, 'These stories are damaging to a world bent on liberation.' Henry Chakava did not bother with this opinion and his own report concluded, 'If this is Marechera's first effort, then he has a great future as a writer.' Nobel Prize winner Doris Lessing said in a review, 'Marechera has in him the stuff and substance that go to make a great writer'.

The colleagues in Africa found new writers. They assessed scripts. They got reader's reports. They criticised the reports I sent from our advisers in Britain. What we learnt to avoid were committee choices. Nobody had a veto. If one of us supported a book strongly enough then it got published. What we needed were enthusiastic and considered voices. The rich outpouring of new writing fed on itself and gave people all over Africa the hope of publication. Manuscripts in various stages of clarity, even in handwriting, poured into the offices in Nairobi, Ibadan and London. A substantial proportion of the manuscripts were sent out for report by readers who were often novelists, playwrights and poets in their own right. It was a time of rapid expansion in African universities and the establishment of departments of literature provided a rich source of reports. The triangle tripled the range of advisers we could actively draw upon.

If the reports were modestly encouraging, copies of the manuscript were circulated to the two other companies in the triangle. Photocopying had only recently become widely available in all three offices, though it was still expensive. The cost of airmail post for manuscripts was high.

Of course most of the manuscripts had to be turned down, but there was an active policy of letting promising writers see reports although that could lead to disagreements. Writing is a lonely business and a plain rejection slip is dispiriting. This policy meant a heavy investment of time, administration, money and concern but it was reinvestment in future authors.

There was almost total agreement between the triangle of Nairobi, Ibadan and London over choosing novels and collections of short stories. Selection of books of poetry depended upon the support for the poet by individual advisers and editors. Plays depended on active producers who could visualise how the scripts could work on stage. Thus Heinemann built an international network of choice.

The potential in oral culture

From his earliest days in the job, Henry Chakava pushed forward efforts to handle oral culture within the written confines of the book. In 1973 he came to London for a six-month training period in the Charles Street office and lodged with the South African exile publisher and editor Ros de Lanerolle, whose name appears on so many reports about manuscripts for the AWS. He may have learnt from me. I certainly learnt from him. My ambition was to show the world that writers from Africa could use the imported form of the novel as inventively as the Irish, the Australians and other writers across the English-speaking world. He wanted to show that the African tradition of oral literature was just as important.

On that visit he began to engage with me on the need for a better representation of oral literature in the AWS through the medium of English. Writers in East Africa showed themselves to be even more inventive than writers in western and southern Africa who also had in various ways engaged with the central problem of how to handle ephemeral oral culture in print. In East Africa Keith Sambrook and I were already beginning to work with Taban lo Liyong who had contacted both East African Publishing House (EAPH) and Heinemann in 1967. We were soon to become his major publishers.

Okot p'Bitek was the most outstanding transformer of the oral tradition into English and his classic *Song of Lawino* had already been published by EAPH. In 1972 Okot p'Bitek approached the Heinemann Nairobi office to discuss a book *Horn of My Love* (1974 AWS 147) which was derived from the oral literature of northern Uganda. Okot p'Bitek's zesty approach showed how there was no need for work to be folksy. So Henry Chakava, with Ngũgĩ, Okot p'Bitek and Taban lo Liyong, had three adventurers in the oral tradition with whom to work.

There is a significant letter from Henry Chakava in which he took up my reservations about collections of folk tales with which to represent oral literature in the AWS:

> We have just received these folk tales from Okot p'Bitek. They are very well written indeed – most are shorter and more concentrated than Mvungi's stories in *Three Solid Stones* [stories from Tanzania]...
>
> I know that generally you are not very keen on folk tales in the AWS. On the other hand I have always insisted, oral literature is becoming more and more important here, and it is quite clear that from 1977 oral literature will form the basis for the teaching of literatures in secondary schools.
>
> It is not quite clear what the requirements for teaching oral literature will be. Last Friday we had a special meeting on oral literature. We decided to approach Mr. Henry Owuor-Anyumba who is the best man in this subject, to write a book tailored to the requirement of the new oral literature syllabus.

New East African writers in the AWS

Nairobi had become a vivacious intellectual and publishing centre by the early 1970s and work by Kenyan and Ugandan authors was appearing.

Books with an East African background were selling well and a popular general market, for African as well as imported books, was being added to the established school market. By now the Nairobi offices of British publishers were becoming competitive in their efforts to sign fiction writers for their lists. The active international marketing of the AWS was its biggest attraction; a writer could get a good sale in Africa but could be confident about also being heard throughout the English-speaking world.

Henry Chakava got off to a good start at Heinemann with the capture of Meja Mwangi. Heinemann's reputation for paying royalties on time and getting books published with some despatch certainly helped attract authors who had experienced the performance of other publishers in Nairobi. Meja Mwangi had had his first novel accepted by EAPH, but Henry Chakava and David Hill managed to get manuscripts from him and Heinemann published his second and third novels before EAPH had published his first one. *The Companion for African Literatures* says: 'Mwangi's work, more than any other Kenyan writer's, provides a representative view of the country as a whole, reflecting its main concerns and the direction of its evolution.' His themes were the underworld, the slums, the working class and the Mau Mau struggle.

Kill Me Quick (1973 AWS 143) was the socially concerned kind of novel which appealed to Ros de Lanerolle, who said (14 December 1972) 'Really quite a find!' *Carcase for Hounds* (1974 AWS 145) was an ambitious novel about the Mau Mau. Ngũgĩ was very interested and in three days produced a critical but constructive report (6 June 1972) with suggestions about rewriting the novel: 'Mwangi writes well. He has material for a good novel ... Action! Would he like to rewrite the novel?' David Hill wrote on 12 January 1973 to say that Meja Mwangi had responded effectively to Ngũgĩ and enclosing a report by Henry Chakava:

> This for me is the first novel which really penetrates the inside organisation and activities of the Mau Mau liberation forces, their strategy, and why the colonial government took so long to defeat the Movement. (Report by HC 12 January 1973)

Going Down River Road (1976 AWS 176) goes back to the world of *Kill Me Quick*. Akin Thomas in Ibadan sent a report by Michael Echeruo which showed clearly that he had been surprised by what he discovered about how authors were writing about the town life of Kenya in a way that was being little done in West Africa:

> ... an important and impressive novel. It is important for what it introduces into modern African fiction in narrative style and in the use of dialogue. It is important, too, for its subordination of the story line to theme, its concentration on locale and mood at the expense of history and plot. It is impressive for its steady candour; its ability to mix the putrid and the gentle not only in a character like Maria but even in a cot like Baby's. [This novel] will, of course, serve for a long time as the guide to Kenya night life (Pilsner, *Karara, Chang'aa* and all) and will be taken (vide Oculi) as an exposé of an aspect of the African scene which brings it much closer to the life-style of the African shanty towns, is meant to leave us wondering what East Africa is really like or going to be. (Report by Michael Echeruo 10 February 1975)

Henry Chakava and I were impressed by a rough manuscript, handwritten on both sides of the sheets of an exercise book, called *The Slums* (1981 AWS 241) by Thomas Akare. He speaks from the centre of the slums and his picture is hard, realistic and unsentimental. We sent positive reports to him and Henry encouraged him to work on it and to resubmit. He laboured on it and we regretted that, when he sent in the revised manuscript, although he had strengthened the plot, his writing had lost some of its vitality. We decided to go ahead and publish and not to endanger the book further by asking him to do yet more revision.

Rebeka Njau was Kenya's first female playwright and a pioneer in the literary representation of women. Her original manuscript 'Alone with the fig tree' had in 1964 won the prize in the East African prize novel competition. She worked on a revision of the earlier manuscript and gave it the new title of *Ripples in the Pool* (1978 AWS 203). It had originally been published by TransAfrica Press. Rebeka Njau asked Henry Chakava to include a subedited and reset edition in the AWS. Henry sent me the perceptive review which he had written of the original publication for a magazine in Nairobi.

> ...In addition to the superb characterization, is the author's use of symbolism. At the centre of these happenings, and possibly influencing them, if not remotely controlling them, is the sacred pool – mysterious, awe-inspiring, divined only by Muthee who watches over it, and endowed with a curse of death or blessing to whoever comes near it ... there is no doubt that this is one of the most outstanding novels to come out of East Africa in the recent past.

Mwangi Ruheni's first novel *What a Life!* when first published by Longman Kenya, was considered to mark a new trend in the Kenyan novel. Henry Chakava and David Hill managed to secure the rights for second title *The Future Leaders* (1973 AWS 139). He went back to Longman Kenya for his third novel but came back to Heinemann for *The Minister's Daughter* (1975 AWS 139). Newspaper reviewers in Britain had begun to realise that the orange covers of the AWS could well lead them to writing that was fresher and more socially concerned than many novels published in Britain. Jeremy Brooks, writing in 1975 in the esteemed *Observer* in London said:

> Mwangi Ruheni is a gentle humourist who extends the rare warmth of his understanding even to his wickedest characters. It is very difficult to pin down in a few words the exact nature of his originality. He has an odd knack of being able to imply the nature of the milieu through the cadences of his prose ... In this witty and engrossing book Mr Ruheni displays the true novelist's gift; he doesn't argue, he shows.

Henry Chakava at about the same time was considering *The Girl from Abroad* (1974 AWS 158) by Samuel Kahiga. Henry Chakava sent 'This superb little novel' to me on 16 August 1973. I acknowledged it guardedly saying that 'I think that it teeters on the edge of banality'. It was the professional novelist Richard Lister who was admiring: 'So it is a simple story of boy meets girl and loses her, and of course with a story as simple as that everything depends on how it is told. And Kahiga tells it superbly'. (26 October 1973).

Henry Chakava was on secondment to the London office at the time and so was able to personally argue for this book to be accepted at the Wednesday meeting of editors and directors. He gave a picture of the liveliness of the fiction market in Nairobi. He and I hoped that there would be new ways of marketing such a popular AWS title in Kenya. Unfortunately Bob Markham was reserved:

> I see no way of obtaining a special order ... [even] if you gave me a special price. I agree that this is the sort of book we should be able to get in to the popular market and by the time Kahiga's book is received we shall be engaged in promoting and selling our own Spear Books for the same market. (30 October 1973).

Reading for entertainment as well as education

Henry Chakava had been quick to persuade Bob Markham that there was a middle-brow popular market alongside the AWS for thrillers and romances in the well-established general book trade in East Africa. So Spear Books was started. It was initially thought that the books would not sell in the education market; the sales director Johnson Mugweru, when he saw nuns at a convent school picking up these titles up from the display in the common room, suggested that they might not be suitable for girls. The sisters laughed and said 'We don't mind what they read as long as they read.' Unfortunately Heinemann in Nigeria did not realise the sales potential for these middle-brow books. Macmillan in Nairobi published a rival popular series called Pacesetters which only sold moderately well in East Africa but took off in Nigeria and often outsold the high-brow titles in the AWS.

Henry Chakava would have been most pleased to publish two thrillers in Spear Books which Meja Mwangi had sold to Longman: I wrote:

> I quite understand the pressures on you to make ends meet. I must say that Henry and I were a little disappointed over the question of the two thrillers for Longman. I am not worried about you writing different books for different markets. That's fine. Many writers have done it. However, don't hesitate in future to consult Henry or myself about your needs. (JC to MM 6 May 1977)

The need for children's books

Spear Books showed how quickly Henry Chakava had realised that there were areas of literary publishing which had to be originated in Nairobi in response to needs in Africa. It was Chinua Achebe who had first made me realise the lack of African children's books. Soon after the Biafran war Chinua Achebe described to me how he had gone into the children's department of a London West End bookshop to find books for his daughter Chinelo. The shelves were full of beautiful books with coloured illustrations but without a brown child in sight. Henry Chakava wrote in 2015 a tribute to Chinua Achebe:

> I was invited in 1986 by the Zimbabwe International Book Fair Committee to chair the opening address at a conference on publishing for children where Achebe and Ngũgĩ were the principal guests ... At the end of the Harare conference I felt the need to start publishing children's books and asked Achebe if he would be willing to come to Nairobi to launch my project. Not only did he agree but he signed over four of his own children's books ... When he arrived in Nairobi in November 1988 we had around 20 new children's books, including his own.

A demand for drama

Drama was an area where the priorities were different for Kenya and London. Keith Sambrook and I had in 1967 established a policy for the AWS that we would publish plays in anthologies or in collections of plays by the one playwright. I did not favour publishing single scripts which were so thin that they got lost on bookshop shelves. When I had been publishing plays in the Three Crowns series at Oxford University Press it had proved difficult to sell single scripts even by writers like Wole Soyinka, J.P. Clark or Joe de Graft.

Henry Chakava saw a gap in the market. He told us how the Kenya schools drama festivals had become very popular and this provided a ready market for multiple sales of single playscripts. He wrote to Keith Sambrook and myself:

> What would be your views if we proposed starting a single play series with Heinemann (East Africa) imprint for which you would have an option to do an AWS edition for the rest of the world? Once started we would get all the local playwrights to publish with us as there is no active Drama series for East Africa (3 August 1976)

Keith Sambrook and I agreed to take *The Trial of Dedan Kimathi* for the AWS. I had written (8 December 1975):

> You should originate the publication because the play is going to have the greatest interest in East Africa. Keith and I feel that this may be the occasion for you to contribute your first title to the AWS.

Ngũgĩ and the question of language

Internationally, Ngũgĩ is famous as a novelist. In Kenya it was his plays, especially in Gĩkũyũ, which were to lead to his detention and ultimate exile. *The Trial of Dedan Kimathi* (1976 AWS 191) which he wrote with Mĩcere Mugo was born out of intense controversy. It made Ngũgĩ realise the power of drama in putting across his message that the new elite was running the country at the expense of the peasantry who had actually fought the liberation struggle.

Keith Sambrook had got Ngũgĩ established internationally with his first four novels. But where was the follow up novel? Many novelists have a struggle to produce their second novel. With Ngũgĩ he was having a struggle with the second phase of his life. Ngũgĩ wrote to Keith Sambrook (23 May 1964) about the new novel *Petals of Blood*: 'Hope alternates with despair.' It was eventually launched in 1977 by, Mwai Kibaki, then a cabinet Minister, at a very grand ceremony at the Nairobi City Hall. Henry Chakava had recently become Managing Director at about the age of thirty. Ngũgĩ with his great sense of drama said, in *Writers in Politics*:

> I would like to start by introducing to this audience the woman who has all along inspired me. The woman who in fact made me go to school to learn to read and write. I am referring to my mother, my peasant mother. (wa Thiong'o, 1981: 94)

A diminutive figure stood by him on the stage. He stated that in future his writing would be in Gĩkũyũ so that people like her would be able to understand his books. He had also invited the actors and builders of the Kamiriithu Centre for whom he had promised, with Ngũgĩ wa Mĩriĩ, the play *Ngaahika Ndeenda*.

As we listened to Mwai Kibaki that evening in July 1977, we could not foresee that members of the administration would be so frightened by Ngũgĩ's writing in Gĩkũyũ that on the very last day of that year he would be detained. He was released eleven months later clutching the script of his novel *Caitaani Mutharaba-ini* written on sheets of toilet paper. The University of Nairobi evaded giving Ngũgĩ his job back and so Henry gave him a desk in his office. It was not just politically and but also commercially brave. Books in Kenyan languages had previously only sold when adopted as set books for exams.

Henry Chakava and his team decided to publish play and novel together in Gĩkũyũ. Johnson Mugweru quietly took orders from bookshops across

Gĩkũyũ nation and got the printer to load books straight into the reps' cars to get the books distributed before any government sanctions were imposed. By the end of 1980, 15,000 copies of the novel and 13,000 of the play had been printed in three impressions.

Henry Chakava and we evolved a new rights relationship for the publication of translations of Ngũgĩ's novels into English. The Kenyan company would have exclusive rights in East Africa and open market rights in the rest of Africa; whichever company took the order would supply the books.

The political risks remained even after Ngũgĩ went into exile in the early 1980s. Alan Hill and Keith Sambrook gave Henry Chakava the right to decide what he should publish whatever the risks. We talked through the dangers with him. We had not imagined that he would suffer personal assault. He and his staff were in the frontline. It was their jobs which were at risk. I believe that the British directors of any other large educational company would have told Henry Chakava to stop publishing such politically sensitive material as it would endanger their school textbook publishing and jeopardise their sales and dividends.

My publishing relationship with Henry Chakava has been of central importance to me. It continued after Clare Currey and I set up James Currey Publishers in 1985. The first book we co-published was Ngũgĩ's *Decolonising the Mind* which is still a good seller after 30 years. Henry could freely talk to me about his struggles with the changing owners and managers of Heinemann before he set up East African Educational Publishers. The international triangle of consultation had disappeared. Henry Chakava ceased to be asked for his opinion about titles for inclusion in the African Writers Series.

References

Chakava, Henry. 1996. *Publishing in Africa: One Man's Perspective.* Oxford: Bellagio Publishing Network.

Clarke, Ayebia and James Currey, eds. *Chinua Achebe: Tributes and Reflections.* Oxfordshire: Ayebia Clarke Publishing, 2014.

Currey, James. 2008. *Africa Writes Back: The African Writers Series and the Launch of African Literature*. Oxford: James Currey.

Hill, Alan. 1988. *In pursuit of Publishing*. London: John Murray Publishers and Heinemann.

Killam, Douglas and Ruth Rowe, eds. 2000. *The Companion to African Literatures*. Oxford: James Currey.

wa Thiong'o, Ngũgĩ. 1981. *Writers in Politics*.

Publisher and Intellectual: The Work of Henry Chakava

By Simon Gikandi

Like the proverbial colossus, Dr Henry Chakava has been an indispensable figure in the politics and practice of publishing in East Africa since the 1970s. He is, of course, now celebrated for having taken over Heinemann Educational Books, one of the most influential publishing houses in East Africa, and for steering it from being an outpost of a global publishing house to a highly valued home product. In addition, Dr Chakava is known and remembered for having introduced East African authors to the African Writers Series (AWS) – without doubt the measure of literary arrival in the world of African letters. He is also admired for having chaperoned dissident writers, most notably Ngũgĩ wa Thiong'o, through the stormy waters of an unforgiving dictatorship in the 1980s. In international publishing circles, few African publishers have achieved the status of a global publisher like Dr Chakava. He is celebrated for his leadership of organisations of African publishers and writers, including the African Books Collective, and the Noma Award for Publishing in Africa. Lesser known perhaps is his role as an intellectual, a philosopher and a critic, a role that has earned him the respect of those of us who have known him for a long time. Dr Chakava may not have played any formal role in the university as an institution of knowledge production, but for those who are privy to his background, there is no doubt that he is a formidable thinker and that his intellectual background has informed his life as a publisher.

Few people know that Dr Chakava was an intellectual before he became a publisher, one of the pioneers of African literature and philosophy, a proud product of the University of Nairobi in that period – the late 1960s and most of the 1970s when it was considered to be a major institution of independent African thinking. He was a participant and witness to the revolutions that took place at the University of Nairobi during this period and an important pioneer in debates about the possibility of an African mode of knowledge, one liberated from the tutelage of colonialism and its institutions. He is, in my mind, the representative of a breed of Africans that has been fast disappearing – the publisher as an intellectual. At least this is one of the capacities in which I have known him, and it is the one I want to highlight on the occasion of his seventieth birthday. Since a *Festschrift* is by its very nature, an act of celebration, my reflections may be subjective but I hope they will locate Dr Chakava in the larger context of the politics of publishing in East Africa and their connection to the formation of writers and intellectuals. I at least hope that I will be able to explain his unique approach to publishing and his unmatched relationship to African writers and intellectuals.

I

I first heard of the name Henry Chakava sometimes in 1974 or 1975. I don't remember exactly how I heard about him, but I was studying for my 'A' level examinations at Kagumo High School in Nyeri County. I was also doing some writing on the side, mostly the kind of plays and poems that an ambitious schoolboy would produce in the back pages of his note book. I think I sent some of these poems to Heinemann Educational Books and the publishing manager, then Mr. Henry Chakava had sent me a rejection letter with some encouragement to continue writing. As it turned out, Mr. Jones Nzeki, the master of my school dormitory (Wilberforce House) and a beloved geography teacher who had shown some interest in my writing, had been a classmate of the said Dr. Chakava at the University of Nairobi. Like all ambitious writers, my driving ambition at the time was to finish high school and leave for the city where, I hoped, I would drink of the fountain of culture, of sweetness and light, and find a vocation as a journalist, an editor, or even university tutor.

As I prepared to leave the provinces for the city after my 'A' levels (in which I had achieved an unprecedented perfect scores in the three literature papers), I had a simple agenda: I would arrive at the University of Nairobi (Idi Amin had made Makerere out of bounds), walk around the great court, drink of the wisdom at its legendary fountain, and explore the stacks of books at the Gandhi Memorial Library; I would then meet the great professors and authors associated with the university, go to the National Theatre, and tour the publishing houses and meet eminent editors. Those were the things that defined the world for me – books, writers, and editors. I was an innocent skinny kid with a big brain and yearned for nothing more than what I imagined to be the immense cultural spaces of the university and the larger than life figures that populated them. I already had a list of the people I wanted to meet as soon as I arrived in the city: John Ruganda, Okot p'Bitek, Ngũgĩ wa Thiong'o, Micere Mugo, Jonathan Kariara, and, of course, Henry Chakava.

It is now easy, in the age of professionalisation and crude materialism to imagine the extent of the idealism – some might say innocence that was to take me to what has turned out to be a long friendship and mentorship with Henry Chakava. But in 1976 the nation was, in spite of its innumerable political and economic problems, still conceived as new, and idealism was an important part of my generation's desire to overcome the terror of a colonial past witnessed in childhood and what Frantz Fanon, whose works I discovered at the time, considered to be the pitfalls of national consciousness. By the time I arrived at the university, the narrative of liberation had atrophied. A year before, J. M. Kariuki, the last and perhaps only defender of the nationalist narrative that had shadowed and haunted my childhood, had been assassinated and his loss had been particularly felt in Nyeri County, our shared place of origin. Increasingly, and in the absence of a political opposition, the university seemed to be the only site of resistance to a nervous postcolonial elite.

When I left home for the 'campus', my father warned me, on the advice of some of our neighbours, to make sure that I didn't associate with those radicals at the university – communists, Marxists, and Maoists, who didn't seem to appreciate the gift of a good and largely free education.

An even larger worry among some of my more conservative neighbours was that I was moving into a field dominated by 'foreigners', people from what they called 'Western', a euphemism for certain Kenyan provinces bordering Uganda. I didn't have the courage or audacity to tell my worried neighbours and relatives that I wanted to go to the university so that I could come to spend more time with these 'foreigners' who shared my interests in language and literature. Forty years later, I can say without hesitation that it was these 'foreigners' who created the conditions for everything that I have done as an intellectual. They introduced me to the real character of a multicultural and cosmopolitan society and enlarged my *Bildung*. In fact, one of them, Dr Chakava, was to become central to my sentimental education.

Arriving at the university and the city was for me, as it has been for many writers and intellectuals, a journey to a certain kind of expectation. At least that is how I imagined it when I boarded a bus bound for Nairobi in October 1976. Some of my peers may have imagined the city as the site of post-adolescent discoveries – Delicious Bar, Florida Night Club and Odeon Cinema, but for me it was the point of entry into literary culture and I had no doubt that Dr Chakava was going to be an important part of this process.

Although I arrived in Nairobi only a few months after he had become the Managing Director of Heinemann Educational Books, Dr Chakava was still associated in my mind with the signature that had sent me a rejection letter with the encouragement to continue writing; but I had taken his words to heart, and in spite of protestations from certain members of my extended family, friends, and even teachers, I had made what was considered to be the foolish decision to read a thing called literature instead of going into the law, the most glamorous field for students in the arts. My late uncle was especially aggrieved by this decision because it had always been his hope that one day I would go into the law and chaperone a family land case against a colonial settler (C.C. No. 22/66 H. D. Poolman v. Kimenju Estate), one that had been going on since 1967. Yet, I chose this thing called literature as a vocation and a desire and those 'foreigners' from 'Western' were to play an important role in validating my ambitions.

Why literature? For one, this thing called literature seemed to be part of the intellectual adventure that would enhance African knowledge in a world experiencing the birth throes of what would later come to be known as globalisation. And, secondly, to be in literature in that period was to be thrust into the middle of an exciting nexus in which editors in publishing houses, journalists, writers, and university lecturers and their students were intimately connected. If Dr Chakava was to become one of my most important mentors, then, it was because he was the link between different sectors in what was then a thriving public sphere, one that provided refuge and support for young writers and critics, especially those who had decided to become writers and intellectuals instead of lawyers and accountants.

A remarkable aspect of this public sphere was not just that it brought people from different backgrounds together, as a proper public sphere should, but that it also established connections between what were supposed to be distinct institutions of cultural production. Indeed, the line between writers, critics, and editors was blurred. Products of Makerere, most notably Jonathan Kariara (at Oxford University Press) and Richard Ntiru (at East African Publishing House) continued to be active poets even as they worked as editors. The playwright John Ruganda had started his career at Oxford before moving to the University of Nairobi. Graduates of the Department of Literature at the University of Nairobi could be found in all cultural sectors: Wangethi Mwangi was starting off what became a distinguished career at Nation Newspapers where Wahome Mutahi would later join him as a columnist; John Sibi Okumu would become an influential figure in publishing; Ciugu Mwagiru was both a short story writer and a high school teacher; John Nottingham, who had moved from East African Publishing House to set up TransAfrica Press, provided advise to aspiring scribes from his small office at Kenwood House.

Among these figures, Dr Chakava stood out in the field of cultural production because Heinemann East Africa housed the imprint – the African Writers Series (AWS), that had come to be identified with African literature. In high school, I had decided that my ambition in life was to be a master of the canon of letters typified by the AWS and I would often use my pocket money to buy the little volumes in orange, hoping to acquire all of them in sequence. By the time I finished high school I had acquired the first thirteen volumes beginning with *Things Fall Apart* and ending with Mongo Beti's *Mission to Kala*. My most urgent task, however, was to enter what I imagined to be the inner sanctum in which authors were made and sanctified. Therefore, sometimes in November 1976 with the hesitant steps of a country boy trying to figure out the city, I made my way across University Avenue, down Koinange Street, Kenyatta Avenue, Wabera Street, until I got to International House on Mama Ngina Street. Having managed to smile my way past the security guard, I took the elevator to the ninth floor, entered the offices of Heinemann Education Books, and asked to speak to Henry Chakava. It was the beginning of a relationship that has lasted for over forty years.

But who was this Henry Chakava who had come to mean so much to me? It was a question that I was asked many times after the publication of my *Reading the African Novel*, my first work of literary criticism, which I dedicated to my parents and to Dr Chakava. Dedicating ones first book to parents or spouses is not unusual, but it is rare that we think of doing so for a publisher just performing his duties. But for me, Dr Chakava was more than a publisher; he was intellectually keen. Indeed, when I started working with him at Heinemann, first as a reviewer of manuscripts and later as an apprentice editor, what he taught me was not just the mechanics of publishing – the choice of typeface, solid copy editing and design, but the importance of extending one's intellectual interest into the books one was reviewing or editing. For Dr Chakava, publishing was not just a business defined by markets and regulation, but also an intellectual and creative enterprise. One of the habits he seemed to have adopted from legendary scholar publishers like William Heinemann and Alan Hill, was to take manuscripts home to read over the weekend and return to discuss them on Monday in an informal book forum at his office. I, too, picked up this habit and I recall with pleasure taking the manuscripts of Nurrudin Farah's *Sweet and Sour Milk* and Dambudzo Marechera's *Black Sunlight* to read in my dorm room at Tom Mboya Hall.

II

When I started reviewing manuscripts for Heinemann, African literature was going through a period of transition, so I found myself, at the tender age of 21, caught in a quiet debate about its future. In *Africa Writes Back,* James Currey has discussed many of these moments where my name and that of Dr Chakava were entwined in debates and disputes about the future of African writing. By turning to me, a very young undergraduate, as a sounding board, Dr Chakava was giving me a second education parallel to the one I was getting at the University of Nairobi. Our literary sensibilities were not always the same – Dr Chakava was more sympathetic to the adoption of oral forms than I was, but we shared a conviction that African writing had to go beyond the genre of the village novel that had given the AWS its identity and authority. Dr Chakava imagined the reformulation of African oral forms as one way out of the village novel; my preference was for the kind of postcolonial modernism I detected in the works of Marechera and Farah. As readers of Currey's book can tell, Heinemann's London office was not initially sympathetic to either an innovative orality or avant-garde, and it is not by accident that experimental African writing was published elsewhere before entering the AWS as a secondary market.

Although Dr Chakava has not spoken or written explicitly about the philosophy behind his works, one can find, hidden in his reflections on publishing in Africa, some important pointers to what made him make the decisions that he made as he tried to negotiate the demand of the market and the claims of literary culture. For example, 'In African Publishing', his 2008 preface to Hans Zell's *Publishing, Books, and Reading in Sub-Saharan Africa,* Dr Chakava set out to provide a retrospective survey on the state of African publishing for several decades marking the key points of transition and establishing the context in which the book trade flourished or floundered. But he was attuned to the political economy of publishing – of the shifts in markets and contexts, as he was to the production of texts and their communities of readers. He did not set out to establish a structural relationship between the politics of decolonisation and the form of African writing; but lying beneath his exploration of the features of the book industry in Africa, he identified the link between the political economy of publishing and the formal aspects of writing. He noted, for example, how the unprecedented production of fiction in Kenya in the late 1960s and 1970s was intimately connected to the existence of close to 30 academic journals that facilitated 'the much needed exchange of ideas' (Chakava, 1996: 27). He also noted how different forms of censorship in Kenya, including the abolition of literature as an autonomous subject of study in secondary schools stifled creativity.

More significantly, Dr Chakava called attention to how the exile of Ngũgĩ wa Thiong'o, the country's most prominent writer, came to affect both writers and readers:

> His absence from the Kenyan literary scene has seriously affected the country's creative atmosphere and has been a great disincentive to young writers. Readers of his books are stigmatized by the state, although none of the titles are officially banned,' (Chakava, 1996: 160).

Dr Chakava would go on to note how the state had managed to infiltrate and control the institution of the university, which had previously functioned as an incubator of writing, and how creativity was stifled through:

> curtailment of literary seminars, journals, and writers' workshops, and a general lack of facilities or incentives to promote and reward academic excellence. There is a lack of intellectual atmosphere and debate on the important issues of the day (Chakava, 1996: 160).

Dr Chakava's work as a publisher was informed by his profound understanding of the inherent connection between the institutions of interpretation, of book production and circulation, and evolving communities of readers. Even in the height of the publishing boom of the early 1970s, he understood the need to have publishers with the requisite capacity to handle materials submitted to them. For Dr Chakava, the absence of an adequate infrastructure for assessing works would appear to have been as important as government censorship or self-censorship in the production of creative writing:

> African publishing houses are swamped with works of fiction for which they do not have capacity to handle. The majority are rejected, either because they do not meet the required standards, but mostly because editors do not have the time and patience to advise authors on how to revise and rewrite to an acceptable level. In other words, Africa's fictional output, and its quality, could rise significantly if African writers were nurtured and guided in the art of writing and script presentation (Chakava, 2008: xxxix).

He also understood the significance of cultural capital in the making of authors, noting that at its peak, the Heinemann's AWS was an attraction and an incentive to African creative writers. The demise of AWS would give rise to local imprints, especially in Kenya, Nigeria, South Africa and Zimbabwe, but these would struggle 'to generate an Africa-wide appeal, and international recognition, such as the AWS enjoyed (Chakava, 2008: xxxix).

In regard to the culture of reading, Dr Chakava often noted that the problem here was not simply one of lower rates of literacy, or even the paucity of reading materials, but the proliferation of poor, or inappropriate, texts:

> There is a paucity of reading material at all levels and those available are, in some cases, badly written, lack variety, or are unattractively produced. Some imported books are culturally inappropriate and normally unavailable, or unaffordable... Well-intention adult literacy programs would often fail because of 'engagement and follow-up reading materials, (Chakava, 2008: xlvi, xlvii).

These insights into the culture of reading would become central to Dr Chakava's own innovations in publishing, many of which are described, in characteristic modesty, in *Publishing in Africa*. One such innovation was the, 'the Spear Books Series':

> When I realized that most of the AWS titles were fashioned for the classroom, I recommended to London, in 1973, that

they should start a new series for leisure reading –romance, adventure, crime, etc. – as we were constantly receiving manuscripts of this kind. The idea was debated at length and turned down in 1974, but I was allowed to start such a series locally if I wished. The first four titles were launched in 1975 to much critical acclaim. Sales wise, they were modestly successful, but I continued with the series, which now has more than thirty titles in print and contains some of our bestselling fiction. Macmillan picked up this idea and launched their 'Pacesetters', gave them their full technical and marketing backup, and achieved instant success. By launching their African Heartbeat Series twenty years later, Heinemann has finally come round to accepting my advice, which, had it been implanted then, would have made them the single source of African creative writing in all its diversity (Chakava, 1996: 52).

Here, we have a perfect example of Dr Chakava's ability to intervene in the culture of publishing and to alter the nature of creative writing: as an intellectual he understood the significance of narrowing the gap between high and low fiction; he understood how popular reading had the capacity to create new readers outside the school. As a publisher, he understood how this kind of literature could create markets outside the state educational bureaucracy.

There were, of course, instances in which Dr Chakava had to make political choices that were to affect the nature of African writing. In fact, for most of the second half of the 1970s and for most of the 1980s, Dr Chakava struggled to maintain a space for creative writing at a time when textbooks were what he described as 'the bread and butter of the Kenyan publishing industry,' (Chakava, 1996: 17). Although he didn't address the issue directly, Dr Chakava understood, perhaps more than any publisher in Kenya that this reliance on textbooks made him dependent on the interests of the state, and that imaginative writing was especially vulnerable to political interference because of this dependence. Writers who were out of favour with the government, most notably Ngũgĩ wa Thiong'o, couldn't have their works adopted as set books for schools, and the publishers of these authors were always at risk of having their general textbooks not adopted at all. As Ngũgĩ's friend and publisher, Dr Chakava was especially at risk from organs of the state whose loathing of the novelist was not a secret.

In retrospect, it could be said that Dr Chakava's major contribution to Kenyan literary culture was his relationship with Ngũgĩ wa Thiong'o. As he notes in a chapter in *Publishing in Africa*, this was a long relationship, one that started at the University of Nairobi at the beginning of the 1970s. Ngũgĩ had returned to the Department of Literature as one of the first African teachers of literature, and Dr Chakava was one of his first group of students. After graduating from the University with a first class degree in Literature and Philosophy, Dr Chakava took on the mantle of publishing Ngũgĩ in the local scene, and what had started as a relation of a tutor and his pupil had now become one of writer and publisher.

This was a relationship of mutual respect, one that would withstand the trials and tribulations of dictatorship, censorship, and the threat of economic ruin; but it was also a friendship built on a shared philosophy. Ngũgĩ was a major influence on Dr Chakava's philosophy on publishing and the politics of African knowledge:

> Ngũgĩ, who was then chairman of the Department of Literature at the University of Nairobi, was constantly reminding me of the need to 'localize' my publishing programme so as to better fulfil the need of the new curriculum. In response, I commissioned the first ever textbook of oral literature ... In addition, I started a series of oral literature studies in Kenya's major languages (Chakava, 1988 : 56).

Conversely, Dr Chakava was influential in the shape and structure of Ngũgĩ's later novels. The example of his critical intervention in the form of *Petals of Blood* is illuminating:

> To demonstrate how responsive Ngũgĩ is to criticism and how he uses it constructively, I once made a casual observation to the effect that Wanja's matatu journey from Nairobi to Ilmorog, which was then identifiably Limuru,

was too long and packed with too many incidents. I made a similar criticism of the delegation of workers and peasants from Ilmorog to Nairobi to meet their 'lost' MP, which I again felt was overstretched and loaded with content that seemed to come out of Ngũgĩ's mouth rather than that of his characters.

He responded to these criticisms by leaving all the incidents intact but 'moving' Ilmorog so that it was now much further away from Nairobi, and its new description had changed from the lush green of Limuru to a drier place resembling Nyandarua, Kinangop, or Lari, or somewhere deeper into the Rift Valley. As for Wanja and her matatu journey, he seems to have edited it out of the novel altogether, later to reuse it in a much more integrated and creative manner in the next work, *Devil on the Cross*, where Wanja becomes Wariinga. Quite frankly, I cannot tell you which edition of *Petals of Blood* is in print, having read several versions of that novel both in manuscript and in proof! (Chakava, 1988: 59)

Later, as Ngũgĩ was harassed at home and hounded into exile, Dr Chakava continued to provide him with material and moral support. More importantly, he protected Ngũgĩ's name from officially-sanctioned slander, which had made its way to the departments of literature at the university, and he ensured that his texts remained in circulation under the government's radar as it were.

III

One question remains to be answered: How did Dr Chakava's intellectual vision affect his practices as a publisher and, by implication, the form of African literature? Again, the relationship with Ngũgĩ holds the key to this answer. As is well known, in 1968 Ngũgĩ and two of his colleagues, Henry Owour-Anyumba and Taban lo Liyong presented a paper to the Arts

Faculty Board of the University of Nairobi, then part of the University of East Africa, calling for the abolition of the English Department. At the centre of this historic proposal was the institution of the oral tradition as an integral part of the imaginative experience in Africa. The trio argued that the study of oral tradition at the university could lead 'to a multi-disciplinary outlook: Literature, Music, Linguistics, Sociology, Anthropology, History, Psychology, Religion, Philosophy' and 'lead to fresh approaches by making it possible for the student to be familiar with art forms different in kind and historical development from Western literary forms'; they also insisted that the students' familiarity with oral literature 'could suggest new structures and techniques; and could foster attitudes of mind characterised by the willingness to experiment with new forms, so transcending 'fixed literary patterns' and what that implies — the preconceived ranking of art forms'. The proposal to adopt a new curriculum was passed and in 1969 Lo Liyong was asked to teach the first oral literature class at the University of Nairobi.

As the first teacher of the course, Lo Liyong was faced with two immediate challenges, which he described in his foreword to *Popular Culture of East Africa*: The first challenge was pragmatic – there was no textbook 'which covered most of the topics, and which was based on cultural materials from East Africa' (vi). The second challenge came from the students' own resistance to oral literature, whose relevance they were quick to question: 'Why are we being taught this now? Hasn't their time passed?' (vi). Lo Liyong's response to these challenges was novel. Instead of waiting for a text to be written in some remote future, he sent his students out into the field to research their own cultures and bring back oral literature as part of the living tradition, not something that had transcended by time. The result of this work was *Popular Culture of East Africa*, edited by Lo Liyong and published by Longman in 1972. The credit for the book, the first systematic collection of oral culture in East Africa, belonged to the students in this pioneering class whose names Lo Liyong listed. One of these he put as H. Chakava (Luyia, Maragoli).

It was a remarkable list of students and future literary scholars, university administrators, distinguished teachers, and editors. Later, as a university student, I had an opportunity to interact with members of this class and the one thing that stood out in their literary and historical work was their fundamental belief in the centrality of oral culture in the decolonisation of African knowledge. Dr Chakava pushed this commitment even further, publishing the first textbook on Oral Literature in East Africa, and fighting for the integration of orality into African creative writing. As James Currey recalls in *Africa Writes Back*, from his earliest days at Heinemann and during his leadership of the company, Dr Chakava 'pushed forward efforts to handle oral culture within the written confines of the book' insisting on 'the need for a better representation of oral literature through the medium of English' (Currey, 2008: 96).

I sensed this commitment during a conversation I had with Dr Chakava in London in the troubled 1980s. He had come to London for the launching of the English edition of Ngũgĩ's *Devil on the Cross* (I had edited the Gĩkũyũ edition for Heinemann before my departure for further studies in Scotland) and I had come down from Edinburgh, where I was a student, to see him. The subject inevitably turned to the recent linguistic turn in Ngũgĩ's writing. Dr. Chakava felt – and I agreed with him, that the disputes about the politics of language had detracted scholars of African Literature from what appeared to be the most radical transformation that had taken place in Ngũgĩ's writing, namely, the rediscovery of Gĩkũyũ oral culture. Later, meeting in another encounter in Boston in 1988, Dr Chakava expressed regret that he had not been able to publish the Gĩkũyũ version of *Matigari* in Kenya then because he considered the novel to be a model of what African literature should have been – an imaginative practice founded on oral expression. Like the works of the many writers who passed through his hands, Ngũgĩ's late style, marked by the indelible sign of orality, couldn't have happened without the quiet cunning of Dr Chakava. We all owe him a debt for this contribution to the world of African letters.

References

Chakava, H. 1996. *Publishing in Africa: One Man's Perspective*. Oxford: Bellagio Publishing Network.

_____. "African Publishing: From Ile-Ife, Nigeria to the Present [an introductory essay]." In *Publishing, Books, and Reading in Sub-Saharan Africa*: edited by Hans Zell. Lochcarron, Scotland: Hans Zell Publishing.

Currey, James. 2008. *Africa Writes Back: The African Writers Series and the Launch of African Literature*. Oxford: James Currey.

lo Liyong, Taban. 1972. *Popular Culture of East Africa: Oral Literature*. Nairobi: Longman Kenya.

wa Thiong'o, Ngugi (James Ngugi), Henry Owuor-Anyumba and Taban Lo Liyong. 1972. "On the Abolition of the English Department." *Homecoming: Essays on African Caribbean Literature, Culture, and Politics*, pp. 145-150, edited by James Ngugi. Westport: Lawrence Hill.

Zell, Hans, ed. 2008. *Publishing, Books, and Reading in Sub-Saharan Africa: A Critical Bibliography*. Lochcarron, Scotland: Hans Zell Publishing.

African Orature: Back to the Roots

An orature epic in prose poetry, commemorating Henry Miyinzi Chakava's 70th birthday

By Mĩcere Gĩthae Mũgo

When we salute daughters and sons of Africa who sheltered African Orature from the protracted drought of colonial education with its whitewashed myths of Africa as a *tabula rasa* and deserted burial ground: a vacant site devoid of history, culture and human rights …

When we celebrate daughters and sons of Africa who reclaimed her, the original home of all humankind, from fraudulent Western historical grave diggers and linked her with all global humanity while affirming her as a site of knowledge and gold mine of the spoken word…

When we commemorate the breed of African intelligentsia that survived the educational, religious, political and cultural containment of colonial and neo-colonial caging classrooms and their strangulating spider webs of lies hanging on tentacles of intellectual pontification …

When we conduct a roll call of African intellectuals who have transcended the lure of academic arrogance and elitist bluff riding on the back of postmodernist jargon and intellectual pugilism, we will find in their midst, a quiet, sober thinker, publisher, writer, trailblazer and innovator ...

Henry Miyinzi Chakava, son of Mama Lena Musimbi and Baba Joram Chakava born in 1946, at Vokoli village, Wondanga location, Sabatia Constituency, Vihiga County in April, the month of heavy rains in Kenya; the month that heralds the planting season, seasonally awaited all year by farmers and communities throughout the land and beyond ...

a season nature-bound to shower us with blessings of water; that year raining upon us a special blessing in human form: Henry Miyinzi Chakava, second born of Mama Lena and Baba Joram. Miyinzi, *mwana wa* Chakava: *Arrive well! Karibu! Umefika! Karibu tena!*

Abantu! Wananchi! Come, let us commemorate one of those who heeded Amilcar Cabral and his liberating call of 'return to the source' – a progressive return and not an indulgence in patriarchal nostalgia of cave culture; a progressive return and never a chauvinistic glorification of the past, nor a justification of retrogressive ethos. Lest we forget it, African orature has its progressive and backward moments. Come all, let us salute a son of the soil, rooted in the orature of his people, nurtured by the orateness of his maternal grandmother, the verbal artistry of his mother and his aunts, and the special story-telling skills of his sister in law.

Henry Miyinzi Chakava, child of orature, we salute you! We embrace you for standing firmly grounded on African soil! Henry Miyinzi wa Chakava, festive star of this festschrift script honorably named '*African Orature: Back to the Roots*'. Henry Miyinzi, quiet sober thinker, publisher, writer, trailblazer and innovator, we pronounce your name again and again and again in ululation of your birth; in celebration of this seventieth year of your life on earth!

You, who have philosophised that Orature enables fast, easy and spontaneous communication of educational, cultural, and entertainment content across communities and generations as it traverses arenas of life and living. You, who have theorised that Orature represents the codified history and wisdom of communities. You, who have applauded Orature as a unique, inexpensive, but effective resource for development in communities that thrive on orate-ness. You, who have embalmed the art of the spoken word in print, giving it wings across the globe.

Henry Miyinzi Chakava of the *asomi* class, your philosophical utterances echo those of a breed of scholars who came into being at the dawn of Africa's independence in the lands of sunrise: Kenya, mythically described as 'the abode of Gods'; Uganda, christened by Winston Churchill, 'Pearl of Africa' and Tanzania, sprawling beneath the lofty, majestic Kilimanjaro. You speak in tune with a breed of scholars who named themselves the East African School in the 1960s and 1970s: former Afro-Saxons who schooled themselves to 'return to the source.'

Abantu, let us embrace scholars of East Africa who refused to become the 'walking lies' of Frantz Fanon's rebuke and became Walter Rodney's 'guerilla intellectuals'. Let us salute scholars of East Africa, for learning to sit at the hearth as apprentices of Orature community artists learning to mine the precious jewels of neglected immemorial communal verbal art. *Wananchi*, let us praise scholars of the East African School for doing away with the 'self-willed amnesia' of Ama Ata Aidoo's chiding; for 'Decolonizing the Mind' with Ngũgĩ wa Thiong'o.

Let us toast scholars of the East African School for raising their voices to a crescendo four decades ago, urging the colonial *literati* to escape from the alienation of Western academia where they sat incarcerated in fortified corridors of elitist privilege; begging them to come 'back to the roots' and not to return to the village just to eat the last chicken in the run, as accused by Okello Oculi, while village children writhe from poverty, hunger and malnutrition.

Let us ululate for the East African School of scholars for climbing down mountains of privilege: Makerere hill, in Kampala, once upon a time the undisputed home of the roaming impala; Dar es Salaam University, inaccessible, in seclusion, sheltered by the rising beatific Pugu Hills! Nairobi, in Maasai, *Enkare Nyirobi*, 'the place of cool waters', but a colonial intellectual desert! Let us salute the universities of Makerere, Nairobi and Dar es Salaam for demystifying academia

High fives to the East African School of intellectuals for abandoning colonial *kasuku* culture; for surviving Okot p'Bitek's Lawino's proverbial forest of books that had smashed Ocol's vitals. At the University of Nairobi, within the first decade of independence, these men and women of letters had replaced self-rejection with a thirst for self-knowledge. They were 'no longer at ease' calling their academic home the Department of English. They no longer took pride in being Anglo-Saxon imitators who had passed a vote of no confidence in their Kenyan indigenous heritages. They had started feeling the judgment of history sitting on their shoulders, accusing them of having failed to enter critical historical moments and intervene, transformer-actively, to honor their human vocation: to wit, naming themselves and their people. They were done with being cogs in the machine of colonial brainwashing with the mission of producing more colonial academic *wanyapara* (overseers) through the continuing miseducation – hear Carter Woodson–of students under their charge. In self-realisation, they abolished the English Department where a British literary diet, with William Shakespeare at the center, had caused severe intellectual malnutrition for the learners since University of Nairobi came into being. They renamed their newly liberated zone: the Department of Literature. They placed African 'Oral Literature' at the core so that the center would hold, followed by African Literature and then the literature of the African Diaspora; closing the circle with literatures from the rest of the World – the English Colonial Mega Master Narrative included, but shorn of its imperialistic self-cloning mission.

Recognising the imperative of re-educating college and high school students from similar mis-education, the new academicians shook Shakespeare and decisively moved him to the periphery in high school and college syllabuses. They replaced him with African 'Oral Literature'; followed by written African Literature; Literature of the African Diaspora and then World Literature, where the Elizabethan man of letters belonged. Organising the learning process to make it move from the known to the unknown, with Orature as the center and pivot, they brought new scholars into being. Scholars rooted in self-knowledge emerged and steered the ship forward. Kenya's orate traditions took root, flowered and bloomed. Since then many scholars have come and gone – too many for us to count on fingers; too many of them for us to list in fear that we might forget some. Many of them have passed on and currently journey in the Hereafter where they have been reunited with myriads of others who went before them. To them we say: walk well in dignity throughout ancestral land and please intercede with our Maker to keep lighting our path in life on this side of existence. *Ashe! Afya Moyo!* You have gone well. Stay well! To those who live on, the poet says: 'May your well of creativity never dry up and may your verbal art create stunning beauty while affirming life by conjuring humanizing visions of justice, love, hope, *utu* and healing for all. *Ashe! Afya! Moyo!*'

In the sixties and seventies at the universities of Nairobi, Makerere and Dar es Salaam, the sun of culture and learning rose and shone with rejuvenating and stunning brilliance from the East of our lives, setting in the West of our colonially imposed perverted HIS-story. New sites of knowledge were gradually excavated: gender-liberated spaces teeming with ordinary peoples' HER/HIS-stories; revolutionary zones were carved out and here, newly found voices dared to utter forbidden terms such as 'feminism' engaging in bold, audacious talk-back on open platforms denouncing xenophobia and homophobia, and all phobias that limit human potential.

It was in these new sites of self-search, self-naming, renaming and collective consciousness that the term 'Orature' was born and popularised by Pio Zirimu and Austin Bukenya at the Colloquium of the Second Black World Festival of Arts and Culture in Lagos, Nigeria.

Oh, who was there at FESTAC 77 in Lagos, Nigeria? Who was there? Who witnessed the gathering of Black scholars, artists, cultural workers and other celebrants as they converged from all corners of Mother Africa, the African Diaspora and Global Africa: scholars, artists and cultural workers gathered under one roof to reclaim Mother Africa as a site of knowledge?

Count me among those witnesses of history and herstory who had sojourned with Kenya's national contingent to play

Woman in *The Trial of Dedan Kimathi*, Kenya's national entry and revolutionary drama shaped by African Orature, commemorating Field Marshal Dedan Kimathi, Kenya's historical hero and Orature's living legend. Count me among the fortunate ones who basked under the brilliance of Wole Soyinka's mind as he provocatively challenged the world's Black intelligentsia to shed off the weight of colonial history and the divisiveness of languages of conquest, and to henceforth actively cultivate Kiswahili as the lingua franca of Mother Africa.

I was there to listen to the eloquence of Pio Zirimu and Austin Bukenya of Makerere as they eruditely and compellingly made the case for 'Orature as a Skill and as a Tool for Africa's Development', advocating its primacy while proposing complementarity between the written and the spoken word, reminding us that since time immemorial Africa has always created and communicated through the twin heritages of the written and the orate, with Orature in preponderance and at the core, teaching us to understand our world first in order to understand the national, Pan-Africanist, international and transnational, celebrating universal peoplehood.

I was present as Zirimu and Bukenya of the East African School of intellectuals at Makerere University expounded the concepts of oracy, orature and literacy, describing oracy as skillfulness and expertise in the art of the spoken word by orate specialists who know how to speak, when to speak and when not to speak. I was there when they hailed orature the highest form of oracy. To wit, oracy in action, culminating in and consummating itself through performance. I was surely there when Zirimu and Bukenya indicted literature for its colonial supremacist criminality in banning and trying to strangle orature, which resisted and survived.

Possessed by the creative muse of the spoken word, fired by the imagination, fanned by the forceful winds of inventive daring, the Makerere School had birthed the term 'Orature,' arguing that since the written word was known as 'litera-ture,' the spoken word should henceforth be referred to as 'ora-ture.' The redundancy and heavy weight of the begging term 'Oral Literature' dropped off our shoulders. No longer would Western-schooled critics burden us and African Orature with definitions and comparisons that imperialistically judged our indigenous heritages by the yardstick of how accurately they fitted into Western literary notions of ethics and aesthetics. No longer would orature be viewed as the younger sibling of literature or as a child hanging onto the apron strings of Mother Writing. Orature was Orature! 'Orature' would henceforth be Orature: an independent, liberated, indigenous art form, with the freedom to define its ethics and aesthetics on/in its own terms; an alternative site of scholarship.

I was on the scene and voluntarily became an initiate of Orature, the imaginative quilt of the orate heritage. I was there, as I am here now, celebrating my double-consciousness as a literate and orate student of the word. The seed that was planted then has matured into a fully grown and flowering plant, yielding seeds that fill the granary with orateness to overflowing. We have harvested and harvested and harvested in short stories; poems; songs; epics; drama; proverbs; riddles and tongue-twisters; dance and music and song; in a panoramic display of ceremonial ritualistic and celebratory performed arts that commemorate birth, second birth, second-naming, initiation and marriage (while learning to critique imposed heterogeneity); arts that revere elders and not ageism; arts that celebrate empowering spirituality. Revolutionary art forms!

But as we feast in celebration of our harvest, we do well to pause and turn our heads back, Sankofa-like, and pay homage to our historical past, even as we engage the present while preparing to plant – Wangari Maathai-spirit-prone – the new communal seed for the future.

We say: ululation in commemoration of African orature: the songs and lullabies that we first encountered while still in our mothers' wombs before we knew how to cry; long before we learnt how to speak. Jubilation in celebration of artistic texts that were composed by our mothers as they carried us on their backs, we, feeling the warmth of their bodies, next to ours–cushioned by their flesh, massaged by contentment and security, rocked to sleep by the rhythm of their songs: lulled by soft lullabies inspired by daily life beats. Hurray for songs that praised us, urging us to carve our space in the world, reminding us to dream of becoming the singers of coming years, daring us to become agents of *African Orature: Back to the Roots!*

Ululation in commemoration of African Orature: stories about the human world; narratives teaching us how to navigate around positive and negative forces in life; tales about nature and the animal world; tales about secrets of the universe; stories of imaginative encounters with creatures from unknown worlds; tales of fright and tales of delight. Horrors about ugly ogres whose sadistic life-mission was to annihilate and swallow whole the world of humans. Stories about the he-elephant and a she-bird that entered the elephant through its anus, then ate up all his insides in revenge for his having killed her children. Stories about the hyena and the greed that made him split in the middle as he walked astride a forking path, trying to arrive at

two feasts simultaneously. Stories about the hare and the rabbit – the 'little people' of Wanjiku Mukabi Kabira's and

Kavetsa Adagala's theorising – whose razor-sharp intelligence was capable of out-witting any bully, however intimidating. Stories about cowards and brave ones. Stories about life and death. Stories about tomorrow and the day after; stories teaching us that the darkest night will always give way to the light of dawn. Stories that educate and humanise.

Ululation in celebration of African Orature: a labyrinth of myths that take us on a journey to rediscover our past while linking us with those who walked the earth before us while unveiling the worlds they inhabited – so different from ours. Myths, a lacework of creations that dare to sound the mysterious depths of the unknown in an attempt to render coherence, continuity, and yes, new meaning to life. Myths, instructive narratives that tell us who we are, how we are and how we came to be; value-laden stories that teach us what went right and what went wrong and why it went wrong. Compositions that unravel how problems came into the world; texts that wrestle with the elusive 'why' in life and demand that we adamantly learn to become weavers of new myths that interrogate false myths as Paulo Freire, Brazilian educator, cautions.

Ululation in celebration of African Orature: the memory, imagination, power and wisdom that ignite legends that connect us with deeds of the past; narratives that carry the his/herstory of our communities while re-capturing the grandeur of days gone by in commemoration of our collective achievements. His/hers/torical narratives that define the community's sheroes and heroes while shaming hyena-like cowards and censuring ogre-prone anti-people bullies

Ululation in celebration of African orature: action-packed epics in lofty poetic utterance, decorated with hyperbole and animated by supernatural drama playing in theaters under leopard skies; roaring thunder; blinding lightening; drowning rain; running mountains and smoking rivers. Spectacular dramas on the extraordinary births of s/heroes who tower over their communities in symbolism of their infinite potential. Action-packed historical accounts of emperors like *Sundiata,* son of Sogolon, the Buffalo woman. Sundiata, unmatched leader who dramatically entered the world stage and transformed ancient Mali into a thriving empire. Ceremonial spectacles such as the *Ozidi Saga,* ritualistically enacted in an open arena for seven days every year as the Ijaw people proudly salute Ozidi, their historical communal hero. Orature creations in the form of the legend of Mwindo, son of Shemwindo, mythologized hero among the Banyanga of the Congo; superhuman being with a body forged in heaven and clothed in iron. Orature wonders about seers of Mũgo wa Kĩbirũ's fame who foretold the invasion by colonials.

Ululation in celebration of African orature … proverbs that Chinua Achebe once called the palm-oil with which the Igbo eat words: deep wells of tested, lived wisdom … riddles that tease the imagination; test reason; exhibit wit and stretch the limits of ordinary conversation … tongue twisters that sharpen focus; stimulate memory; complicate oracy and teach the tongue to say the unsayable by pushing speech beyond the boundaries of familiarity … family trees that remind the young that to survive, the branches of a tree must connect to a sturdy trunk supported by strong roots that reach deep, deep, deep into the soil. Communal texts that philosophise: 'I am because you are and since you are, therefore I am,' hear John Mbiti, in affirmation of *Utu;* Wise sayings that declare: 'I am well if you too are well,' listen to the Shona people's greeting.

Ululation in celebration of African orature that has flowered since time immemorial, that we have harvested and stored away in the granaries of books and films, in preservation of our verbal cannon. Special ululation in praise of enslaved people's narratives, known as *Slave Narratives* that remind us the Trans-African Slave Trade never succeeded in capturing the souls of enslaved Africans; stories that bear testimony to resistance and struggle as the captured foughtslave raiders; as the enslaved suffocated in the baracoons; as Africans were chained together in crowded ships braving the terror of the Middle Passage; as 'slaves' sweat on the plantations defying hard labor and the lashes of the overseer's whips, resisting; as the enslaved escaped and created liberated zones that they named *quilombos*, as they established *maroon* communities and carved mazes of escape routes and corridors across the Americas, culminating in the Underground Railroad through which the enslaved walked to freedom. Stories of stoic resistance; songs of rebellion; poems of sorrow and hope; dramas of tragic pain, juxtaposed with epics of self-assertion and ultimate victory, proving that no enslaver, however powerful, can chain oppressed people's imagination. Hail to these Orature creations that became literature!

And now in ululation of African Orature, we celebrate you, Henry Miyinzi, *mwana wa* Chakava; Henry Chakava, innovative publisher and trailblazer of orate and written texts, for preserving spoken texts in print. We salute you, High school Orature progeny of Mwalimu Henry Owuor-Anyumba; Chakava, University student of Professor Taban lo Liyong. Miyinzi wa Chakava, childhood initiate of the spoken word at the feet of Vokoli Village professors of verbal art, we greet you at seventy years of age. We greet you, orate Elder. We greet you, nationally-decorated Moran of the Burning Spear! We greet you Star of this festschrift script named *'African Orature: Back to the Roots,'* a garland of verbal art for you, Elder at seventy!

Henry Miyinzi wa Chakava, celebrated 'Father of Kenyan Publishing', accept this garland!

6

The Dominance of the Textbook in African Publishing

By Ayo Ojeniyi

Introduction

The three major categories of books are: general books, specialist books and educational textbooks. Publishers embark on one or all of these categories depending on their socio-political and economic environment as well as their publishing policy. Their capacity and vision also play a role in determining the category of books that they publish. It is, however, evident that the availability of large consumer markets for books and profitability go a long way in influencing the dominance of textbook publishing in Africa.

Book publishing in Africa came about through the export market drive and activities of well-established multinational publishing outfits in Europe coming to Africa to set up sales outlets. Following independence in many African countries and the expansion of educational opportunities through increase in the number of primary and secondary schools, these multinational publishing companies transformed their sales outlets to full-scale publishing outfits to meet the local demands for textbooks that take into consideration the peculiar cultures, traditions and history of these former colonies. According to Obanya (2005:247):

> In the early days, most of today's big publishing companies were sales outlets of multinationals of the same name.

In essence, the initial and primary concern was the production of educational needs of the newly-independent states in Africa. These publishing houses became the first generation of book publishing companies in Africa from which new generation of indigenous publishing companies learnt the art of book publishing. It is against this background and other social-economic and political factors that we shall, in this paper, be examining the issue of dominance of the textbook in African publishing, using some African countries as case studies.

History and development of African publishing

The term 'African Publishing' simply refers to the activities or business of producing books, magazines, journals and other instructional materials for public distribution by publishers based in Africa. Usually, these materials are tailored to meet the special needs of the various peoples of the continent.

Nigeria

In Nigeria, early publishing efforts were associated with the activities of missionary printing presses. As aptly observed by Adelekan (2005: 186):

> Most of the active Christian missions had by the mid-19th century established presses in Africa for the purpose of printing religious literatures. However, over time their activities extended beyond the narrow areas of interest to embrace general publishing with evangelical objectives.

Christian missionaries in Africa played an important role in the development of Western education and inculcation of Western culture. The introduction of Western education in African countries and the early publishing activities served as precursors to the eventual arrival of the more organised European commercial houses to take on the task of producing books on a wider scale.

The foundation of publishing was laid in Nigeria in 1859 when *Iwe Irohin Yoruba* was printed in Abeokuta by the missionaries of the Church Missionary Society (CMS) led by the Reverend Henry Townsend.

Similarly, around the same period, a printing outfit had been established in Calabar by 1846. This was some 70 years before the birth of Nigeria in 1914 and some 500 years after John Gutenberg first printed the Bible. In fact, about 50 newspapers were founded between 1859 and 1940 including the *Daily Times*, which was first published in 1926. Newspapers, political and religious literature constituted the bulk of publishing activities in Nigeria for nearly a century until 1949, when Oxford University Press established a sales outlet in Nigeria. Even then, no local book publishing took place until around 1956 when a few indigenous authors-cum-printers wrote and printed their *Questions and Answers* pamphlets, etc., which they distributed themselves. They took advantage of the expansion in education (i.e. free primary education and establishment of modern schools) in the old Western Region to engage in some form of publishing business. The Onitsha Market Literature also flourished around this period.

Other major publishing houses which established their presence in Nigeria in the late 50s and early 60s included Heinemann, Longman, Thomas Nelson, Macmillan, Cambridge University Press, London University Press and Evans. About the same period, indigenous publishers such as Onibonoje, Ilesanmi, Aromolaran, Tabansi, etc., also established very strong presence in the educational market. The *New Nigerian* newspaper started to produce small pamphlets for the purpose of mass literacy. Regional Ministries of Education also published mass literacy books and established Adult Education classes in almost every village. Although there are today about 200 registered member-firms in the Nigerian Publishers Association, it is estimated that over 750 publishers exist in Nigeria. This number is very small in the light of the needs and population of Nigeria, estimated to be about 180 million, especially with the massive expansion at all levels of education in Nigeria since 1955.

Ghana

The story of Ghana, another Anglophone West African country, is almost the same as that of Nigeria. The publishing industry in Ghana took its root from the missionary activities of the mid-19th century when Basel and Bremen missionaries published Twi spelling and reading books. About the same period, the Methodist Mission established a printing press in Cape Coast. The expansion in education in the fifties and sixties culminated in the establishment of the Ghana Publishing Corporation in 1965. Its establishment served as impetus for the emergence of indigenous publishing houses thereafter. In both countries, these early efforts were aimed essentially at training clergymen for missionary activities and clerks for the British trading companies (Ojeniyi 2004).

Kenya

Unlike Nigeria and Ghana, the history and development of publishing in Kenya in particular and East Africa in general could be traced to certain individuals who met in Dar es Salaam in 1925. This led to the establishment of the East African Literature Bureau (EALB) in 1933. Thirty years later, the East African Publishing House was founded in Kenya and it was closely followed by prominent British publishing firms which established their presence in the country. For example, Longman established a sales outlet in 1950, Oxford University Press (OUP) in 1952, and Thomas Nelson, Evans Brothers and Heinemann in 1965. These publishers concentrated on publishing primary and secondary textbooks (Ikoja-Odongo, 2004: 70-72).

Historically, most of the first generation companies which currently engage in publishing in Africa were offshoots of multinational publishers that came to take advantage of the boom in education and the attendant textbook demand following the independence of countries in Africa. In Nigeria for instance, apart from these multinational publishing companies, indigenous and equally successful publishing companies later sprang up to compete for space with their older and more experienced counterparts. Examples include Spectrum Books, Literamed Publications, and Africana-First Publishers, to mention just a few.

The issue of dominance of textbook publishing

Uwalaka, as cited in Tiamiyu (2005:143) comments on the performance of the Nigerian book industry between 1975 and 1995, observing that,

> Educational publishing dominated the industry, accounting for 80% and 77% of publishers' total output

and booksellers' sales, this contrasted with percentages of less than 15% in US and UK in 1992'. In the same vein, Nwankwo (2005:173) also asserted that, 'Publishing in Africa is heavily dependent on the bread-and-butter textbook market.

In many countries, textbook publishing is the engine of the book publishing industry. Statistics provided by the World Intellectual Property Organisation (WIPO, 2001) suggests that one out of every three books published world-wide is a textbook. The preponderance of textbooks or educational titles in African publishing is therefore not unusual. The reasons for this are historical and economic. Following the education explosion that occurred between 1960-1970, educational publishing became the most lucrative and economically viable line of publishing business in Africa. However, according to Ogunleye (2005:92),

> The concept of educational books has ceased to be confined only to school textbooks and paperbacks, which are a sub-division of general books that are now extensively used as supplementary materials in teaching especially English.

In this sense, the famous African Writers Series (AWS) conceived by Heinemann UK and popularised by Heinemann Educational Books, Nigeria and its sister East African company in Kenya can be regarded as educational books. Many of the titles under this series were used and are still in use as supplementary readers for examination purposes. The 'immortal' *Things Fall Apart* and others fall into this category of school books used for teaching and examination purposes. Some of the issues relating to educational publishing, according to Ogunleye (2005: 93-94), include the following:

1. 'The market for educational books is easily identifiable and wide and allows for large print-runs which guarantee low production cost and low selling prices.

2. The prices of educational books are not usually printed on the cover. Educational book potentials attract the lowest trade discount in the industry because of their market potentials.

3. Mass-marketing approach in both promotion and distribution is ideal for educational books to ensure massive publicity in the mass media and wide distribution in all distribution channels.

4. The distribution channels include available bookshops, the authors themselves, bookstalls in urban and village markets and even book displays at pavements of mosques and churches during services. Many traders veer into selling textbooks during the book seasons.

5. There is need for generous use of sample copies in order to stimulate the adoption of books. Any marketer who is miserly with sample copies of educational books does so at his own peril.

6. Another lucrative subsidiary of educational books is the so-called 'Examination-Aids', which include 'Questions and Answers' books. These are 'self-selling' as students consider them as tools that boost their exams preparedness.

7. It is sometimes alleged that the educational book review and adoption processes of the Ministries of Education are political and favour particular publishers, irrespective of the quality of the books adopted.

8. There is fierce competition among educational book publishers and cases of piracy and plagiarism are rampant. Piracy, which is a 'thriving business' for intellectual robbers but a scourge to publishers, has gone beyond the age-long reasons of high price, and unavailability and scarcity of educational books despite a huge demand for them. It is usually perpetrated by independent traders who desire to make fast profits during the book seasons.

9. The seasonal nature of the business of educational books makes educational publishing rather precarious. Once the season is over, the sales slump to trickles and such publishers usually have cash-flow problems. Similarly, because of competition, one publisher's books are usually adopted as instructional texts only for a short period, say, three to five years at the end of which they will be replaced by another publisher's books, thus, alternating the years of prosperity among the publishers.

10. Federal and State Governments in Nigeria have often intervened in the distribution of educational books through bulk book purchases for distribution to public schools. But some of these governments have sometimes defaulted in paying for such books, thus compounding the financial problems of such publishers.

It must, however, be stressed that this issue of dominance of the textbook in publishing in Africa is limited to pre-primary, primary and secondary school textbooks. The story is different with regard to tertiary institutions where textbooks in use are mostly imported, written and published by foreign authors and publishers respectively. And yet, the importance of textbooks, especially those authored and published in Africa, cannot be over-emphasised. Ferrel and Heyumann (1988) and Philip Altbach and S. Gopinathan (1988) harped on the importance and relevance of textbooks as being central to the curriculum in higher education, as well as being integral to education at the primary and secondary school levels. They also stressed that textbooks are universal and influential as they remain the key element of the educational experience of students.

In many Nigerian tertiary institutions, because the imported titles are expensive and very hard to come by, students resort to photocopying of materials or rely mainly on lecturers' notes and hand-outs. For example, in Nigeria, Adesina (1990) observes four basic anomalies that characterise the book situation in tertiary institutions as follows:

1. Book famine or book crisis, a reference to the general book scarcity and the prohibitive cost of books when available.

2. Acute shortage of essential books and non-availability of some of them particularly in the professional areas such as Medicine, Law, Business Administration, Architecture, Pharmacy, Engineering, etc.

3. Unfavourable impact of foreign input and influence, which came as a result of the massive importation of books in the 70s and 80s.

4. The lack of relevance of available books to the Nigerian environment.

Provision and distribution of textbooks in Africa

The development of education, literacy, national culture and dissemination of knowledge is a basic element in the knowledge acquisition process of any nation. The publishing industry, whose primary role is to produce and distribute books, is the engine of that process. Unfortunately, only a few African political leaders understand that books are the basic tools of education, which in turn, are the basic investment for socio-economic and technological development.

The importance of books and their relevance to national development have been excellently captured in the words of Anthony Read, former Director of the United Kingdom's, Book Development Council, as follows:

> Books, especially textbooks, are perhaps the most vital element in educational programmes of developing countries. Books have the economy, the ease of handling, the ease of access and the ability to be shared which make them by far the most cost effective tool for development. They provide essential knowledge and knowhow, they supplement the teacher and make self-help possible; they are essential to literacy and understanding science (Read 1980: 77-78).

The need for textbook development as a strategy for educational growth has continued to generate concern among stakeholders in the educational sector and also among governments and non-governmental agencies. This concern arises from the fact that Africa is contending with the dearth of appropriate and relevant textbooks to conform with the ever-changing educational needs and dynamics of the societies.

As part of the efforts to arrest this trend, a conference was held at the University of Ile-Ife, Nigeria, in 1973, to look at publishing in Africa in the 1970s and beyond. The problems confronting African publishers were identified and solutions proffered. Ten years later, in 1983, when the World Congress on Books was held in Lagos, most of the problems identified in 1973 still remained – and they persist even today. The inconsistent fiscal and educational policies, weak publishing infrastructures, the heavy dependence on government patronage and near total control of education by African governments have negative impact on African publishing at various points. It is against this background that collaboration among African Ministers of Education should be encouraged to support the development of coherent national book policies that adequately cover equitable and transparent procedures for book production, selections, procurements and distribution. Let us now examine the issues region by region.

West Africa

Nigeria

As part of the control measures to ensure qualitative education, especially at the primary and secondary school levels, State Ministries of Education, especially those in Southern Nigeria, call for the review of textbooks every six years at the primary school level, and every three years at the Junior Secondary School (JSS) and Senior Secondary School (SSS) levels. This is with a view to streamlining books to be adopted and used in schools. Publishers are expected to submit four or even six copies of each their titles and pay certain amount for the review exercise. The Nigerian Publishers Association (NPA) has been able to peg the review fee to ₦5000 (equivalent of 25 US dollars), even though some states do ask for something higher. Furthermore, some state governments sometimes buy bulk copies of relevant textbooks for their schools. The problem is that payment for the books is very slow. Some publishers are still being owed huge sums of money for books supplied some thirty years ago!

In the mid-70s, some state governments in South-Eastern Nigeria and certain subject associations such as the Science Teachers Association of Nigeria (STAN) had joint publishing ventures with selected publishers to produce and market course books in core primary school and JSS subjects, using examples from the immediate environment of the children.

It was not until the launch of the Universal Primary Education (UPE) scheme in 1976 and later, the Universal Basic Education (UBE) Programme in 1999, that the Federal Government of Nigeria started to intervene in the supply of educational materials to schools. Another involvement of the Federal Government was the licensing of JSS titles, 'under duress', to the Federal Ministry of Education's Books Acceleration Programme in 1992. The films of books to be produced by litho printing were given to pre-selected printers while the publishers whose books were involved were rewarded with token licence fees and royalties. The scheme was a huge disaster as production quality was jettisoned (i.e. four-colour books were produced as 2-colour) and the costs of printing turned out to be higher than the published prices of the books!

The Nigerian Educational Research and Development Council (NERDC), a parastatal of the Federal Ministry of Education, also came up with a Tertiary Book Acceleration Project in the 90s. This involved the Council soliciting for academic works from university dons. The manuscripts were originated to camera-ready artwork by NERDC and publishers were commissioned to produce bound copies. Unfortunately, the project really never took off.

The United States Information Service (USIS), in an attempt to introduce American books to tertiary institutions in Nigeria, similarly launched its Tertiary Books Reprint Programme about the same period. USIS was responsible for the off-shore payment of licence fees and royalties and, in addition, guaranteed the bulk-purchase of almost half of the print-runs. The programme, which involved some selected publishers, was successful to a point before it was scrapped by USIS owing to the hostile political environment. The programme was 'understandably' limited to the social sciences, politics and governance.

On a happier note, the World Bank Primary Education Project (PEP 1) and Petroleum Trust Fund (PTF) National Educational Materials Procurement Programme have contributed immensely to the capacity building of publishers in Nigeria. The Federal Government secured a World Bank Loan of $120 million in 1991 to revamp primary education in the areas of curriculum development, teacher training, rehabilitation of classrooms and infrastructures, and provision of reading materials. The component relating to the procurement of books was to the tune of $40 million. The intervention was in four subject areas, i.e. Social Studies, Mathematics, Science (in English and selected Nigerian Languages) and English Language for primary classes 1-6. It contributed over 75 million books into the school system between 1994 when publishers began the distribution of the books and 2000 when the programme ended.

The PTF local intervention in the production and supply of books and other educational materials, such as exercise books, ball pens, graph books, etc., to primary, secondary and tertiary institutions also led to the printing of some 40 million books across-the-board in 2000/2001. But for the scrapping of PTF, the scheme would have been a continuous, revolving one. Meanwhile, the Education Tax Fund (ETF), another government parastatal which manages the funds accruing from the 2% education tax of profits from companies operating in Nigeria, is intervening in the stocking of books for university libraries and a few primary and secondary schools. The ETF has now metamorphosed into the Tertiary Education Tax Fund (TETFUND) and intervenes in the construction of facilities and provision of books and journals in tertiary institutions, while the Universal Basic Education Commission (UBEC) does the same at the primary and secondary school levels.

In April 2000, the Federal Government secured another credit of $55 million for the Second Primary Education Project (PEP II). Out of this, a sum of $7.32 million was earmarked for the provision of supplementary readers, i.e. picture, reference, fiction and non-fiction books in 30 focus schools, in each of the 36 states of the country and the Federal Capital Territory. This project involved the procurement and distribution of some two million supplementary readers to 1,110 focus primary schools in Nigeria. The books were sourced from Africa and Europe.

All these book projects are expected to provide the book base for the Universal Basic Education (UBE) programme. One would like to say, concerning foreign interventions that while foreign loans are desirable to solve short-term problems in the production and distribution of books, the long-term and more sustainable solution is for government to assist in developing the publishing infrastructures, train publishing personnel in such areas as electronic publishing, e-commerce and internet advertising, relax import duties on raw materials such as paper, printing ink, plates, etc., and grant soft loans to Nigerian publishers for mass production of books for the nation's educational needs. That, in our view, would be more productive than depending on foreign hand-outs for our book needs in the country.

The curriculum and book development efforts of the Nigerian Government became an important issue again when the Universal Basic Education Commission (UBEC) in collaboration with the Federal Ministry of Education (FME) launched the Primary and JSS Books Project in 2007. The Nigerian Educational Research and Development Council (NERDC) also introduced new Universal Basic Education curricula about the same time. These curricula, which are supposed to stabilise basic education in Nigeria have since been revised about three times – all, needless to say, to the detriment of publishers.

The Book Procurement Project, which has slowed down somewhat in 2015, has provided a much-needed breather for some publishers. While it lasted, some 100 million textbooks in Basic Science, Basic Science and Technology, English, Mathematics, Social Studies and supplementary readers have been distributed to primary and junior secondary schools throughout the Federation. At the secondary school level, the NERDC has shifted attention to entrepreneurial education by designing various subjects which are meant to enable the senior secondary school students to be self-reliant after leaving school. The gap in the local provision of tertiary books is gradually being filled by publishers who are in tune with the needs of the various institutions and in touch with course co-ordinators and lecturers who develop books with local contents.

Ghana

Ghana shares a similar experience with Nigeria in terms of textbook development, provision and distribution along the lines of private sector participation. This is evident, for example, in the production and distribution of four million supplementary readers in English and local languages to 12,000 public primary schools by twenty-five publishers under the Basic School Book Supply Scheme in 1999.

The Textbook Development Policy, which became operational in 2001, was a departure from the old practice in which the government controlled most of the textbook market in Ghana. Under this policy, publishers are free to develop textbooks in line with the curriculum. Independent assessors within and outside the Ministry of Education would assess the various publishers' textbooks and those which conform with the syllabuses would be approved for each subject and class while those that do not cover the syllabuses are turned into supplementary and resource materials. Of course, the publishers are responsible for the marketing and distribution of their books, but in case of bulk-purchase by government, only three out of the approved textbooks per subject are purchased. From the information available with respect to the Gambia and Sierra Leone, the production and distribution of textbooks are controlled by the government (Nwankwo, 2001:211 – 212).

Francophone West Africa

Book publishing in the francophone West African countries follows a different pattern where the book trade is still largely in the grip of French multinationals. The three Nouvelles Editions Africaines (NEAs) which used to be a partnership between the governments of Senegal, Cote d'Ivoire and Togo and French firms have gone their different ways. However, each NEA is still being controlled by its individual government. In Cameroon, its Publishers Association was engaged in a tug of war for many years with the government which wanted to grant the monopoly for the production and distribution of primary and secondary school books to a French firm. Now, publishers have secured a reprieve. They submit their books to the Cameroon Book Commission in Yaounde for assessment after which publishers will market the approved textbooks that are in line with the syllabuses in schools and colleges. In Mali, and with the help of the government, publishers have achieved considerable success in the textbook business in the face of serious competition with French multinational publishers.

On the whole, primary and secondary school textbooks account for some 80% of the books produced in the region. The predominant languages of publication are English and French in anglophone and francophone countries respectively. Unfortunately, publications of school texts and general books in indigenous languages are still trailing behind the foreign non-African languages (Nwankwo, 2001:211-212). In Nigeria, for example, although local language publishing is gradually getting attention, not more than 15% of the book outputs are in the indigenous languages. The haphazard implementation of the National Policy on Education, which prescribes that the medium of instruction should be the mother tongue, at the lower basic education level, has not helped the publication of books in these languages which would have promoted learning, teaching and research in the indigenous languages.

The West African Examinations Council (WAEC) which conducts senior secondary certificate examinations in Nigeria, Ghana, Liberia, the Gambia and Sierra Leone should normally serve as a veritable platform for a single large market for textbooks in anglophone West Africa, but the peculiar and different teaching syllabuses within those countries and the trade barriers across borders undermine such a tantalising prospect.

Southern Africa

Some of the countries in the Southern African region, of which South Africa is our focus, have peculiar approaches towards the publication of textbooks. Nevertheless, textbook publishing accounts for more than 60% in the region. With the cut on expenditure in textbooks by South Africa in the 90s, the fortunes of educational publishers not only nosedived, the entire publishing industry shrank. This situation opened the eyes of the publishers in the direction of trade and general publishing (Impey, 2001:197, 200). On the other hand, Botswana, Lesotho and Swaziland had a common Integrated Science curriculum and worked with Heinemann UK to produce the outstandingly successful Boleswa Integrated Science project for the junior secondary schools in Bostwana, Lesotho and Swaziland. (*Boleswa* was coined from Botswana (Bo), Lesotho (Le) and Swaziland (Swa)).

It is instructive to note that educational publishing and the textbook trade has since picked up substantially in South Africa. The annual publishing industry survey by the Publishers' Association of South Africa in 2013 showed that educational publishing increased by 26% while trade and academic publishing fell by 2.6% and 5% respectively. Indeed, textbooks accounted for 66% out of the 98% total domestic turnover while the export turnover was just a mere 2%. There is, however, a threat to textbook publishing in the country as government has proposed a single textbook policy which would abolish a booklist of eight textbooks per subject per class and replace it with one book per subject per class. Apart from adversely affecting the quality of education delivery in terms of content and pedagogy, the policy is most likely to impoverish those publishers who are not lucky to have their books on the list (IPA Country Report, 2015).

It is worth noting that innovation in educational publishing has enabled small publishers, whose lists have some textbook potentials but who lack marketing and distribution facilities, to go into profit-sharing deals with larger publishing companies for maximum exposure of their books. The arrangement will also enable small publishers not to lose out in the production and distribution of large textbook orders. This is in the light, for example, of the EU funding, sometime ago, of textbooks and materials supply to educationally disadvantaged institutions which favoured foreign publishers, to the detriment of local publishers (Impey 2001:200).

East Africa

It is estimated that textbook publishing in Kenya, our focus in the East African region, contributes some 95 per cent of the total revenue of the publishing industry, which is put at about 12 billion Kenyan shillings (equivalent of 150 million US dollars annually (Waweru, 2013). It should be stressed that the unity that existed in the major anglophone East African countries (i.e .Kenya, Tanzania and Uganda) several decades ago in terms of the economy, agriculture, tourism, education, etc., can still be felt today. As a result of the deep knowledge of the terrain and, lately, the common language of Kiswahili, publishing companies in Kenya, for example, could establish publishing outfits in Uganda and even in the Central African country of Rwanda in order to take advantage of favourable textbook policies and intervention by governments and donor agencies for large textbook orders in the host countries.

In Kenya, the national policy on textbook which deals with the publication, procurement and supply of textbooks, limits the role of government to curriculum development and quality assurance, as against the old government policy after independence up to the nineties, which gave government almost total control over the publishing industry. Consequently, the book publishers play a prominent role in book development by producing various textbooks from which the Kenya Institute of Curriculum Development (KICD) selects the ones adjudged to be in conformity with the curriculum.

The textbook policy in Uganda, like in Kenya, Tanzania, Malawi, Ethiopia and Ghana was controlled by government in the early years of independence. Just like Kenya, the Ugandan government backed down on state control of textbooks and enacted a policy in which publishers produce the books while government acts as the regulator. Apart from the governments, the World Bank, DFID, USAID, the Irish Government, etc., have at various times provided financial support for the procurement of textbooks, especially at the primary school level (Ikoja-Odongo and Batambuze 2008).

The Maghreb

Publishers in the Maghreb countries of Algeria, Morocco and Tunisia are struggling to forge an identity distinct from the dominance of French publishers. This dominance is evident from the fact that the Maghreb Des Livres Book Fair was held not in the Maghreb, but in Paris, in February 2015! Despite the fact that there are 240 publishers in Algeria, 40 in Morocco and 30 in Tunisia, French publishers still flood the Maghreb with both educational and general books.

After the revolution in Tunisia in 2011, interest in books seemed to have waned generally as the populace appeared to have become more interested in non-fiction and essays on current affairs in order to keep abreast of developments after the revolution. It is expected that government will eventually settle down to determine what textbooks would be adopted and used in its schools and colleges. The situation is similar in Morocco where there is little aid for the book industry. On the other hand, the Algerian government has been involved in the support and development of its fragile book industry for over a decade (Snaije 2015).

Challenges of textbook publishing in Africa

The challenges that have always confronted textbook publishing and, indeed, the knowledge industry in Africa do not appear as if they are about to go, even fifteen years into the twenty-first century. Inconsistent educational and fiscal policies, infrastructural deficiencies, socio-economic, environmental and political factors and current trends constitute challenges to textbook development and publishing in Africa.

Despite the expansion in education and the spirited efforts to eradicate illiteracy in Africa, there can be no comparison in the number of books produced in the whole of Africa in ten years and those produced in the advanced countries in a single year (Ondari-Okemwa 2007:6). For example, the developed countries a few years ago produced 500 titles per one million of their inhabitants while Africa produced 40. In fact, African countries are producing fewer books than the other developing countries in Asia and South America. The reasons for this are not far to seek. I proceed to list some of these reasons – and it is not an exhaustive list:

1. *Printing:* Only few big presses are available and most African countries cannot cope with the rapid technological changes in printing. As such, most large print-runs of textbooks are printed abroad in China, India and Malaysia.

2. *Paper:* This is perhaps the most important factor in book production. The three paper mills in Nigeria are moribund. Despite the paper mills in Zimbabwe, Egypt, Angola, Algeria, Ethiopia, Kenya, South Africa, etc., most African countries depend on imported supplies which make paper and cover boards to be scarce and expensive.

3. *Publishing personnel:* There is a dearth of trained, experienced and ICT compliant editors, artists, illustrators, typesetters and marketing personnel. Formal training is not readily available as few universities

and polytechnics offer publishing courses. However, occasional training courses are arranged from time to time by national publishers associations and regrettably, the defunct African Publishers Network (APNET).

4. *Language:* Most African languages do not have developed orthographies to generate sufficient publishing interest.

5. *Inconsistent educational and fiscal policies:* In Nigeria, an example was the decision by government some years ago to scrap Modern Mathematics in the primary and secondary schools, after the same government had nurtured and patronised the change to modern mathematics. Publishers were left with thousands of modern mathematics textbooks which became suddenly obsolete! Also in the last seven years, the Basic Education Curricula have been revised three times, with publishers stuck again with obsolete books. In South Africa, the publishers are fighting for survival in the face of the proposed single textbook policy, as against the existing eight textbooks per subject per grade.

6. *Piracy:* It is a social and economic menace which, like malaria, if not rolled back, has the potential of killing authorship and the publishing industry in Africa. It is estimated that publishers lose some 40% of the textbook market to pirates annually. The copyright laws across nations in Africa, therefore, need to be strengthened and enforced to contain the menace.

7. *Poor promotion and distribution network:* It is no exaggeration to say that distribution is perhaps the weakest link in the book chain in Africa today. The retail and distribution outlets in form of bookshops and mini-depots are very few. As a result, most publishers deal directly with schools on 'sale or return' basis, with attendant late payments, loss of books, and books not returned in mint condition. Henry Chakava, one of Africa's foremost publishers, alluded to the neglect of marketing and distribution by publishers when he said:

> As far as I am aware, there is no African publisher who produces advance publicity on new and forthcoming

titles. Few bother to print promotional leaflets. Only a handful produce annual catalogues. Most catalogues have incomplete and outdated information. Blurbs could do with a little editorial intervention. Essential bibliographic information, such as ISBN, year of publication, price and marketing restriction, etc., maybe missing (Chakava, 1996:111-113).

This does not apply, of course, to all African publishers but the fact remains that most publishers sit back as soon as books roll out from the press. And in the absence of adequate marketing, promotion and distribution of books, especially textbooks, sales opportunities are lost while authors complain that their books deserve better visibility.

In spite of it all, a significant progress has been made by the self-help and co-operative initiative founded by African publishers in 1989; that is, African Books Collective (ABC) which is based in Oxford and distributes African publishers' books to the developed countries of the world, especially in Europe and the Americas. While this is a welcome development, ABC is of little help in textbook distribution because textbooks do not flow across freely across geographical and cultural boundaries due to the restriction of curricula. Of course, the initiative and creativity of authors and publishers to make the textbooks attractive to read to all and sundry are restricted also owing to the specific demands of curricula.

Prospects and impact of textbook publishing in Africa

The massive expansion in education at all levels and mass literacy programmes are an indication that the publishing business generally and textbook publishing in Africa more specifically have bright prospects. The public and private schools, colleges and universities and student enrolments continue to increase in leaps and bounds over the last five decades and textbooks are required to facilitate the educational process. Even tertiary and scholarly publishing, which is seen as not too viable, has caught the attention of some textbook publishers who see it as a diversification strategy to boost the income they derive from their primary and secondary school textbook publishing.

The democratisation process which is taking place all over Africa has thrown up an enlightened citizenry that is thirsty for education and demand for human rights. Parents and the general public who are desirous of education for their wards and themselves will be asking for not just textbooks, but as time goes on, general and leisure books as well. The population explosion has a marked effect on the demand for textbooks and other reading materials. Similarly, the establishment of paper mills and relaxation of fiscal measures such as zero import duty on books and reduction of tariffs on paper, printing materials and machinery will enable books to be produced cheaply and help to build capacity for publishers and printers.

The developments in Information and Communication Technology (ICT) have opened opportunities to transform and display textbook contents in CDs, eBooks, ePub, etc. Apart from enhancing pedagogy, these formats will bring in additional revenue to publishers. For example, ePublishing in India is growing at a rate of 35% per annum, while the sales of eBooks in the United States have overtaken paperbacks by over 200% since February 2011. The development in ICT notwithstanding, both print and digital publishing will continue to go hand in hand, with no threat to the former in the nearest future (Eyitayo, 2011).

Despite the weak purchasing power due to the poor economic climate in the continent, there is still a ready, guaranteed and substantial market for textbooks. Most parents make efforts to buy textbooks to enhance quality education delivery for their wards, especially in private schools. Also, interventions by governments and donor agencies in the procurement of textbooks, especially in the core subject areas, have gone a long way in ameliorating the shortage of textbooks in public schools and generated considerable print-run orders for textbook publishers. This, of course, is at the detriment of other areas of publishing like creative writing, biographies, autobiographies, journals and tertiary and scholarly publishing. This leads to the question of the poor reading culture in Africa.

Poor reading culture or low readership is not just about the scarcity of reading materials. Several factors, including the high percentage of air time being devoted to entertainment content on our radio and television and invasion by the internet also play a role in this. The famous African

Writers Series attained the level of success it enjoyed not because of a good reading culture but because some titles in the series were adopted for use in the teaching of Literature-in-English in schools. Most pupils do not read books for leisure but concentrate on textbooks to pass examinations. Obviously, general motivational and leisure books are *sine qua non* to intellectual development. As Robertson Davies (1913-1995), a Canadian novelist and critic, cited in Aina (2014:80), once put the case, A truly great book should be read in youth, again in maturity and once more in old age, as a fine building should be seen by morning light, at noon and by moonlight. Leisure and general books develop the intellect of the mind and make readers become leaders.

Conclusion

Publishers in Africa currently lack the capacity to meet the textbook requirements of the continent and, therefore, it is necessary to enhance their capacity to meet the textbook demands of the different countries on the continent. With respect to Nigeria, for example, Professor Emmanuel Nnolue Emenanjo, as cited in Ajeluorou (2014:21), has observed that,

> Nigeria produces less than one percent of her actual books needs, which should stand at some 200 million books per year. This calculation is based on a modest estimate of 4 to 6 books per child in the primary school for 20.4 million pupils, 8 books per student in the secondary school for 6.4 million students and 8 books per student for over 1 million students in tertiary institutions.

This is a grim prospect for the country's educational development and the book industry. Many African countries are in this same pathetic situation.

The World Bank study reported in 2008 that Anglophone Africa tended to develop country specific textbook publishing at the secondary school level which is more expensive in terms of price, yet more relevant to the immediate environment. The Francophone Africa, on the other hand, encouraged secondary school textbook publishing to suit transnational curricula. This is, of course, cost effective with large print-runs. For example, the average unit cost per book in Uganda was US $11.10, Cameroon US $8.85 and Togo US $9.47(Ikoja-Odongo, p.73).

An enabling environment should be created for books and other resource materials to be available in the right quantity, quality and variety for effective teaching and learning in African schools. In this regard, the governments and their agencies should make material inputs in publishing available and affordable. Also, the issue of poor reading culture should be tackled headlong. To achieve this, African governments, public-spirited individuals, civil societies and corporate organisations must invest in the knowledge industry by, among other things, building and stocking school and public libraries with physical and virtual books backed with Internet facilities and equipment for eBooks, etc.

It is pertinent to note that more than 50 per cent of Africa's youth are either illiterate or semi-literate. Without education, knowledge and skills, decent jobs and prospects of a meaningful future are dim (Oteng 2015:38). As Africa's youth is Africa's future, and in order to rescue the continent from the shackles of poverty, corruption, under-development, insurgency and backwardness, the African Union and governments, through education, human capital development and entrepreneurship, need to empower the youth to unlock the abundant resources in Africa. Therefore, our attitude towards education and books must change. It is then that African countries can join their counterparts in other parts of the world in the journey towards sustainable development.

References

Adelekan, A.I. 2005. "Government Policies and the Development of the Book Publishing Industry in Nigeria". In *Issues in Book Publishing in Nigeria-Essays in Honour of Aigboje Higo at 70*, pp 185-196, edited by Festus Adedapo Adesanoye and Ayo Ojeniyi. Ibadan: Heinemann Education Books.

Adesina, Segun. 1990. "The Educational System and the Book Situation in Nigeria" *Education Today,* Vol. 4 No.1.

Aina, Dolapo. 2014. "Reading Culture and Mental Magnitude of Nigerians", *The Guardian* (Nigeria), 12 May, 2014, p. 80.

Ajeluorou, Anote. 2014. "Opportunities, Challenges of Book Publishing as e-books Take Root", *The Guardian* (Nigeria), 21 February, 2014, pp. 20-21.

Altbach, Philip G., Amadio A. Arboleda and S. Gopinathan, eds. 1985. *Publishing in the Third World: Knowledge and Development.* London: Heinemann Educational Books.

Altbach, Philip G. and S. Gopinathan. 1988. *Indian Book Industry* Vol. XXXVIII No. 283 (May-June 1988).

Chakava, H. 1996. *Publishing in Africa: One Man's Perspective*. Oxford: Bellagio Publishing Network.

Echebiri, Azed. 2005. "Book Production in Nigeria in the New Millennium: What Prospects?" In *Issues in Book Publishing in Nigeria-Essays in Honour of Aigboje Higo at 70*, pp 197-218, edited by Festus Adedapo Adesanoye and Ayo Ojeniyi. Ibadan: Heinemann Education Books.

Eyitayo, S.A. 2011. "Technology and Infrastructural Development: What the Future Holds for the Book Industry in Nigeria". Paper presented at the Nigeria International Book Fair, Lagos, Nigeria, 10 May, 2011.

Ferrel, Joseph P. and Stephen P. Haynemann, eds. 1989. *Textbooks in the Developing World*. Washington DC: The World Bank.

Ikoja-Odongo, J.R. 2004. "Publishing in Uganda with Notes from Africa: A Review", available at: www.scribd.com/doc/9082/807, pp 1-91, retrieved on 27 October 2015.

Ikoja-Odongo, J.R. and Charles Batambuze. 2008. "Educational Publishing and Book Distribution in Uganda", available at: http://docs.mak.ac.ug, retrieved on 27 October 2015.

Impey, B. 2011. "Book Marketing and Distribution in Southern Africa". In *Book Marketing and Promotion: A Handbook of Good Practice,* pp. 197-209, edited by Hans Zell. Oxford: INASP.

IPA. 2015. "Publishing in South Africa 2015, International Publishers Association (IPA) Country Report", available at: http;//www.internationalpublishers.org/market-insights/count... South-Africa, 28 April, retrieved on 24 October 2015.

Nwankwo, Victor. 2001. "Book Marketing and Distribution in West Africa". In *Book Marketing and Promotion: A Handbook of Good Practice,* pp. 211-223, edited by Hans Zell. Oxford: INASP.

Nwankwo, Victor. 2005. "Print-on-Demand: An African Publisher's Experience". In *Issues in Book Publishing in Nigeria-Essays in Honour of Aigboje Higo at 70,* pp. 173-183, edited by Festus Adedapo Adesanoye and Ayo Ojeniyi. Ibadan: Heinemann Education Books.

Obanya, Pai. 2005. "EFA/UBE as a Challenge to the Publishing Industry". In *Issues in Book Publishing in Nigeria-Essays in Honour of Aigboje Higo at 70,* pp. 239-257, edited by Festus Adedapo Adesanoye and Ayo Ojeniyi. Ibadan: Heinemann Education Books.

Ogunleye, Bisi. 2005. "Marketing the Nigerian Book: Beyond the Local to the African and the World". In *Issues in Book Publishing in Nigeria: Essays in Honour of Aigboje Higo at 70,* pp. 81-111, edited by Festus Adedapo Adesanoye and Ayo Ojeniyi. Ibadan: Heinemann Education Books.

Ojeniyi, Ayo. 2004. "The Need for Textbook Writing for the Use of University Students in Nigeria", paper presented at the Two-day Workshop on Textbook Publishing for University Students organised by Obafemi Awolowo University Press Ltd, Ile-Ife, Nigeria, 9-10 February.

Ojeniyi, Ayo. 2015. "African Youth Empowerment through Book for Sustainable National Development", paper presented at the International Conference of the Nigeria International Book Fair at Lagos, Nigeria, 12 May 2015.

Ondari-Okemwa, Ezra. 2007. "Scholarly Publishing in Sub-Saharan Africa in the Twenty-First Century: Challenges and Opportunities", *First Monday*, Volume 12 No. 10 (2007): 1-15.

Oteng, Seth. 2015. "Voice is Fine – but Needs to be Heard", *Development and Cooperation International Journal,* Vol. 42 No. 3 (2015): 38-39.

Read, Anthony. 1980. "Problems of International Book Distribution". In *The Future of the Book (Part 1),* edited by P. Oakesholt and C. Bradley. Studies on Books and Reading No 8. Paris: UNESCO.

Smith Jr, D.C. 1990. *A Guide to Book Publishing – Revised Edition.* Lagos: University of Lagos Press.

Snaije, Olivia. 2015. "Publishing in the Maghreb Challenged by Colonial Legacy". Available at: http://publishingperpectives.com, retrieved on 11 November 2015.

Tiamiyu, N. 2005. "Prospect of Nigerian Book Publishing in Electronic Age". In *Issues in Book Publishing in Nigeria: Essays in Honour of Aigboje Higo at 70,* pp. 143-157, edited by Festus Adedapo Adesanoye and Ayo Ojeniyi. Ibadan: Heinemann Education Books.

Waweru, David. 2013. "Why Publishing in Kenya is Tougher than Boxing". Available at: http://publishingperpectives.com, retrieved on 24 October 2015.

WIPO. 2000. Report of Seminar in Reprographic Reproduction Rights, held in Accra, Ghana, 3-4 April, 2000. Geneva: World Intellectual Property Organisation.

7

Popular Fiction Publishing in Africa: Does it Have a Place?

By David Maillu

I

When does a work of fiction become popular or serious? Who decides what qualifies for popular or serious fiction? Every genre has its own conventions. Popularity, simply responds to the fundamentals of people's cultural waves. Seriousness on the other hand is what qualifies for literary analysis, criticism and basis for theories of literature. What people read may make them relate to others within the society on a more personal level. Popular fiction therefore appeals to what the society holds: people's beliefs, feelings, wishes and morals. Specifically, by reading works of popular fiction one is able to reveal higher traces of sensitivity to various societal goings-on. However, as Nick Hornby as quoted by Catherine, R.S., (2014 : 14) laments,

> One of the problems, it seems … is that we have got it into our heads that books should be hard work, and that unless they're hard work, they're not doing us any good.

Nevertheless, fiction, popular or otherwise simply refers to the plot-driven literary works written with the intent of fitting into a specific literary genre, in order to appeal to readers and fans already familiar with that genre. Some literary critics argue that popular fiction is less worthy to read than serious fiction. Nonetheless, it is subjective to judge one creative piece as serious and the other as 'less serious' as there is no consensus yet setting exact parameters or conventions of any genre as either.

From the foregoing it is clear that fiction, popular or serious is fundamentally meant to respond to people's social, cultural, economic and political realities. Therefore one may argue that popular fiction is not simply fiction that aims to be popular, or just entertain but that it addresses the same issues as serious literature, though differently. For instance, two authors may choose to write on the theme of political intolerance in a nation but their approach in displaying their thematic concerns is captured differently. This could be explained by the fact that serious fiction targets adult and mature readers while popular fiction seeks the audience of teenagers and young adults. Popular fiction usually cuts across fiction genres such as crime, thrillers, romance, mystery, science fiction, fantasy among others – all of which affect society in many ways. It includes the kind of books you see in airport bookshops, along African city roads – the books that make you laugh or cry, and simply take you away. The prime aim of popular fiction is to entertain readers and keep them turning pages far into the night because they can't put the book down – while still keeping them informed on the issues affecting their person and society.

II

African stories were existent before the mid-1970s. Though embedded in orature and the general folklore, popular African fiction took various forms. The irrefutably famous ogre and hare stories were in fact popular fiction for children. That is why every society told theirs differently: in rhythm with cultural values and beliefs. Therefore, the introduction of popular literature as defined by Western parameters was in its very sense decolonising African thought of fiction and paying tribute to the African concept of storytelling. The philosophy of popular fiction opened up an African stream of culturally founded style that is here to stay and develop. Having taken its roots in the early 70s with the launch of Heinemann's Spear Books Series, by 1980s the storm of popular fiction had crystalised and gained substantial ground in the fight against the imported concept of literature.

Perhaps, the talk about the rise of popular fiction in Africa is best captured by Prof. Bernth Lindfors who taught East African and Caribbean

Literature. In the Introduction of his book *Early East African Writers and Publishers*, he states:

> It is the output of a large group of literary newcomers from East Africa who expressed themselves in large and popular literary forms not only in English but also in a number of indigenous languages …

Then Lindfors, perhaps based on his lack of understanding of the foundation of African cultural expressions, added:

> The early literature that emerged in East Africa in tone and quality from that produced in West Africa was addressed to a resident mass readership interested in entertainment than in serious engagement with social and political issues. The result was a growing body of popular literature aimed at eliciting laughter rather than exciting protest.

In the above, Lindfors implies that in order for literature to be serious and excite protest, it has to be delivered in serious sounding words. That is not true, for seriousness can be expressed in simple language. Even in ordinary life, you do not have to look serious to say serious things. You can act comically yet express profound seriousness. You can educate and entertain using simple or funny words – that is what stand-up comedies do.

To employ serious sounding words in literature in order to deliver excitable and protesting reaction has been the philosophy of western literature. Such kind of literature is in most cases coloured by class-consciousness; hence the division between the haves and have-nots. For example, there emerges a distinction of literature for the educated or high-class consumption and literature for the less-educated or low-class consumption. Operating in a class-conscious status, one becomes susceptible to expressing themselves in certain ways, which gives them the sense of belonging to that class; for birds of the same feather flock together. Hence, the Queen's English and commoner's English.

Colonial administration in Africa made every effort to show that traditional Africa had neither tangible nor intangible history. Literature, History, Philosophy, Architecture including all other disciplines that the West has been associated with, were imported to Africa in style by colonialism. The school was fed with curriculum from Europe, and the concept of literature, for example, was given foreign interpretation. That foreign interpretation was presented at the expense of traditional interpretation. What literature presentation emphasised was the Oral Literature, perceived as a primitive communication tool. It is against this backdrop that the school literature set books and class readers are termed as serious literature while the rest are referred to as popular literature.

However, it is worth noting that in Africa, written literature has a long history. Take for instance the following excerpt translated from the Pharaonic Period: 2780 to 330 BC, and cited by Prof. Theophile Obenga in his book *African Philosophy*:

> If you wish a friendship to last, in a house you enter as a master, brother or sister, wherever you may go, take care not to get close to the women. Whatever they meddle with ends badly. No creature is safe from their wiles, and thousands of men have thereby been misled from goals useful to themselves. One loses one's reason for a body cold as porcelain, which then changes into burning carnelian. The pleasure lasts a short moment, then one gets killed for having known them.

Or consider another Pharaonic *Song of the Hearts Sublime*, (Song 1) that reads:

> The only one, the beloved, the incomparable one;
> World's most beautiful
> Behold her, brilliant as the New Year's star
> At the start of a splendid year
> She whose face sparkles, whose skin glows
> She whose eyes look out brightly
> And whose lips speak softly;
> Never uttering a word too many

> She, the long-necked one of the radiant bust
> Has hair of true lapis
> The lust of her skin surpasses gold
> Her fingers are like lotus petals
> She of the delicate waist and slender hips
> She whose limbs affirm her beauty
> Whose every step is full of dignity
> My heart is afire with desire for embrace
> She makes every man's head turn to see her.
> Whoever she greets is filled with joy
> Feeling himself first among youth.
> When she steps out of her house.
> One dreams he sees the lone star ...

Does that sound African? Does it have 'serious' words? Any one reading this with a Western scholar approach to literature would jump to a classic claim that, after all, the Egyptians were not black people.

But compare the mood of the above pharaonic song by revisiting Okot p'Bitek's *Song of Lawino* which was developed and translated from Acholi Songs, a traditional and oral genre resembling so much others that cut across traditional Africa:

> My husband
> Now you despise me
> Now you treat me with spite
> And say I have inherited the stupidity of my aunt
> Son of Chief
> Now you compare me
> With the rubbish in the rubbish pit
> You say you no longer want me
> Because I am like the things left behind
> In the deserted homestead
> You insult me
> You laugh at me
> You say that I do not know the letter A
> Because I have not been to school
> And I have not been baptized

As in *Song of Lawino*, most sung poetry geared at criticism in traditional setting was the most effective tool for women in disciplining men. When a village received information from a family member or from anyone else that a certain man was exercising a serious anti-social behaviour, the matter became something of great concern to villagers. Villagers were brought up to act responsibly in upholding community values. In order for the villagers to push the man into reformation, they decided to compose ridicule songs with which to put him to shame in the public eye. This is what pop fiction was meant to achieve in Africa: Maintain discipline, morals and order in the society. The use of simple 'less serious' words notwithstanding, the fiction delivered on its objective.

Therefore, a music composer would be approached and commissioned to compose the song. Even if the man's wife was the composer, or she participated in singing him out in the ridicule, the husband would have no base for punishing her. Any attempt to punish her may even invite a worse song of ridicule about him. 'It's not me who sings about you, but the public,' she would defend herself.

The aim of the song is to deliver the information directly and most effectively. Simplicity, therefore, is crucial. In order for the song to hit the victim most successfully, emotional and vulgar words were not even spared in the composition of the song.

It is from this premise that one should read and understand that part of *Song of Lawino* and the following part from *After 4.30* by David G Maillu:

> I'm fisherwoman of men
> When I catch them
> I club them on the head to kill
> The bait on my hook
> Has the favourite food for men
> I don't shake when a man tells me
> He loves me
> Even drunks say that
> All rogues and murderers
> Say that when erect

> I've seen many one-night loves
> It touches me no more
>
> When a man calls me
> Sweetheart, darling, and says
> He loves me beyond bounds
> In a love that dies with one ... [night]

In traditional Africa seriousness can be expressed in many dramatic ways. It can be presented through organised public expression where drama, dancing, and even crying are employed. For example, whereas in the western world religious expressions, such as in church choirs, people would sing without bodily movements, the African singing would be accompanied by dancing in order to involve the entire personality in the delivery. This is the cue that popular African fiction follows. Using simple words to address serious social-economic immoralities and keeping society in check.

Perhaps this was the perception that Prof. Gareth Griffiths in *African Literature in English* had when he said:

> The works of David G Maillu illustrates how a popular, self-published writer can continue to exploit a local taste for literary styles with clear and obvious links to indigenous forms. Maillu is one of a small group of African writers whose marketing model has been the Western best-selling author. His novels sell at African airports and bookshops, alongside those of writers like Arthur Hardley, Robert Ruark or Wilbur Smith. The successful life-style has inspired a number of other writers to develop similar popular forms. Yet, Maillu's work is far from being merely a copy of Western styles and genres. In a text like *After 4.30*, he shows that, for East African readers, the long poem can be successfully used to structure a modern, popular narrative.

III

The place of Henry Chakava in African popular fiction

Henry Chakava's gallant approach to publishing and his passion for innovative solutions to African publishing is immeasurable. His contribution to the moulding, training and bringing to literary platform African writers, editors and other publishing professionals is cross-generation. Since his entry into the publishing scene in 1972 as an editor, Chakava took it upon himself to identify and nurture African authors and literary works. With the responsibility to carry on the mantle of expanding the African Writers Series (AWS), he did not disappoint – his impact on the growth of the iconic AWS is evident.

However, Chakava's passion to address readership needs across age and class culminated when, on realising that the AWS catered only for 'serious reading', he made a 'surprising' but convincing recommendation to Heinemann's London office. As captured in his book, *Publishing in Africa: One Man's Perspective,* he says:

> ... I recommended to London, in 1973, that they should start a new series for leisure reading–romance, adventure, crime, etc. – as we were constantly receiving manuscripts of this kind. The idea was debated at length and turned down in 1974, but I was allowed to start such a series locally if I wished. The first four titles were launched in 1975 to much critical acclaim.

It is this recommendation that gave birth to the Spear Books Series. The series that harbours all African pop fiction books published by East African Educational Publishers. The series succeeded in not only addressing the local socio-cultural issues but was also a market hit.

Forty years later the series has expanded and sales are still worth appreciating. It is home to many budding authors with a bug of creativity and enthusiasm to tell the African story. Though not a candidate for school set book category, the series offers an opportunity for leisure reading, vocabulary development and general appreciation of the African fiction work.

As if Chakava opened a window of popular fiction publishing, currently, many African publishers and publishing houses publishing in Africa have pop fiction series to cater for the ever expanding market.

IV

Popular fiction in the digital age

Since the advent of the Information and Communication Technologies (ICTs), fiction has changed a great deal in both presentation and delivery. However, the question begs: What is the place of African pop fiction in this arena? A casual visit to such online book marketplaces as Amazon, GoodReads, SlideShare, Bushbaby Books, and eKitabu paints not a very encouraging picture of this.

Moreover, a general search for 'African pop fiction' on Google is shocking. There is very little, if anything at all written about the subject. Does it mean that there is no research done on this genre? If that's the case, why? Not having studies, writings or commentaries about a subject online in the 21st Century is not only shocking but also worrying. It could of course mean either of the following: that the subject has not been studied at all, or that none of the studies is available in digital format. Whichever is true about African popular fiction, does not offer any reprieve to a genre so deeply rooted in African culture. A genre whose demise is too expensive to imagine.

All is not lost however, as there is big opportunity in Wordreader. Using the digital resource, the ePub, Wordreader has transformed how stories are told across the African continent. ePub version allows for access of the book on mobile devices such as the Kindle and smartphone. It is therefore suitable for an 'on-the-go' reading and African authors and publishers should take advantage of such technology to spread popular fiction to the remotest part of the continent.

In Kenya, eKitabu provides a suitable platform for African fiction to be accessed. Using the Portable Document File format of the eBook, eKitabu acts as the gateway for both self-published and traditionally published authors to share their stories online. With its Digital Rights Management System, eKitabu infrastructure provides a safe and secure environment for selling books. It has contributed greatly by giving opportunities to young budding authors to exercise their creative prowess by telling stories that could otherwise have not been heard.

Conclusion

In spite of the criticism it has endured, African popular fiction, has a long history and its future is promising. Its foundation is in the history of African traditional style of expression. The reawakening of African values is putting more light in the importance of cultural integrity. Popular fiction therefore is not going anywhere. If anything, it is destined to expand and acquire more diversity and sophistication.

Henry Chakava's contribution to the birth and development of the African pop fiction cannot be overemphasised. By pioneering a series purely dedicated for popular fiction, he succeeded in building base for what would later become an avenue for young authors to tell stories that could have otherwise not been read. We believe that this precedence will see more publishers take up the challenge and introduce other African-relevant series that cut across gender and age.

With the digital publishing realities sinking in and African governments throwing weights behind them, the future is exciting. However, a lot needs to be done for African pop fiction to occupy its space in the digital world – in both quality and quantity. This is the challenge the current digital savvy writers should take up and ensure its full realisation.

Fiction, popular or otherwise should be fanned and developed to meet readers' needs.

> And as Daphne de Jong argues, Readers of 'serious' fiction expect to be challenged and like to be entertained; while readers of popular fiction expect to be entertained

and like to be challenged. They're often the same readers in a different mood.

In fact, one may argue that pop fiction and serious fiction are Siamese twins: separated at birth but connected by their DNA strands, and that their place in African culture and literary contribution should be self-complementing.

References

Achebe, Chinua. 1963. *Things Fall Apart*. London: Heinemann.

p'Bitek, Okot. 1972. *Song of Lawino and Ocol*. Nairobi: East Africa Publishing House.

Catherine, R.S. 2014. *The Pleasures of Reading*: A Booklover's Alphabet: Libraries Unlimited, California, USA.

Chakava, H. 1996. *Publishing in Africa: One Man's Perspective*. Oxford: Bellagio Publishing Network.

Currey, James. 2008. *Africa Writes Back: The African Writers Series and the Launch of African Literature*. Oxford: James Currey.

Lindfors, Bernth/ 2011. *Early East African Writers and Publishers*. Trenton, NJ : Africa World Press.

Maillu, David. 1974. *After 4.30*. Nairobi : Comb Books.

8

East African Publishing and the Academia

By Emilia Ilieva and Hillary Chakava

One of the manifestations of Africa's marginalisation in the current context of globalisation is its minimal presence in the arena of global knowledge. Africa consumes far more knowledge from centres of knowledge production outside its borders than it produces and disseminates itself. Even research on Africa and knowledge about Africa is for the most part produced and published not in Africa, but in the UK, USA or France. This is not a neutral fact. The 'locations, identities, and ideologies of those who produce, categorise, disseminate, and safeguard knowledge on Africa, or any other region, have and will always matter'. Skewed as these currently are, they perpetuate 'relations of dominance of Africa by the West' (Zeleza, 1994: 182, 183). To come out of this state of subordination, African people require knowledge that is relevant to their experiences and aspirations, which alone can empower them to transform their lives in the directions they desire.

It is African scholars – especially those located in universities – who have the mandate to do research and create knowledge. And it is through publishing that this knowledge can be organised and disseminated so as to benefit the society. Thus knowledge production and scholarly publishing are two processes whose successful integration to a large extent determines Africa's emancipation from external dependency as well as its progress.

East Africa offers an example of some remarkable achievements in the collaboration between publishers and academicians as well as brings to light some problems that need to be resolved. In East Africa, the creation of specialised academic knowledge began in earnest in the 1950s and 1960s as part of the professionalisation of the major disciplinary fields within the newly established university colleges. Publishing houses within the region, some of them established during the same period, immediately took it upon themselves to publish this knowledge, releasing an impressive number of books and launching a broad range of journals and magazines. The 1960s and the early 1970s were particularly fruitful in this respect as the colleges and later universities grew in leaps and bounds. Moreover, the determination of young scholars to expand the frontiers of knowledge redoubled in the face of evidence that their input was needed as part of the larger effort to build the new nations emerging from colonialism.

These heady days were, however, soon over. The late 1970s presented numerous challenges of underdevelopment and revealed the lack of political will to deal with them effectively. These were exacerbated by the recessions in the global economy and the encroachments of political liberalism. Economic constraints and ideological dictates began to erode the role of universities as important institutional sites for the production of scholarly knowledge. In the course of the 1980s, another bout of global recession resulted in the imposition of a free-market capitalism, which was extreme in its manifestations and its unsuitability to the developmental state. Universities were particularly hard hit, having been declared practically irrelevant by the architects of the imposed Structural Adjustment Programmes (SAPs).

The 1990s signalled relief, as the wind of democratisation brought back the possibilities for free speech and inquiry, and scholarly research and publishing seemed to have gained a new lease of life. But it soon became clear that political democratisation, accompanied as it was by economic liberalisation, could not guarantee the resources universities required to function properly. In fact, universities were called upon to adopt a new corporatist ethos in which their financial survival took precedence over all other concerns. The gross deficiency of public funds for universities meant that the freedom to pursue independent research was curtailed. In addition, there was little time for fieldwork, and graduate supervision, writing and publishing were neglected. This decline in academic activities was so immediate and drastic because the universities did not have 'long histories and traditions of scholarly production and the protective networks of generations of generous alumni' (Zeleza, 2003: 400). Publishers had little content to publish and, as they themselves were adversely affected by the economic downturn, they could not act as a stimulating force either. The particular histories of knowledge production and dissemination in East Africa show in concrete terms how the mechanism linking publishing and the academia works.

History was perhaps the discipline that asserted its significance most strongly in the three colleges that constituted the University of East Africa (1963-1970) – Nairobi, Dar es Salaam and Makerere. At the University College of Nairobi, 1964 marked a turning point, with the appointment of Bethwell Allan Ogot as Professor and Head of the History Department. Ogot came with the clear mission to fashion the discipline of history in such a way as to restore humanity to the African people, whom the colonial library had represented as lacking in a historical past. Writing and publishing were immediately employed by him as strategies to realise this mission. Thus, he authored *History of the Southern Luo* and 'Reintroducing the African Man into the World: Traditionalism and Socialism in African Politics'. Both were published in 1967 by the just launched East African Publishing House (EAPH); the first as a book, the second as an essay in the new *East Africa Journal*.

Knowledge production was Ogot's major concern and he ensured that it emanated from within the process of teaching and learning. Thus he insisted that the honours undergraduate students write dissertations based on local histories. The first of these, published in 1969 by EAPH under the common title *NGANO*, included the excellent essays of William Ochieng', Kenneth Ali Mude, K. M. Okaro Kojwang, T. W. Bonaya, S. C. Langat, P. K. arap Magut, J. B. Ndung'u and Simon Baitwababo (Atieno Odhiambo, 2002).

Regular departmental seminars until 1980 gave faculty and graduate students the opportunity to present findings from their ongoing research work and set the ground for future publications. The Historical Association of Kenya, founded in 1967, held annual conferences at which scholars and high school teachers engaged in lively debates about research and pedagogy. The proceedings of some of these conferences were published in the *Hadith* series. This series, whose first issue came out in 1968, was also published by EAPH. Through it, research findings were quickly disseminated to eager students in schools and tertiary colleges. The association also edited the *Kenya Historical Review*, which soon gained prestige and became the coveted outlet for publication of Kenyan historical scholarship by authors from within Kenya as well as from the rest of the world. The History Department also hosted and edited the *TransAfrican Journal of History* from 1971.

To stimulate this productivity further, another scholarly entity was set up in 1964. This was the East African Institute of Social and Cultural Affairs, with presidents Julius Nyerere, Milton Obote and Jomo Kenyatta as its patrons. It was this institute that set up the East African Publishing House, which was to have a tremendous impact on knowledge production in the region.

One of the priorities of EAPH was the publication of scholarly monographs. Some of the titles published between 1967 and 1974 were G. S. Were's *History of the Abaluyia of Western Kenya*, Isaria Kimambo's *History of the Pare*, M.S.M. Kiwanuka's *The Kings of Buganda*, and Ahmed Idha Salim's *History of the Swahili Speaking Peoples of the Kenya Coast*.

> These works collectively revolutionised the historiography of the region, turning the gaze of scholarship away from 'East Africa and Its Foreign Invaders' trope of Sir John Gray and Kenneth Ingham to the production of history of the Africans by the locals (Atieno Odhiambo, 2002: xiv).

EAPH also published the *East Africa Journal*, which encompassed the entire thought-world of East Africa. The journal not only enriched the historiography of the region through the publication of historical essays, but provided the marketplace for ideas regarding the futures of the new East African nations while it lasted (1964-1972). The role of the intellectual in nation building preoccupied Ali Mazrui and Tom Mboya.

The issue of corruption in Kenya's cooperatives attracted early attention. Ogot and Okot p'Bitek vigorously debated the topical issue of African epistemologies. Pumla Kisosonkole, Grace Ogot and Miria Obote started discussions on the so-called Woman Question as early as that time. Following his work in the commission into Kenya's education system, Simeon Ominde wrote the essay, 'Education in Revolutionary Africa'.

EAPH also undertook the publication of the Historical Association of Tanzania papers and generally facilitated the remarkable output from the new History Department in Dar es Salaam, inaugurated in 1964. Within a short time, the became well known for its innovative approaches and tangible contributions to the teaching and writing of African history. It did not have a colonial pedigree and was set in an institution that thrived in a radical intellectual atmosphere. By 1967, the department's staff included three Tanzanian historians – Isaria Kimambo, Arnold Temu and Gilbert Gwassa, all specialising in East African history (Brizuela-Garcia, 2006).

Historians at Dar es Salaam were keenly focused on the 'African initiative' in history; that is, on the centrality of Africans in all aspects of the historical life of peoples, especially their opposition to such external forces of oppression as colonialism. Thus Kimambo's first three books – *A Political History of the Pare of Tanzania, ca 1500-1900*; *Mbiru: Popular Protest in Colonial Tanzania*; and *A History of Tanzania* (edited with A. Temu) – focused on this theme. Kimambo also joined hands with other historians working in Tanzania in the 1960s to demonstrate the validity of oral traditions as sources of historical knowledge. A major contribution in this respect was a volume edited by Andrew Roberts entitled *Tanzania Before 1900*, to which Kimambo contributed (Mapunda, 2005). All these works were published by EAPH between 1968 and 1971.

Gilbert Gwassa (1939-1982) published outstanding work, which made him a world authority on the Maji Maji uprising. EAPH published his 'The German Intervention and African Resistance in Tanzania' (1969), *Kumbukumbu za vita vya Maji Maji 1905-1907* (1969), *Records of the Maji Maji Rising Part One*, which Gwassa edited with John Iliffe (1967). Gwassa's *The Role of Religious and Traditional Beliefs during the Maji Maji War* (1970) was published by the University of Dar es Salaam (Beez, 2008).

Other works which originated from scholars of the University of Dar es Salaam and were published by EAPH included: *Recording East Africa's Past* by Andrew Roberts, *West Africa and the Atlantic Slave Trade* by Walter Rodney, *The East African Slave Trade* by E. A. Alpers, *The Making of the Karagwe Kingdom* by Israel K. Katoke, *Nyungu Ya Mawe* by Aylward Shorter, *The East African Coast* by J. E. G. Sutton, *The African Churches of Tanzania* by T. O. Ranger, *Portrait of a Nationalist* by G. R. Mutahaba, and *Early Trade in Eastern Africa* by J. E. G. Sutton. EAPH also launched the series on the Maji Maji research papers with the publication of *The Maji Maji War in Ungoni* by O. B. Mapunda and G. P. Mpangara.

At Makerere, history teaching had originally started in 1944 and focused on British and European history. Once a good number of African staff had been hired by the late 1960s, Makerere also took the path of placing African history at the core of studies. At the Makerere History Department, the major research enterprise was the three-volume History of Uganda project, which endeavoured to produce 'a new history of Uganda which will bring East African history more closely in line with modern historiographical standards' (Rockefeller grant allocation, quoted in Sicherman, 2006). Although the disruption of scholarly activities under Idi Amin put an end to work on this project, Ugandan historians who participated in it turned their prospective contributions into significant books, articles, monographs, and dissertations. Three books stood out: *A History of Kigezi in South-West Uganda* (edited by Donald Denoon), published in 1972 in Kampala by the National Trust Adult Education Centre; *The Iteso during the Asonya* (edited by J. B. Webster, C. P. Emudong, D. H. Okalany and N. Egimu-Okuda), published in 1973 by EAPH; and *The Central Luo during the Aconya* by J. M. Onyango-ku-Odongo and J. B. Webster, published in 1976 by the Nairobi branch of the East African Literature Bureau (Sicherman, 2006).

The progress made in the study of African history in the East African universities did not continue throughout the 1970s. The stagnation that set in towards the end of that decade was part of the general deterioration of historical studies in African universities 'in the midst of widespread scepticism about the value of professional academic history for the economic and social development of African societies' (Brizuela-Garcia, 2006: 150). This was accompanied by the overall reversal of gains made in the social, economic and political sphere of the three East African countries, as well as in the rest of Africa.

Under these circumstances, the New Dar School of Historiography took a sharp turn from the nationalist historiography of the 1960s and presented a strong criticism of it. Discussions veered towards philosophy and theory of history. This emphasis, as Kimambo explained retrospectively, was occasioned by the difficult political circumstances at the time. 'From the historians' point of view, the two decades of debating theory did mean lost opportunity to produce historical knowledge for almost a whole generation' (Kimambo, 1993: 15). At Nairobi, as well as Dar es Salaam, budgetary cuts eventually had negative effects on both research and teaching in history, while history at Makerere was shattered by the violence into which Uganda descended.

Publishing also suffered. The collapse of the East African Community in 1977 brought to an end such joint enterprises as the East African Literature Bureau, which since its inception in 1948 had been the major publisher of scholarly work in the region. The performance of the EAPH began to decline, until it was declared insolvent in 1984 (Chakava, 2007: 67). Nonetheless, the production of historical knowledge, though adversely affected, has continued, and the publication of scholarly titles in history, though diminished, has not stopped. East African Educational Publishers (EAEP), Kenya Literature Bureau (KLB), in Kenya; Mkuki na Nyota, in Tanzania; and Fountain Publishers, in Uganda, have done great service to the discipline. Thus, EAEP has to its credit: *Decolonization and Independence in Kenya, 1940-93*, edited by B. A. Ogot and W. R. Ochieng, the *UNESCO General History of Africa*, among other publications. KLB has published such works as F. E. Makila's *An Outline History of the Babukusu* and Henry Mwanzi's *A History of the Kipsigis*. Mkuki na Nyota has released, among other titles. Issa Shivji's *Pan-Africanism or Pragmatism. Lessons of the Tanganyika-Zanzibar Union*; *Yes, In My Lifetime. Selected* Works *of Haroub Othman*, edited by Saida Yahya-Othman; *Indian Africa. Minorities of Indian-Pakistani Origin in Eastern Africa*, edited by Michael Adam; *Custodians of the Land: Ecology and Culture in the History of Tanzania*, edited by G. Maddox, J. Giblin, and I. Kimambo; *East African Expressions of Christianity*, edited by Thomas Spear and Isaria Kimambo. Fountain Publishers has on its long list Samwiri Rubaraza Karugire's *A Political History of Uganda*; Bertram Mapunda's *Contemplating the Fipa Ironworking*; and Apolo Nsibambi's *National Integration in Uganda 1962-2013*.

Academic presses have also been involved in the publication of historical knowledge. The University of Nairobi Press has, among its titles, *Decentralization and Devolution in Kenya: New Approaches* by Thomas Kibua and Germano Mwabu, *Governance and Transition Politics in Kenya* by P. Wanyande, M. Omosa and C. Ludeki. Dar es Salaam University Press has issued *Humanities and Social Sciences in East and Central Africa: Theory and Practice*, edited by Isaria Kimambo, *Settlements, Economies and Technology in the African Past* by F. Chami, G. Pwiti and C. Radimilahy. Currently,

> calls for the 'Africanisation' of knowledge reveal deep anxieties in a field that has retained much of its intellectual vibrancy and commitment to innovation, but has also become largely disconnected from African institutions and thus, African societies. (Brizuela-Garcia, 2006: 159).

Falola (2006) has outlined specific themes and topics that African historians need to pursue in deepening and diversifying the study of national history and in connecting national history to 'global history' if the current 'crisis' in African historiography is to be overcome. It is the task of the East African historians of today to work on this scholarly agenda. They can only bring it to fruition with the involvement of East African publishers.

Moving to the discipline of literature, in the mid-1960s, the newly hired African staff in the three colleges of the University of East Africa set out to overhaul the literature curriculum they inherited from the 'English' departments in which they found themselves. This 'revolution', which placed African literature at the centre of study, played a significant role in 'decolonising the imagination' (Ngũgĩ, 1993: xiv), and led the way in the 'constitution of African literary study as a legitimate academic discipline' (Jeyifo, 1990: 43) in Africa. Apart from Africanising the curriculum, the other major task of the young lecturers was the development of African critical standards and theoretical models which would constitute an enabling critical tradition for the study of the growing body of modern African literature.

> The stage was set in the 1960s-1970s for a series of continuous confrontations between an emergent African critical establishment and an active Euro-Africanist establishment over critical standards, modalities of institutionalisation and canonisation of African literatures. (Adesanmi, 2006: 104).

It was in the course of such confrontations, animated debates and polemical discussions, as well as in the midst of actual critical practice, that new critical standards were beginning to emerge. Literary forums yielded seminal papers and these papers were published without undue delay by publishing houses within the region.

In 1971, a Festival of East African Writing was held at the University of Nairobi, whose proceedings were published in two volumes. The first volume, *Black Aesthetics in East Africa* (EALB, 1973), edited by Pio Zirimu, contains papers on such topics as aesthetic dualism, Negritude, beauty, and black identity. Zirimu had first made a call for the development of an African poetics that would examine the connections between ethics and aesthetics on pages of the literary magazine *Dhana* (Zirimu, 1973: 51). The second volume, *Writers in East Africa: Papers from a Colloquium* (EALB, 1974), is based on the writers' workshop, in which the particular problems of writers in different genres were discussed.

In 1980, the anthology, *Viewpoints: Essays on Literature and Drama*, was published by KLB, edited by Majola Mbele. It contains papers prepared for the literary magazine produced under the auspices of the Literature Department of the University of Dar es Salaam. The common stand taken in all these papers is the affirmation of the political nature of art, against what was described as bourgeois aesthetics.

Individual critical contributions to the development of East African literary studies were also published by the East African Literature Bureau and its successor, the Kenya Literature Bureau. These included Peter Nazareth's *Literature and Society in Modern Africa* (1972) and *The Third World Writer: His Social Responsibility* (1978), Micere Githae Mugo's *Visions of Africa* (1978), and Chris Wanjala's *The Season of Harvest: A Literary Discussion* (1978) and *For Home and Freedom* (1980).

Major journals like the *East Africa Journal*, the *Journal of the Language Association of East Africa*, and *Transition* (the latter published in Kampala by Rajat Neogy between 1961 and 1975), and a number of smaller magazines contributed to this literary vibrancy. *Ghala* was the special literary issue of *East Africa Journal*. It was started in September 1966, but acquired that name in the July issue of 1968. Devoted mainly to creative writing, it also carried critical articles and reviews. *Zuka: A Journal of East African Creative Writing* included short stories, poetry, critical essays and book reviews, as well as occasional articles on African art. *Busara*, formerly *Nexus*, was published under the auspices of the Department of Literature of the University of Nairobi, and presented original creative writing and critical articles, including material discussed at the University's Writers' Workshop. *Joliso: East African Journal of Literature and Society* included short stories and articles, and aimed to provide a platform for criticism, analysis and comment, not only for the literary critic, but also for social scientists, historians, philosophers, and educationists. *Umma* (formerly *Darlite*) was the journal of the Department of Literature at the University of Dar es Salaam. It published short stories, plays, and poetry, both in English and in Swahili. *Dhana* (successor to *Penpoint*) featured creative writing from East Africa together with critical essays and book reviews.

Nearly all these journals and magazines ceased publication in the late 1970s and early 1980s. At the same time, the study of literature also took a downward slide. At Dar es Salaam, a national and ideological crisis reversed the achievements made since 1967. In Nairobi, Ngũgĩ's concept of 'committed' writers and critics was dying in the mid-1970s. At Makerere, Amin brought all scholarly aspirations to a standstill in 1977 by the grisly murder of 150 students and the injury and imprisonment of others (Mamdani, 1982: 128).

The strong beginnings, however, have had a measure of continuity in the production and publication of literary knowledge in the 1980s and 1990s. EAEP published such works as Ngũgĩ wa Thiong'o's *Decolonising the Mind*, Adeola James' *In Their Own Voices: African Women Writers Talk*, *Readings in African Popular Fiction* (edited by Stephanie Newell), David Kerr's *African Popular Theatre*, Marlin Bahan's *African Theatre in Development*, and Josef Guster's *African Film: Re-imagining a Continent*. The University of Nairobi Press has issued Marjorie Oludhe Macgoye's *The Composition of Poetry* and *Creative Writing in Prose*. At present,

> the development of viable critical models, the institutional inscription of African literature, and the methods and modalities of its entry into global circuitries of dissemination and legitimation ... constitute the sites in which African literature continues to be subject to extraneous determinations and imperialist preferments. (Adesanmi, 2006: 103).

East African scholars need to rescue African literature from such 'preferments' and recapture its study through ground-breaking critical works, which need to come out of local publishing houses. They have also made a significant contribution to the indigenisation of the study of African religions. As a lecturer and professor at Makerere between 1964 and 1967, John S. Mbiti produced some of his most influential works: *Concepts of God in Africa* (1970) and *Introduction to African Religion* (1975). Although both were originally published outside Africa, they were conceived at Makerere. The second expanded edition of *Introduction to African Religion* (1991) was published by EAEP in 1992.

Okot p'Bitek criticised the early scholars for employing Judea-Christian terminology and Hellenising African religions in *African Religions in Western Scholarship*, which was published by EALB in 1971. More recently, EAEP has published J. N. K. Mugambi's *Critiques of Christianity in African Literature*; James Currey, Fountain Publishers, EAEP and Ohio University Press have co-published Heike Behrend's *Alice Lakwena & the Holy Spirits: War in Northern Uganda, 1985-97*. University of Nairobi Press published J. N. K. Mugambi's *A Comparative Study of Religions* in 1990.

Philosophy as an academic discipline also emerged out of the publications of East African scholars in the 1960s and 1970s. These scholars tackled the two major tasks facing the African academic at the time: 'to articulate the tenets of the traditional African culture in Western academic terms' and 'to formulate theories, interpretations, and criticisms of their own' (Gordon, 2006: 422, 423). In *African Religions and Philosophy* John S. Mbiti offered an analysis of African people's conception of time as a key to understanding their religious beliefs and attitudes of mind. This book was a direct outcome of Mbiti's teaching, and extensive research and fieldwork at Makerere. Originally published in 1969 in London and New York, it was later reissued by EAEP.

Henry Odera Oruka not only became the founding chairman of an independent Department of Philosophy at the University of Nairobi in 1980, but offered advancement and criticism of such developments as ethno-philosophy, nationalistic-ideological philosophy, professional philosophy, and sage philosophy. He worked to distinguish sage philosophy from 'philosophic sagacity', which was his particular research project. The second edition of his book, *Punishment and Terrorism in Africa*, was published by KLB in 1985. *Ethics: A Basic Course for Undergraduate Studies* came out the University of Nairobi Press in 1990, while *Practical Philosophy: In Search of an Ethical Minimum* was published by EAEP in 1997, after the author's death.

D. A. Masolo, who also taught at the Department of Philosophy, University of Nairobi, published extensively locally in the 1980s, before he moved to the USA. *Philosophy and Cultures*, which he co-edited with Odera Oruka, was published by Bookwise Publishers in Nairobi. 'Ideological Dogmatism and the Values of Democracy' was a chapter he contributed to a book published by Heinemann Kenya. His *magnum opus*, *African Philosophy in Search of Identity*, was co-published by EAEP and Indiana University Press in the USA, in 1994.

In the sciences, Makerere was the main centre of research in East Africa in the 1950s and 1960s. The expatriate lecturers published mostly in international journals and through foreign publishing houses, and their work had little local relevance (Opiyo-Odongo, 1992: 95). But publications in the form of departmental Occasional Papers had both local pertinence and international reach. The fields in which research began earliest were agriculture and medicine, then other fields, such as zoology, joined in.

> Some of the researchers were concerned with more than conveying their subject matter to students. They wanted to show them how knowledge was produced, and, in some cases, to involve them in the actual production of knowledge, in order to attract talented undergraduates to academic or research careers and to help others to understand research findings that they might encounter later in their professional lives (Sicherman, 2006).

But the decline which started in the late 1970s reversed this trend.

The *East Africa Journal* served as a publishing outlet for scientists too. T. R. Odhiambo and William Banage published articles on what they called the 'Crisis of Science' or 'The Scientific Revolution in East Africa'. An early issue edited by Douglas Odhiambo, Mohammed Hyder and Wilbert Chagula was devoted to 'Maintaining and Expanding Research in East Africa'. Reuben Olembo's was concerned with 'Science, Scientists and Society: Bridging the Development Gap through the Sciences'. East Africa's only woman medical doctor at the time, Dr Josephine Namboze discussed 'Priorities in Health Planning'; while Dr Hilary Ojiambo interrogated the realm of indigenous knowledge with an article on 'The Psychology of Witchcraft', and another on 'New Perspectives on Medical Education' (Atieno Odhiambo, 2002). For a long time after the *East Africa Journal* ceased publication, scientists had no forum to discuss their ideas and research findings. The launching of *Innovation and Discovery* by the Academy Science Publishers in the early 1990s, provided some welcome opportunity.

East African publishers have not been keen on publishing books in science, but such titles exist. For example, in recent years, Mkuki na Nyota has published *Managing a Changing Climate in Africa: Local Level Vulnerabilities and Adaptation Experiences*, by Pius Zebhe Yanda and Chipo Plaxedes Mubaya; Fountain Publishers have published *Design of Appropriate Agroforestry Interventions in Uganda* by M. Bukenya Namirembe, A. Zziwa and D. Waiswa; the University of Nairobi Press published the third revised edition of *Medicinal Plants of East Africa*, by J. O. Kokwaro, a much needed record of indigenous knowledge.

The above survey shows that the East African region is heir to both a brief but distinguished past of close collaboration between the academia and the publishing enterprise, in which a vast and diverse corpus of scholarship was produced and made available to East Africa and the larger world, and a longer and more recent past of dismantling of that relationship, due to a weakening of each of the two entities, and the consequent stagnation in the production of knowledge, to the detriment of the region. A look at the present moment reveals a plethora of new challenges.

As far as the academic environment is concerned, the difficulties have to do with the massive expansion of higher education in the last two decades and the consequent underfunding and understaffing of universities, their inadequate infrastructure, and the crisis of quality in teaching and learning. A new institutional culture has evolved whereby intellectual concerns have been displaced by financial and administrative exigencies. Under these circumstances, research and the standard of publications have declined.

Academicians are not hapless victims of this state of affairs as they have generally been acquiescent and complicit in the entrenchment of the prevailing status quo. Driven by mercantilism justified as dire need, they have largely abdicated their responsibility to scholarship and lost the mental energy and intellectual passion that could make them 'snatch a triumph from adversity'.

Spurred by the pressure to 'publish or perish', East African academicians have often opted to sacrifice quality for quantity, which has resulted in an 'inflation of publications', rather than the 'expansion of knowledge' (Veney and Zeleza, 2001: 12). Their publications mostly appear in journals launched by selfish founders among themselves with the sole aim of meeting immediate promotional needs. Such journals are typically of low standard and their life-span is predictably short. Yet without the production of strong, influential journals, scholarship cannot thrive.

Irregularity of publication is what undermines the reputation of even promising journals. This is the shortcoming of nearly all journals currently published in Uganda, for example. These include old ones like *Uganda Journal* (1934), *Makerere Medical Journal* (1964) and *Mawazo* (1968), as well some re-started and new ones like *Makerere Law Journal* (1975), *African Crop Science Journal* (1993), *Dialogue* (1994), *Uganda Environmental and Natural Research Management Policy and Law* (1992), *African Journal of Peace and Human Rights* (1995), *PIC News* (1998), *East African Journal of Peace and Human Rights*, *Journal of African Religion and Philosophy* (1989), *Education Journal* (1998), *Makerere University Research Journal* (2006) (Ikoja-Odongo, 2009). In Kenya, the *Journal of East African Natural History*, published by Nature Kenya/ East African Natural History Society since 1910, is the exception rather than the rule in longevity and regularity of publication.

The serious among academicians, dissatisfied with the status of local journals, seek publication abroad. But by so doing, they only make the vicious circle complete: weak journals become weaker through the constant supply of weak submissions. Committed and competent editors, as well as a 'professional culture of scholarly publishing and management' are sorely missing (Zeleza, 2003: 409).

On the positive side, research output in scientific publications has been on the rise over the last decade. According to the UNESCO Science Report

(2015), the three East African countries dominate scientific publishing in sub-Saharan Africa. Overall, the growth in scientific publications in East African countries reflects greater political support for science and technology. All the three East African countries have in place development plans – Kenya's Vision 2030, Tanzania's Vision 2025 and Uganda's Vision 2040 – which seek to leverage on science, technology and innovation to spur rapid economic growth (UNESCO, 2015).

Kenya remains the leading country in scientific publications and research impact in the region. The INASP report on Africa's scientific activity indicates that between 1996 and 2009, Kenya registered a total of 11,420 scientific publications, which were cited 126, 919 times over the same period; Tanzania registered 5,239 publications which were cited 8,858 times; while Uganda had 4,395 publications cited 49,796 times (INASP, 2012). Kenya's publications are mainly in the areas of agriculture, biological sciences and medicine. Tanzania and Uganda publish mostly in medicine, agriculture, biological science, immunology and microbiology (UNESCO, 2015; INASP, 2012).

Apart from university presses, research agencies and government departments are also active in academic publishing within the region (INASP, 2012). Makerere University leads in total output of scientific publications. Other non-university leaders include Kenya Medical Research Institute, Allied Sciences (Tanzania), International Livestock Research Institute (Kenya), Uganda Ministry of Health, National Institute for Medical Research (Tanzania), World Agroforestry Centre (Kenya) and Kenya Agricultural Research Institute (INASP, 2012). In all, African Journals OnLine (AJOL), the world's largest collection of peer-reviewed, African-published scholarly journals, based in South Africa, hosts 28 Kenyan journals, 18 Tanzanian journals, and 12 journals from Uganda, all in the sciences.

Turning to the East African publishers of today, 'in general', they are 'continuing to cut back their academic publishing programmes' (Chakava, 2007: 74). EAEP is the only house that has continuously published academic books for the last 50 years, first as the Kenya branch of Heinemann, then as Heinemann Kenya, and now as EAEP. The company has over 200 academic books in print. Working in the same spirit are Fountain Publishers, which, since its inception in 1988, has published over 700 titles, with a significant number of them in politics, economics, culture, and education, and Mkuki na Nyota, established in 1991, which has published over100 scholarly titles.

The East African university presses, such as the Dar es Salaam University Press, established in 1979, Nairobi University Press (1984), and Makerere University Press (1997), have, on the whole, not fulfilled the 'lofty mission' of university presses the world over: 'to publish and disseminate the best possible scholarship' (Greco, Wharton & Estelami, 2009:76). Thus, the present moment demands a change that would revamp the collaboration between the academia and publishers and expand the creation and dissemination of knowledge in East Africa. The change must start with the producers of knowledge – the academicians. They need to rededicate themselves to their duty to constantly study, teach, research and write. They need to do so in the context of the revitalisation of their universities, which they must spearhead themselves.

One major component in this task is to improve the quality of their publications. Measures in this direction have already been taken elsewhere on the continent. Thus, the Academy of Science of South Africa (ASSAf) has set up a scholarly publishing programme to strengthen research publishing in South Africa and to contribute to the national system of innovation. Within that programme, publicly adopted best-practice guidelines are followed by editors and publishers throughout South Africa, especially insofar as effective peer review and objective editorial decision-making are concerned. ASSAf is mandated to carry out external peer reviews and other quality audits of all South African research journals in five-year cycles, in order to make recommendations for improvement in content and management. In addition, there is a discipline-based peer review of all South African journals, managed by the academy's Chair of the Committee on Scholarly Publishing in South Africa. It recommends journals that qualify to be placed on a national, online, open access platform and also suggests ways to improve journals that are operating below the expected standard (Taole, 2010). Such measures can be adopted in the East African region.

There is also the need for East African scholars to address the new challenges to their intellectual integrity and commitment. Scholars like Amina Mama have elaborated the idea of ethical research in Africa and insisted that the manifestation of globalisation in higher institutions requires that Africa's scholarly community needs 'to proceed beyond declaring an ethical commitment to freedom, to actually working to contribute to it in the course of our professional lives and our knowledge-building and teaching practices', that is, to deal with the methodological implications of their research (Mama, 2007: 18). Publications by East African scholars must be a reflection of such ethical research.

Furthermore, East African scholars, whether residing in the region or in the diaspora, must strive to publish in the first place with publishers and journals within (East) Africa. As has been observed, the tendency to publish 'internationally' 'is not a sign of the African academics' confident universalism but of their insecure provincialism, reflecting a desperate search for intellectual legitimation from academic systems and epistemological traditions that have historically dismissed and infantilised them' (Zeleza, 2003: 410).

Scholars like D. A. Masolo have shown the way. Although based abroad, Masolo wrote the Foreword and contributed an article to the inaugural issue of *Thought and Practice: A Journal of the Philosophical Association of Kenya* in 2009, and continued to write for the 2010 and 2011 issues of the same journal. He also participated in the special issue of the *Maseno University Journal* of 2012, dedicated to the memory of the historian E. S. Atieno Odhiambo.

Regarding publishing models generally, two basic propositions have been made: one is to make commercial models more sustainable; the other is to retain the publication and dissemination of scholarship within the realm of academia (Schroeder and Siegel, 2009). The two need not be mutually exclusive, but can in fact complement one another. What can East African trade publishers and their counterparts in universities do to reengage the academicians?

Commercial publishers need to explore such opportunities as co-publishing, electronic publishing, and Print On Demand (POD) technologies (Chakava, 2007). They also need to heed Henry Chakava's call that:

> 'It is not so much the strength of your bottom line but the contribution that you make to the academic and cultural welfare of your society that will be remembered' (1996: 142).

University presses need not endlessly lament their pecuniary troubles. They are not an exception. The truth is that 'scholarly publishing isn't financially feasible as a business model – never was, never was intended to be, and should not be'. But if scholars believe in the value of scholarship, they 'must devise the best ways to support university press publishing and rally the support of the profession as a whole' (Davidson, 2009: 37, 39). Various concrete proposals have been made for university presses in Africa. Darko-Ampem (2003) has recommended a consortium of African university presses. Chakava has spoken of the possibility of university presses within East Africa going into 'partnership with commercial textbook publishers ... such as Fountain Publishers, KLB or EAEP, to handle the trade side of the business, leaving them to concentrate on getting the books published' (Chakava, 2007: 72).

Publishers need also to be more demanding regarding the quality of manuscripts they accept for publication. In addition, they need to head-hunt for the brilliant minds quietly at work on university campuses, and 'extract' from them the manuscript they are forever revising or are simply reluctant to write. They must discover the Henry Owuor Anyumbas of our time and persuade them to put their ideas on paper.

Academicians and publishers have no other choice but to close ranks and, together, restore the dignity of East African people in the vital area of knowledge production. As has been observed,

> For Africa to depend on external sources for knowledge about itself is a cultural and economic travesty of monumental proportions. ... The real challenge, then, is not simply to fill empty library shelves and acquire

gadgets for faster information retrieval, but to produce the knowledge in the first place, for Africa to study, read and know itself, to define itself to itself and to the rest of the world, and to see that world through its own eyes and not the warped lenses of others. There is no substitute for a vigorous intellectual system, of which publishing is an integral part (Zeleza, 1997: 80-81).

This vigorous intellectual system must be the vision to which East African publishers and the academia aspire.

References

Adesanmi, Pius. 2006 "Third Generation African Literatures and Contemporary Theorising." In *The Study of Africa, Volume I: Disciplinary and Interdisciplinary Encounters,* pp. 101-116, edited by Paul Tiyambe Zeleza. Dakar: CODESRIA.

Atieno Odhiambo, E. S. 2002. "Introduction: Bethwell A. Ogot and the Crucible of East African Scholarship, 1964-1980." In *The Challenges of History and Leadership I Africa: The Essays of Bethwell Allan Ogot,* pp. vii-xxii, edited by Toyin Falola and E.S. Atieno Odhiambo. Trenton, NJ: Africa World Press.

Beez, Jigal. 2008. "Gilbert Clement Gwassa 1939-1982: A Tribute to the Founder of Tanzanian Maji Maji Research." *Habari Infobrief des Tanzania Network 2008* 4, pp. 64-67. Available at: http://nbn-resolving.de/urn:nbn:de:0168-ssoar-216162, retrieved on 12 November 2015.

Brizuela-Garcia, Esperanza. 2006. "African Historiography and the Crisis of Institutions." In *The Study of Africa, Volume I: Disciplinary and Interdisciplinary Encounters,* pp. 135-167, edited by Paul Tiyambe Zeleza. Dakar: CODESRIA.

Chakava, H. 1996. *Publishing in Africa: One Man's Perspective*. Oxford: Bellagio Publishing Network.

Chakava, Henry. 2007. "Scholarly Publishing in Africa: The Perspective of an East African Commercial and Textbook Publisher." In *African*

Scholarly Publishing Essays, pp. 66-75, edited by Alois Mlambo. Oxford: African Books Collective Ltd.

Darko-Ampem, K. O. 2003. "Scholarly Publishing in Africa: A Case Study of the Policies and Practices of African University Presses." PhD thesis presented to the Graduate School of the University of Stirling. Available at: *https://www.google.com/?gws_rd= ssl#q=darko+ampem+publishing.* Retrieved on 20 November 2015.

Davidson, Cathy N. 2009. "The Futures of Scholarly Publishing." In *The State of Scholarly Publishing: Challenges and Opportunities,* pp. 35-47, edited by Albert N. Greco. Piscataway, NJ: Transaction Publishers.

Falola, Toyin. 2006. "Writing and Teaching National History in Africa in the Era of Global History." In *The Study of Africa, Volume I: Disciplinary and Interdisciplinary Encounters,* pp. 168-186, edited by Paul Tiyambe Zeleza. Dakar: CODESRIA.

Gordon, Lewis R. 2006. "African Cultural Studies and Contemporary African Philosophy." In *The Study of Africa, Volume I: Disciplinary and Interdisciplinary Encounters,* pp. 417-442, edited by Paul Tiyambe Zeleza. Dakar: CODESRIA.

Greco, Albert N., Robert M. Wharton, and Hooman Estelami. 2006. "The Changing Market for University Press Books in the United States: 1997-2002." In *The Study of Africa, Volume I: Disciplinary and Interdisciplinary Encounters,* pp. 49-81, edited by Paul Tiyambe Zeleza. Dakar: CODESRIA.

Ikoja-Odongo, J. R. 2009. *Publishing in Uganda with Notes from Africa: A Review.* Kampala: Nabotu.

INASP. 2012. "Scientific Development in African Countries: A Scientific Approach 1996-2009". Project Report. Available at: http://www.inasp.info/uploads/filer_public/2013/06/20/scientific_development_in_african_countries.pdf. Retrieved on 25 February, 2014.

Jeyigo, Biodun. 1990. "The Nature of Things: Arrested Decolonization and Critical Theory." *Research in African Literatures,* Vol. 21, No. 1 (1990): 33-48.

Kimambo, I. N. 1993. *Three Decades of Production of Historical Knowledge at Dar es Salaam*. Dar es Salaam: Dar es Salaam University Press.

Mama, Amina. 2007. "Is It Ethical to Study Africa? Preliminary Thoughts on Scholarship and Freedom." *African Studies Review*, Vol. 50, Issue 01 (2007): 1-26.

Mapunda, Bertram B. B. 2005. "A Critical Examination of Isaria Kimambo's Ideas through Time." *History in Africa*, Vol. 32 (2005): 269-279.

Mamdani, Mahmood. 1982. "The Makerere Massacre." In *The Debate (University of Dar es Salaam Debate on Class, State & Imperialism*, pp. 128-132, edited by Yash Tandon. Dar es Salaam: Tanzania Publishing House.

wa Thiong'o, Ngugi. 1993. *Moving the Centre: The Struggle for Cultural Freedoms*. Nairobi: EAEP.

Opiyo-Odongo, Joseph M. A. 1992. *Designs on the Land: Agricultural Research in Uganda, 1890-1990*. Nairobi: ACTS Press.

Ranger, T. O. 1969. "The Recovery of African Initiative in Tanzanian History." Inaugural Lecture at the University College, Dar es Salaam, Inaugural Lecture Series No. 2.

Schroeder, Robert and Gretta E. Siegel. 2009. "A Cooperative Publishing Model for Sustainable Scholarship." In *The State of Scholarly Publishing: Challenges and Opportunities*, pp. 219-229, edited by Albert N. Greco. Piscataway, NJ: Transaction Publishers.

Sicherman, Carol. 1998. "Revolutionizing the Literature Curriculum at the University of East Africa: Literature and the Soul of the Nation." *Research in African Literatures*, Vol. 29, No. 3 (1998): 129-148.

Sicherman, Carol. 2006. *Becoming an African University: Makerere 1922-2000*. Kampala: Fountain Publishers.

Taole, Nthabiseng. 2010. "Towards Improving Research Inputs and Outputs in South Africa: The Initiatives of the Academy of Science of South Africa." In *Scholarly Publishing in Africa: Opportunities and*

Impediments, pp. 15-23, edited by Solani Ngobeni. Johannesburg: Africa Institute of South Africa.

UNESCO. 2015. *UNESCO Science Report: Towards 2030.* Paris: UNESCO Publishing. Available at: http://unesdoc.unesco.org/images/0023/002354/235406e.pdf, retrieved on 20 November 2015.

Veney, Cassandra Rachel and Tiyambe Zeleza, eds. 2001. *Women in African Studies Scholarly Publishing.* Trenton, NJ: Africa World Press.

Zeleza, Paul Tiyambe. 1994. "African Studies and the Disintegration of Paradigms." *African Development,* Vol. XIX, No 4 (1994): 179-193.

_____. 1997. *Manufacturing African Studies and Crises.* Dakar: CODESRIA.

_____. 2003. *Rethinking Africa's Globalization. Volume 1: The Intellectual Challenges.* Trenton, NJ: Africa World Press.

Zirimu, Pio. 1973. "Questioning the Makerere Modes of Criticism: One Man's Irritations." *Dhana,* Vol. 3, No. 2 (1973): 457-53.

9

Publishing in East Africa: A Close Examination of Uganda (1985-2015)

By James Tumusiime

Introduction

Book publishing in East Africa has a history that is closely tied with the continent's colonial experience. Although early books came from Arab caravan traders, it was not until the spread of Christianity and the attendant missionary activity that literacy, books and related publications, gained new ground in East Africa. Church presses in the region and books imported mainly from Britain serviced the education system. Most of the imported books came from British publishers based in the UK and later, some set up office in the region particularly in Nairobi. To publish locally generated books, the East African Literature Bureau (EALB) was founded in 1948. Its creation improved and advanced literacy and literary production. Headquartered in Nairobi, the EALB had branches in Kampala and Dar es Salaam from which plenty of work in literacy and book development was done especially in indigenous languages. As the book industry continued to grow, nearby institutions like churches also propelled writing and publishing. Alongside the EALB, newspapers also provided an outlet for new forms of knowledge that the colonial enterprise depended on to inform society of its varied policies.

It is important to note that throughout the East African colonial experience most of the publishers who entered the industry were foreign-based, especially with bases in London and they treated East

Africa like one region. These publishers included Oxford University Press, Macmillan, Longman, Thomas Nelson and Evans. Some of them eventually established offices in the region, especially in Nairobi. In other cases local investors gradually bought into some of them. For example, in 1965 Heinemann and Cassel, both of London, merged to form Heinemann Publishers Kenya in Nairobi and provided groundbreaking literary publications in the region. With the East African Community (EAC) in place, and the three countries sharing the same school curriculum, and the same examination syndicate at O and A-level, school books easily crossed borders, and were shared across the whole region. It was mostly the multinationals and EALB that supplied books in the region. Books like *East African Mathematics*, *The Nile English Course*, and *Oxford English Course*, etc. were common names across the region. However with President Amin declaring the 'economic war' in 1972 and the subsequent collapse of the EAC in 1977, the region abandoned calls for more integrated development. The EALB also broke and each country went separate ways. Tanzania strengthened the Tanzania Publishing House (TPH) and Kenya set up the Kenya Literature Bureau (KLB), while publishing in Uganda gradually died.

In Uganda, throughout the Amin regime (1972-1979), there was hardly any book publishing. The entire book industry collapsed. Even the multinational publishers who often supplied books in Uganda also stopped following the turmoil brought about by Amin's economic war. Consequently, schools and other book buyers and readers then resorted to few imported books, photocopies and cycle-styled pamphlets from teachers.

With the collapse of the Amin regime in 1979, and a semblance of stability returning to the country, the book industry in Uganda started to show signs of recovery. From around 1982, international publishers started coming back to survey the available opportunities, and books produced in Nairobi were again being imported into the country. However, through the 1980s and early 1990s multinational publishers dominated the publishing scene and the local publishers had no voice in the market or the book trades. The few multinationals who were able to win book tenders in the donor-funded recovery programme of the Obote II days and the early years of Museveni's government entrenched themselves in the education system.

The space for local publishers

Starting from 1990 grumbling voices from local publishers and some of the multinationals that had lost out in the donor funded textbook bonanza of the 1980s and early 1990s grew louder. Around this time, two main publishing houses had been established in Uganda: Fountain Publishers and Crane Publishers. Both companies were young and did not understand the publishing terrain really well. Recording steady successes with its maiden (politically appealing)[1] publications, Fountain Publishers ventured further afield. Interested in becoming a complete publishing house, it put out its first textbook for ordinary level – *Revision Mathematics*. Reviewers, especially teachers, received the book well. Encouraged, Fountain sought to circulate it widely, a thing that could happen by selling it to the Ministry of Education's National Curriculum Development Centre (NCDC) . They were met with rejection: By some dubious arrangement, international publishers had acquired monopoly of supplying school books to the Ministry, which the latter distributed to schools.

In many former colonies, publishers based in former colonising countries had monopolised the textbook publishing business. The multinationals had come up with a sort of racialised homogenous characterisation that all Africans looked the same! One book would be published in the UK to serve all African and Caribbean countries without respect for local context. So they would carry the same illustrations in books to be sold either in Ghana or Uganda. When they wanted to sell them in Uganda, they would work with a couple of people at NCDC to indigenise the books. This meant replacing foreign names with Ugandan names, and foreign places with names of villages in Uganda. At the front cover, these publishers would say, 'Published by National Curriculum Development Centre,' indicating the NCDC as the publisher. On the title pages of these books, the names of

---

1 One of Fountain's first books was *Who is Who in Uganda* (1990) and the book became a sensation because it rhymed well with the information-starved populace, especially on the men and women running the country.

the teachers that had participated in the adaptation would be inscribed – as if they had been the authors. As Nancy Rose Hunt has noted, this stage-management was geared towards denying the initiative and progress of particular peoples across history so as to enable the transmutation of their history to become that of Europeans in Africa.[2]

There was little, if any, concern for promoting local publishers. Foreign-owned publishers had influenced their way right to the top and it would be very difficult to dislodge them. While this trend of publishing was commonplace in many countries, some of those that cared about their citizen's interests would make sure that a window was open for the local publishers, which was not the case for Uganda. I want to think the entire political establishment and government bureaucracy did not understand the importance of having a strong local publishing industry in their countries – so was publishing as an idea. Similar attitudes were prevalent in Kenya in the 1970s and 1980s. However, this was only to a degree. For some time, foreign-owned companies including Macmillan, Longman, Heinemann, and Oxford had dominated the Kenyan publishing industry. These brought in the professional skills and expertise. Since these foreign-owned companies relied heavily on Kenyan nationals especially in the mid-level management positions, they had empowered the nationals as professionals in the book and newspaper industry. One of these professionals was Henry Chakava who continued to fight for more indigenisation of the industry. Ugandan professionals continued learning from these encounters with the Kenyan industry, and these lessons would soon bear fruits.

Trying to push a book into the Ministry of Education opened the eyes of Fountain Publishers, perhaps the most established local company at the time. Serendipitously, around this time, the Canadian Organisation for Development of Education (CODE) had started working in Uganda, and was keen on developing local publishers. They had opened shop in Tanzania and were working to reach other countries in the region. Aware that multinationals suffocated local publishers, one of CODE's

---

2 See Hunt Rose Nancy (2002), 'Tintin and the Interruption of Congolese Comics' in Landau P.S. et.al. (2002), Images and Empires: Visuality in Colonial and Post-Colonial Africa, University of California Press: Berkeley.

senior personnel suggested strengthening the publisher's association so that they could put up a united front as local publishers. It happened that a few months earlier, Fountain Publishers and Crane Publishers had started the Uganda Publishers and Booksellers Association (UPABA). Crane Publishers' Managing Director Mustapha Mutyaba had worked for years with Longman and had a good sense of the industry and also had understanding of the workings of multinationals. CODE offered to help local publishers find their footing. It offered to give them exposure to African countries whose publishing industries were much advanced, and with local players having central positions.

In 1992, CODE funded Fountain Publisher's James Tumusiime and Mustapha Mutyaba of Crane Publishers for trips to Nairobi and Harare. In Nairobi, the two met Henry Chakava who had just become owner of Heinemann (Kenya) and had renamed it East African Educational Publishers (EAEP). Chakava was incredibly insightful about the politics of the industry in Africa. He explained how the Kenya publishing industry, which was the most advanced in the region, worked and how it had managed to strengthen local capacity. At the end, he offered to support the Ugandan struggle to publishing independence.

In Zimbabwe, the experience was different but equally liberated. Twelve years after independence, the country was buzzing with life, the economy was booming – and everyone was deeply excited about generating and acquiring knowledge. They had an efficient system of publishing where government helped local publishers. All books written by the different publishers and taken to the Curriculum Development Unit (CDU) were received on the understanding that neither was to be rejected. In this effort, the CDU would advise publishers on how to improve their manuscripts before having them printed. Because books were bought continuously, publishers were not judged on the basis of winner take all. In this case, those who did not make it on the first round were given a second chance. When members of UPABA returned from their trips, they sought meeting with President Museveni and in 1992, together with the representatives of multinationals met the President at State House. Despite acknowledging that local publishers did not have the capacity to produce books for schools, local publishers demanded opening of the supply of school books. Despite the potential that this meeting possessed, it did not bring about any immediate tangible benefit.

Enter USAID

It is still interesting that while European-based publishers were bent on continuing to dominating Uganda's publishing space, American donors became keen on opening space for local publishers. It started when personnel from the Project Implementation Unit of the Ministry of Education supported by the World Bank picked interest in the local publishers fight. An internal report on a study in education in 1989 indicated that the World Bank spent $28 million on a five-year project to improve education and most of this money was spent on buying books since 1982. It also indicated that the beneficiary schools had ignored the books delivered to them. The problem: the books were out of touch with the realities on the ground. The books were too foreign to attract any attention from their intended readers. Around the same time, the United States government was in advanced stages of funding a project in education called SUPER (Support to Uganda Primary Education Reform). Valued at about $100 million, it was meant for supporting teacher training, buying books and building classrooms.

With this report, UPABA, energised by the motivation from EAEP's Henry Chakava, and ideas from the newly formed Harare-based African Publishers Network (APNET), sought audience with the education advisor at USAID. At the end of the meeting, USAID stepped back a bit noting that they would only carry on with the project unless the supply of school books was done in a transparent manner. With further studies on publishing in the region, USAID called a conference for a conclusive roadmap.

The Lweza Conference

In early 1993, stakeholders in Uganda's publishing industry met at a church facility in Lweza – a town off Entebbe road – to deliberate on the future of book publishing and selling in Uganda. Perhaps this will remain one of the most important conferences in Uganda's publishing history. Stakeholders included publishers and booksellers under their association,

UPABA, directors from the Ministry of Education, including the head of the National Curriculum Development Centre, the head of the Uganda National Examinations Board (UNEB). They also included the Commissioner for Education. USAID played the observer's role. With facilitators coming from the Kenya Institute of Education (KIE), the conference assumed a regional configuration as heated deliberations ensued.

At the end of a very long and heated exchange, Ministry of Education officials and the representatives of multinationals effortlessly conceded to opening up the procurement process. The conference ended with a policy that stipulated, among other things, the need to create an Instructional Materials Unit (IMU) in the Ministry of Education, which hitherto did not exist, but which would now oversee a transparent system for vetting books used in schools. In mid-1993, the Ugandan government promulgated the national textbook policy. The policy among other things, after the bidding process, allowed three best-evaluated publishers per subject to supply books in all the schools. This meant competition improved in the industry allowing publishing to thrive – with many players including local ones. Although this policy opened the door for local publishers to participate in book tenders in the Ministry of Education, none of these companies had the capacity to compete with the well-established multinationals. The only alternative available for the local was to form partnerships with the more established companies especially from Kenya and Ghana. One of the most renowned cases was the partnership between Fountain Publishers and EAEP. This partnership produced coursebooks for primary science – *Fountain Primary Science for Uganda*. Ugandan and Kenyan authors wrote these Coursebooks jointly. The book proved a spectacular success and inspired further collaboration between publishers in Uganda and other countries.

In the publishing history of Uganda, this is regarded as the 'Golden Era'. Many publishers set up offices in Uganda and engaged Ugandan authors in all subjects. That way, teachers, editors, and illustrators and other book-related professionals in the country got opportunities to participate in the now vibrant local books industry. Many books were thus published, and many bookshops were opened in different parts of the country.

Challenges

Presently, there are over 20 registered publishers in Uganda. Some of these are indigenous while others are regional or international. A number of them are seasonal – appearing only during book tender submission time. By 2015, only nine of these were registered with Uganda Publishers Association (UPA). That said however, the publishing environment is yet to realise its full potential. Across the region, the publishing industry is still dogged by multiple challenges. These range from a poor reading culture, uncertain investment climate, poor book buying policies, and a weak book chain (see for example, Makotsi and Nyariki, 1997; Mlambo, 2007). In the first instance, the stakeholders in the book industry – government, parents, the examination board, libraries, bookshops, and the inspectorate of education are barely talking to each other neither do they understand what the other is doing. Parents and schools have remained shy to appreciate publishing as a major component of education sector, and government has remained unsupportive. That aside, the investment climate in East Africa has still failed to harmonise the three intrinsically related components of publishing – with pedagogical, financial and industrial. Away from issuing tenders, government has kept aloof from appreciating the other components of publishing, which need regulation and help (see for example, Makotsi and Nyariki (1997) discussion of the absence of the loan facility for publishing without collateral). Indeed, although publishing mostly looks like a service industry concerned mostly with making sure good content books are provided to the country's readers, it is also an industrial enterprise in the sense that printing and binding of books is a core aspect of the business, and is very industrial in this sense. These require huge financial investment requiring the help of government.

In Uganda for example, government's flip-flopping policies on books is a cause for uncertainty, which continues to stifle the industry. In 1993 when the book policy was opened to allow local publishers to compete with the multinationals, the policy on tenders allowed at least three publishers to supply books per subject. They would then be asked to compete in the market amongst each other convincing schools to buy their books.

When that policy was in place, many publishers had some assurance that some of their books would be bought. This encouraged them to venture into publishing in different subjects even outside prescribed textbooks. It also forced them to be creative and quality conscious in order to present more appealing books to the now empowered teachers – empowered in the sense that they did the selection. In 2002, however, government adopted the winner-take-all policy even when it was clear it had potential to kill the industry. When a winner-take-all policy was adopted, it meant if one publisher won on a subject – whether the winning was based on a technicality or pricing and not necessarily content – it meant all the others had to pack their bags and leave, for a period of five years or longer depending on the lifecycle of the curriculum! In the end, the industry suffered from the absence of competition, while at the same time, competing publishers were stifled. It is highly likely that the adoption of the winner-take-all policy also contributed to the departure of many publishers especially from Uganda because the environment became uncertain.

The other challenge facing the industry is a weak book chain – publishers, printers and bookstores. Composed of authors, editors, illustrators, graphic designers and reviewers, publishing continues to suffer from a dearth of these highly professional skills. With the exception of the illustrators, many people of these professionals have been self-taught especially from sister-professionals. For instance, teachers of English language often give the industry editors, while experts of different areas work as reviewers. For a while, Fountain Publishers had to hire expatriates for editors and reviewers. With the absence of high quality printing in the industry, Uganda has continued to rely on Kenya and further afield such as India and Malaysia for printing. The challenge is compounded by a small number of bookshops and libraries across the country, and schools failing to build a strong reading culture. Put together, with the absence of avid readers in schools, it ends in an absence of both writers and editors, which impacts the amount of books that come out at the end of the day, which has effect on printing and overall investment in the industry. A study done in 2013 showed that slightly over 20 titles were published annually in the entire country from recognised local publishers (more books are being self-published, although this has challenges of quality).

Other challenges across the region have included the failure to appreciate publishing as a small part of a larger process. According to Janssens-Andrejew and Bakker (2012), the challenges of publishing in East Africa must be situated in the larger problem of the poor research climate in the region since it is research and writing initiatives that feed into the publishing industry.[3] The challenges seem enormous: poor reading culture among the reader base, inadequate training in research initiatives, and inadequate skilling of educational programmes' reviewers, among others.[4] Yet, Bakker and Janssens-Andrejew highlight the findings of Adam, King and Hook (2010) who noted that the challenges of publishing in Africa were reflective of a larger research malaise:

> the volume of activity remains small, much smaller than is desirable if the potential contribution of Africa's researchers is to be realised for the benefit of its populations. The challenges that the continent faces are enormous and indigenous research could help provide both effective and focused responses (Adams et al, 2010: 5).

In light of these findings, it would seem that alleviating the challenges of the publishing industry in East Africa is closely entwined with surmounting the obstacles to effective research initiatives and managing the literary culture, all of which feed into each other to form a complex web of relations, which publishing is an integral part.

Conclusion: Moving forward

The idea of a book flood – where learners are 'showered' with reading material, say ten books against one learner – could help straighten matters a great deal by producing a community of readers who would have a ripple effect in the book chain. This policy is credited with the uplifting

---

[3] Anne Bakker and Floris Janssens-Andrejew, *Opportunities and Challenges: Academic and Digital Publishing in Tanzania* (Dodoma: St. John's University of Tanzania, 2012), p.5.
[4] Ibid, p.8.

of the educational standards in the Asian Tiger economies of Malaysia, Singapore, South Korea and Thailand. Although this might not cost too much money (considering the experience of other countries that have done it), governments are yet to come to terms with such a suggestion. As regards the place for bookselling, the few publishers who are locally-based have moved beyond the traditional bookshops by seeking other outlets to get their books to the reading public. Most of the major supermarkets in Kampala and other major towns – Nakumatt, Tuskys, Shoprite, and Capital Shoppers – nowadays have book sections on different topics including textbooks. This is a promising trend. Even smaller stores around the city have spaces for bookselling. More and more places for selling books are opening, and indication of a rising interest in books, and a growing culture of reading.

With the expansion of the East African Community where Burundi and Rwanda came on board, with the latter switching to an English curriculum, the East African publishing industry got a boost. Rwanda has prioritised education and has borrowed heavily from the experiences of the other East Africans to build its industry. As a result many publishers have set up shop in Rwanda and are working with Rwandan professionals to produce books for schools, and the general public. This is an equally important development for the regional industry.

In spite of these apparent successes, all the countries in the region are still bogged down with unclear book policies. This makes it hard to predict the future success of the industry. This calls for a more favourable and transparent business environment. The space within which publishing works to give its final products to clients calls for clarity of guidelines. Publishing houses, the public and government agencies are all partners in this endeavour and must contribute in the debate on how to improve the sector. However, governments must provide the leading role by improving budgetary allocations to the improvement of schoolbook supplies and the research initiative climate that can ensure creativity among writers, sensitise the public on the significance of literacy and a good reading culture.

References

Adams, Jonathan, Christopher King and Daniel Hook. 2010. *Global Research Report Africa*. New York: Thomson Reuters.

Bakker, Anne and Floris Janssens-Andrejew. 2012. *Opportunities and Challenges: Academic and Digital Publishing in Tanzania*. Dodoma: St. John's University of Tanzania.

Hunt Rose Nancy. 2002. "Tintin and the Interruptions of Congolese Comics". In *Images and Empires: Visuality in Colonial and Post-Colonial Africa*, edited by Paul Landau and Susan Griffin. Berkeley: University of California Press.

Mamdani, Mahmood. 1996. *Citizen and Subject: Contemporary Africa and the Legacy of Late Colonialism*. Kampala: Fountain.

Mamdan, Mahmood. 2008. "Lessons from Zimbabwe," *London Review of Books*, Vol. 30, No. 23.

Makotsi Ruth and Lily Nyariki, eds. 1997. *Publishing and Book Trade in Kenya:* Nairobi: East African Educational Publishers.

Meister, Robert. 2011. *After Evil: A Politics of Human Rights on South Africa*. New York: Columbia University Press.

Mlambo, Alois, ed. 2007. *African Scholarly Publishing*. Oxford: Africa Book Collective.

Waweru, David. 2013. "Why Publishing in Kenya is Tougher than Boxing, Publishing Perspectives", available at: http://publishing perspectives.com/2013/01/why-publishing-in-kenya-is-tougher-than-boxing/#.VoKlNprpfmI. Retrieved on 30 December, 2015.

10

Indigenous Publishing in Africa: The Need for Research, Documentation and Collaboration

By Hans M. Zell

From the Scottish Highlands to Nigeria

This writer recently donated a substantial collection of books, monograph series, journals, articles, and many other documents on publishing and book development in sub-Saharan Africa to a university institution in Africa.[1] The collection was shipped from its previous location in Lochcarron, a small remote village in the Northwest Scottish Highlands, to the still very young Kwara State University Library in

---

1 The collection consists of the following material: (i) Books, monograph series, essay collections, conference proceedings, book sector studies, book industry training manuals, theses and dissertations, as well as reference works. (ii) A large number of journals including, for example, complete runs of *The African Book Publishing Record* since it was first published in 1975, APNET's *African Publishing Review*, and the *Bellagio Publishing Network Newsletter*; as well as complete runs or back issues of a number of book professional journals, such as the *Journal of Scholarly Publishing* and *Logos. Forum of the World Book Community,* that have contained frequent articles on publishing and book studies in Africa and the developing world. Much of this material was contained in the reference resource *Publishing, Books & Reading in Sub-Saharan Africa: A Critical Bibliography*, published by Hans Zell Publishing in 2008, in both print and electronic formats. A very substantial number of new records have been added to the online database since publication of the print edition. (iii) Also part of the collection are a large number of box files containing over a thousand periodical articles, press clippings, reports, studies, and surveys on many aspects of publishing and the book world in Africa, together with some unpublished material and ephemera.

Nigeria, in October 2015. Another component of the donation is a rich online database currently containing over 3,000 for the most part fully annotated records, making it the most comprehensive documentation, and ongoing analysis, of the state of the book sector and the 'book chain' in Africa. The physical collection covers the twenty-year period from 1996 to 2014, and is a continuation of an earlier collection and archive (for the 1960-1995 period) that was donated to the African Publishers Network (APNET) in Harare in 1995.[22]

The most recent donation follows an invitation to several institutions in Africa and elsewhere to express an interest in acquiring the collection, and submit a proposal for the continuation and hosting of the database. Strong expressions of interest were received from a total of eight institutions, in Ghana, Kenya, Nigeria, South Africa, Zimbabwe, and the UK. After careful review of all submissions, Kwara State University Library in Malete, Nigeria, was chosen as the recipient of the collection, and as the new hosting institution for the online database.

Kwara State University submitted a detailed plan describing the implementation process of moving the database to a more dynamic digital platform, by which the existing database is being exported from its current solution, thereafter normalised and structured by a software development organisation, before finally being imported into a Drupal based database.[3] This migration – which will lead to a huge enhancement of the database in terms of its functionality and utility – will take place sometime during the course of 2015 or early in 2016.

Prompted by these developments, Kwara State University intends to set up a Book Institute or Centre for the Book, which will form part of its academic and research plans to establish a range of research centres that will also incorporate a Nigerian Film Institute and a Centre for Ilorin Manuscripts and Culture. This is very good news, and it has given me

---

2   Unfortunately this earlier collection donated to APNET is no longer accessible, and its precise status is not known.

3   Pending its migration to the new hosts in Nigeria the current database is now freely accessible at *http://www.hanszell.co.uk/cgi-bin/online/pbrssa.shtml*. The Drupal based database is: *https://www.drupal.org/* open access/open source content management platform

a measure of satisfaction to see the collection and the accompanying database finding a new home in Africa, where the work which I started over four decades ago will now be carried on. The new Nigerian hosts hope that the online database can continue to be further developed and expanded through collaborative curation with institutions elsewhere in Africa, as well as by enlisting the assistance of some of the major African studies libraries in the countries of the North.

The need for research and analysis about the African book sector

There is a vital need for research, analysis, documentation, and systematic gathering of reliable data and statistics on the whole book sector in Africa. Such reliable data is essential to reinforce advocacy and fundraising for African book-related programmes and new book sector initiatives.

Kelvin Smith, in a book review essay of the print edition of *Publishing, Books and Reading in Sub-Saharan Africa*[4] eloquently articulates the arguments for the building of a dynamic state of the art digital resource, as well as the need for more North-South collaboration and research links. He argues that if publishing and information professionals, NGOs and civil society organisations in Africa are going to be successful in advocating the importance of their work for the greater development goals, then more data and rigorous analysis will be required. The preservation and further development of research resources available through digital networks will be vital to this. Moreover,

> A programme to develop a North-South research group could also include training opportunities in Africa on rights and digital publishing issues that are so important in the global publishing landscape. It could provide an incentive to establish long-term partnership programmes that would be of equal benefit to researchers in and out of Africa. It could provide the additional benefit of including African

---

4 Hans M. Zell, *Publishing, Books and Reading in Sub-Saharan Africa: An Annotated Bibliography*, with an introductory essay by Henry Chakava (Lochcarron, Scotland: Hans Zell Publishing, 2008), p. 762p. Online edition available at: *http://www.hanszell.co.uk/pbrssa/index.shtml*.

publishers and libraries in more public-commercial digital partnerships with partners worldwide, and give experience in new digital publishing methods. The engagement of the university and industry research sectors in the development of this resource would add weight to advocacy activities in support of book development. (Smith, 2006: 187)

... In global terms this is a small task, and the costs are also small when compared to research networks in other fields — think of how quickly Google could do this. There could be other benefits. In addition to ensuring the continued development of the research base, it would also be a way of showing that African documentation, too often ignored, is important to the worldwide research community. Where better to show this than in relation to publishing, books, libraries and reading? (Smith, 2006: 187).[5]

North-South and South-South collaboration for publishing education and training

There are currently only six university institutions in sub-Saharan (English-speaking) Africa with departments of publishing and book studies, two in Ghana, one each in Kenya and Zimbabwe, and two in South Africa (see Appendix for full details). In developing a North-South research group it could well be beneficial for these African institutions to seek collaboration or partnerships with publishing and book studies departments in the countries of the North, notably the UK, where two of the leading centres for publishing education are the Oxford International Centre for Publishing Studies at Oxford Brookes University and the Stirling Centre for International Publishing and Communication at the

---

5   Kelvin Smith, 'A Magnum Opus on African Publishing.' *Logos. Forum of the World Book Community* 19, no. 4 (2008): 184-187. Freely accessible at *https://www.academia.edu/2700335/A_magnum_opus_on_African_Publishing*. Kelvin Smith is a former Principal Lecturer at the Oxford International Centre for Publishing Studies at Oxford Brookes University.

University of Stirling in Scotland.[6] These two institutions have attracted a sizeable number of African students over the years, for both undergraduate or masters programmes in publishing. Graduates from the programmes have gone on to a range of publishing or publishing-related careers in the commercial as well as not-for-profit sectors in Africa. There are also a small number of institutions in North America who have shown a special interest in publishing in the developing world, for example the Master of Publishing Program at Simon Fraser University in Canada.[7]

So it would make sense to establish research links, or the formation of a research cluster, bringing together suitable academic and research institutions in Africa, Europe and in North America, and which, as Kelvin Smith suggests, might then also include training opportunities in Africa or elsewhere on digital publishing and rights issues. Equally desirable of course would be active South-South collaboration and research links between the six African institutions mentioned above, and/or links between publishing training institutions in English-speaking Africa and those in the francophone regions of the continent, such as the Tunis-based Centre Africain de Formation à l'Édition et à la Diffusion (CAFED).[8]

It ought to be added that, for institutional collaboration to be effective and productive, and for long term benefits to accrue to participating institutions, all parties will need to be convinced of the value of their collaboration, which must be oriented towards long-term sustainability

---

6   Oxford Brookes University: *http://publishing.brookes.ac.uk/*; University of Stirling in Scotland: *http://www.publishing.stir.ac.uk/*. With the support of the UK Department for International Development, the Oxford International Centre for Publishing Studies earlier carried out an exchange programme with the (then named) Department of Book Industry at Kwame University of Science and Technology in Kumasi, Ghana, from 1998 to 2001. This also involved collaboration on course development, and the development of teaching and learning materials.

7   Details on Simon Fraser University is available at: *http://publishing.sfu.ca/master-of-publishing/*. See also, for example, *http://tkbr.ccsp.sfu.ca/pub802/2014/01/electronic-book-publishing-where-is-its-place-in-developing-countries-2/*, and also its useful list of publishing schools worldwide at *http://www.lib.sfu.ca/help/research-assistance/subject/publishing/schools*.

8   Centre Africain de Formation à l'Edition et à la Diffusion (CAFED), 9, rue Hooker Doolitle, Tunis Belvédère, Tunisia (other address: *not* verified, Immeuble Intilak, 1082 Cité Mahrajène, Tunis, Tunisia) cafed@email.ati.tn or *cafed@topnet.tn*, no website at this time. Principal contact: Ridha Najar, Technical Director/CEO.

goals. While seeking international collaboration, it is likewise important that there is more interaction between university institutions with departments of publishing studies and the book professions at the local level. And that these academic institutions should become more pro-active to establish book industry links, as well as actively engaging with their national book trade associations, book development council, national library board, and other stakeholders in the book sector.[9] Additionally, university institutions involved in publishing education should seek to enhance their profile and visibility – both locally as well as internationally – by publishing the results of research undertaken by members of staff, and making this available online on their websites.

Finally, in the light of the demise of the African Publishers Network,[10] there is now a need for an African book promotional organisation, or a library or research institution in Africa, to accept responsibility to act as a centre of knowledge about African publishing: systematically acquiring and collecting new material pertinent to the book sector, conducting research, generating reference resources and building up databases, archiving and digitising collections, and making these widely accessible to the African book professions, as well as to those elsewhere undertaking research into the many aspects of publishing and book development on the continent.

Can a new organisation or institution – that has the will, the capacity, and necessary commitment – be found to take on the role of research and documentation about the African book sector?

---

9 This is already happening to a large extent in South Africa, but there is not much evidence elsewhere of such book industry links, and active collaboration between the academic institutions involved in publishing education and the local book industry.

10 The African Publishers Network (APNET), the pan-African organisation founded in 1992 and established to strengthen indigenous publishing throughout Africa, brought together national publishers associations and publishing communities. Unfortunately it has been dormant for several years now, and although there is still a governing board there are no signs of activities of any kind (as at October 2015), and its website has been shut down.

Generating book industry data and statistics

An important component of such an organisation's activities would have to include the systematic gathering of statistical data about African publishing output, analysis of book imports and book exports, readership surveys, as well as research about book buying and reading habits, in print or digital formats.

The need and availability of reliable book production statistics is perhaps particularly acute. In much of the literature on publishing in Africa numerous writers of articles and reports on the state of the book sector in Africa have raised the issue of Africa's total book production, comparing it with that of the rest of the world. Almost always they have cited the figure to be between 2-3 per cent of the world's publishing output. This is the figure that has been cited perpetually for the last two decades at least. When quoted over the years, the figure has been static and has neither shown an upward trend, nor a decrease. The figure is based on analysis from the UNESCO Institute of Statistics (UIS) and those figures, in turn, came from the statistical data presented in the 'Culture and Communication' domains in the now discontinued UNESCO Statistical Yearbooks from 1963 to 1999, and which, as I have demonstrated in a recent article,[11] have unfortunately been chronically patchy and suspect for a number of reasons. For example, books in the major African languages, published in many parts of Africa, were not represented in the UNESCO data, and all those titles remained invisible in the statistics.

The UNESCO Statistical Yearbooks provided worldwide figures for the production of books in English, French, German, Spanish, and Russian. As far as the figures for African countries are concerned, the flaws in the data gathering process, and the lack of responses to questionnaires, has probably been the main reason for significant gaps in the statistics, as well as the relevance of the data collected and published. If non-responding countries had provided the requested information, the statistics would most likely have shown increasing production of books in the countries

---

11 Hans M. Zell, 'How Many Books are Published in Africa? The Need for More Reliable Statistics.' *The African Book Publishing Record* 39, no. 4 (2013): 397-406. Pre-print version, freely accessible, at: *http://www.academia.edu/4549278/How_many_books_are_published_in_Africa_The_need_for_more_reliable_statistics*.

of Africa. Over the years the quality of the UIS databases were probably also affected by diminishing UNESCO resources for data verification and documentation. Thus, UNESCO/UIS publishing and book production data for Africa has regrettably always been highly inconclusive for several reasons, and the bottom line is that reliable figures of book publishing output for the continent of Africa, or sub-Saharan Africa more specifically, simply, and lamentably, do not exist.

Even the UNESCO Institute of Statistics would now seem to concede that its figures were unreliable, and that presumably was also the reason why publication of statistical data was discontinued. The view from the UIS[12] is that one needs to look at several key issues when talking about the production and dissemination of book statistics: the first is the capacity of countries to produce reliable statistics in this field, generated by both the public and private sectors. They assert that without reliable national data it is not possible to have reliable international data, and the primary reason why international data for the African continent is lacking is because there is a lack of data at the national level. In addition to many methodological constraints in the gathering and publication of book-related data, the other key issue in book production statistics is the changing environment in which books are nowadays produced and consumed. Technology and the Internet have dramatically changed the whole book industry landscape, and present a formidable challenge in measuring publishing output in a timely and well-coordinated manner.

In a useful UNESCO-commissioned study undertaken in 2008, *A Methodology to Collect International Book Statistics*,[13] the authors set out convincing reasons why book statistics are a crucial key to sustain the quality and diversity of books. In that study Africa and its 46 sub-Saharan countries are seen,

> as the prototype for a data-poor region. With the exception of
> South Africa, national statistics for the book industries and

---

12 José Pessoa, Programme Specialist & Head of Culture Statistics, UNESCO Institute for Statistics (UIS), personal communication, 17 October 2013.
13 Rüdiger Wischenbart and Holger Ehling, *A Methodology to Collect International Book Statistics. Framework–Indicators – Methodology & Strategies – Groundwork for a Test Run* (Paris: UNESCO, 2009), p. 28; available at: *http://unesdoc.unesco.org/images/0018/001824/182475e.pdf*.

its sectors are either not compiled or are seemingly without relevant relation to the economic truth. From our knowledge and recent discussions with industry participants on the development of the publishing industries in these countries we conclude that the industries as such are growing, especially in the educational sector, but there are no tangible data to back up this assessment. The most recent serious approach to collecting book industry data on a continental basis was undertaken by APNET and ADEA at the turn of the century. For this, the national publishers' institutions were issued with a detailed questionnaire, which asked for data on a range of 29 topics, from demographic to taxes. Just over 20 countries responded to this questionnaire, and a qualified follow-up concerning data research or training of respondents was not undertaken. This has led to the ADEA/APNET report being seriously flawed (Wischenbart and Ehling, 2009: 22).[14]

The Association for the Development of Education in Africa (ADEA) Working Group on Books and Learning Materials, had recommended that APNET should facilitate the sharing of information between national publishers' associations as it relates to the different procedures that need to be followed when exporting books from/to a particular African country, and with which all publishers and booksellers need to be familiar when embarking on the export of their books to another African country. Each national book trade association was asked to complete a detailed questionnaire setting out current procedures, and the legal and fiscal regulations in each country. A total of 29 national book trade associations responded and completed questionnaires. Each country response offers information not only on aspects of book export/import procedures and financial aspects (e.g. customs tariffs on imports, exemptions, tax systems on inputs, other taxes such as VAT, export regulations, cost of financial

---

14 As the authors of the above UNESCO study do not cite precise publication details of the 'ADEA/APNET report' published 'at the turn of the century' it is not clear from their comments which report, precisely, they found flawed. It should be added that, in 2009, APNET published a 42 page report about the *APNET-ADEA Study Project on Intra-African Book Trade* http://www.african-publishers.net/images/stories/downloads/adea_apneta_study.pdf [page no longer accessible, website withdrawn].

transactions such as bank transfers, etc.), but also a variety of information on the 'book chain' in each country, for example number and type of publishers, printers, booksellers and book distributors, public libraries, legislation on copyright, book trade associations, national book policy situation, and other information relating to the state of the book in each country. Albeit slightly flawed here and there, this study was a valuable and information-rich resource. Unfortunately the report is no longer available online, or in printed form.

Wischenbart and Ehling (2009: 22) go on to say that 'the lack of reliable data has been a negative factor constraining both the development of the individual publishing industries as well as the private and public (donor/NGO) investment in the sector. However, it has to be recognised:

(i) that data collection for its own sake is unlikely to be productive if it arises from a perceived rather than an actual need, and

(ii) that there are huge challenges and complexities in the goal of collecting data for book industry surveys.

Extracting the survey data can be a highly time-consuming process for those contributing to such data gathering efforts. Moreover, systematic collection of data is not likely to succeed without the full collaboration of national publishers and book trade associations, national library boards, as well as individual publishers.

A great deal of thought must also be given to the survey process, the methodology of collecting and integrating data, and the choice of indicators, for example categories (of books, by subject), publishers (number of), annual turnover (of publishers/publishing markets), book exports (by publishers), distribution (number of booksellers/retailers), book sales (sales of combined publisher direct sales and through retail channels), book imports (via the retail book trade and by publishers), libraries (number of), and possibly other cultural, media and information indicators. Such data gathering amounts to a formidable task, but with the active support of all players in the local 'book chain' it should be achievable, as indeed has been effectively demonstrated by the wealth of data that has been collected and published for the South African book industries.

Whose responsibility?

Whose responsibility, then, should it be to gather national book-related data? Through their national bibliographies, several national library boards in Africa have, over a number of years, made valiant efforts to produce statistics relating to national publishing output in their countries; but these activities now seem to have ceased, and most national libraries in Africa unfortunately remain seriously and chronically under-funded. National bibliographies could indeed be used as the basic source for creating book production statistical analysis, but national bibliographies for many African countries either don't exist, or where they exist they are currently dormant, or seriously lag behind in publication, sometimes by several years, or even decades. More than 20 countries in Africa still have no national bibliography. Only a few countries currently offer digital databases recording national publishing output and, like the print versions, they tend to lag behind in their publication schedules.

An added problem is that legal deposit in Africa – the act, and legal obligation, by publishers of depositing free copies of their published material in their country's national library – is still inadequately enforced, and probably also still poorly understood by some publishers; and sometimes the procedures for obtaining ISBNs or ISSNs from the national agency are unnecessarily laborious or bureaucratic. Moreover, unless legal deposit copies are properly catalogued and included in the country's national bibliography, there is little incentive for publishers to supply free copies.

In the absence of book industry data, use of the ISBN system is often suggested as a possible approach to obtain book publishing statistics for any country. While this sounds attractive in theory, it does not normally work in practice, and for the reasons which I have set out in an earlier study.[15] Principally because blocks of ISBNs are usually obtained from local ISBN agencies in advance, but it may then take the publishers several years to use them up and allocate a unique ISBN for each new title or new edition as they are published; and some may never in fact be used. Therefore the relation between ISBNs issued and books published can be highly skewed.

---
15 Hans M, Zell, 'How Many Books are Published.' op cit. p. 7.

Collecting book industry data would seem to be an obvious activity for national book development councils (or their equivalents), which now exist in several African countries. Unfortunately only a small number of them are currently active — National Book Development Council of Cameroon, Ghana Book Development Council (GBDC), National Book Development Council of Kenya (NBDCK), Book Development Centre (Nigeria-part of six academic centres of the Nigerian Educational Research and Development Council/NERDC), Nigerian Book Foundation, Centre for the Book (South Africa), National Library of South Africa, National Book Development Council of Tanzania (Baraza la Maendeleo ya Vitabu Tanzania-BAMVITA) Tanzania, and National Book Trust Uganda, with such regional organisations as East African Book Development Association and African Publishers Network (APNET).[16] Book development councils have also been established in Lesotho, Malawi, Namibia, Zambia and in Zimbabwe, but they are all currently dormant and have no Web presence. The survival of the existing councils is primarily because their funding is based either on government support, or dependent on continuing external assistance from donor agencies. Apart from the South African Book Development Council, none of them would appear to offer any publicly accessible book sector data, certainly not on their websites.

Some might well argue that it is not the job of national book development councils to collect and disseminate book industry data and statistics, that they have a great many other priorities to promote literacy, books and reading, and that, instead, this should be the responsibility of national publishers and book trade associations. There are now national publishers associations

---

16 Contacts for these councils are: National Book Development Council (*http://www.cambookcouncil.org/*, not accessible as at 17/11/15); Ghana Book Development Council (*http://gbdc.gov.gh/*); National Book Development Council of Kenya (*http://www.nationalbookcouncilkenya.org*); Book Development Centre (*http://nerdc.ng/academic-centres/book-development-centre* and *http://nigerianbookfoundation.webs.com/* (not accessible as at 17/11/15); Centre for the Book, National Library of South Africa (*http://www.nlsa.ac.za/index.php/about-us*); South African Book Development Council (*http://www.sabookcouncil.co.za/sabookcouncil/index.html*); National Book Development Council of Tanzania (*http://www.bamvita.or.tz/default.asp* (not accessible as at 17/11/15), and National Book Trust of Uganda (*http://nabotu.or.ug/*). Regional organisations include East African Book Development Association (*http://eabda.or.ke/book-development-organizations*) and APNET (currently the website is no longer accessible/withdrawn).

in most African countries, although some are currently dormant or their activities heavily curtailed. Like the book development councils, and again with the exception of South Africa, none of them would appear to offer any book production statistical data and analysis.

Analysis of annual book publishing output on a national basis is only available for a few North African countries – albeit patchy and not always reliable – and, in sub-Saharan Africa, only for South Africa, where that country's Print Industries Cluster Council (now merged with the South African Book Development Council) has published a wide range of valuable annual surveys and reports relating to the book and printing sector, including the retail trade.[17] Other reports published include an investigation into the factors that affect the cost of books in South Africa, studies relating to the development of a national book policy, as well as a national survey of the reading (e.g. of newspapers and magazines), book reading, and book buying habits of adult South Africans. The latter was an important milestone as it provided, for the first time in South Africa, quantifiable measures on the state of reading and book reading in that country.

To the best of this writer's knowledge, such profiling of the population in terms of demographic and psychographic analysis has thus far only been attempted in South Africa, yet national surveys of this nature as a source of data can form a significant component in, for example, understanding readership trends, and personal or household expenditure on books and other reading materials. These valuable, meticulously compiled, and highly detailed surveys are a continuation of a series of book industry profiles that form part of a systematic data collection exercise and central database developed and housed at the Department of Information Science (Publishing Studies Division) at the University of Pretoria. The reports and surveys aim to provide a mechanism to track changes in the South African 'book value chain', and which can also be used as a tool to monitor the

---

17 These reports can be freely accessed at the 'Research and Development' pages of the South African Book Development Council at *http://sabookcouncil.co.za/?page_id=22*. Other data and statistics has been published by the Publishers Association of South Africa *http://www.publishsa.co.za/*, for example its *Annual Book Publishing Industry* surveys published since 2008, the latest is for the year 2013, published in December 2014 *http://www.publishsa.co.za/downloads/2013_Annual_Publishing_Industry_Survey.pdf*.

impact of the country's national book policy. The South African Booksellers Association produces a variety of statistics relating to the retail sector, as well as publishing annual trade reports in its journal *Bookmarks*.[18] It has commissioned and published a series of useful annual book retail industry surveys. Nielsen BookScan South Africa in association with BookData SAPnet publishes annual sales analysis designed to provide an overview of the trade sector of the South African book industry.[19]

That South Africa is the leader in statistical and survey data on their book industries is not surprising, as that country has had a much longer publishing history than is the case elsewhere in sub-Saharan Africa, where indigenous book publishing on any scale did not emerge until the mid-1960s or early 1970s. However, what is now needed is much more vigorous and coordinated action by African book trade associations or national book development councils to systematically collect, analyse, and publish a wide variety of book-related data on an ongoing basis, in order that the continent of Africa is no longer viewed as a 'data-poor region', and reliable and authoritative sources become available to monitor African book publishing output.

Collaboration and knowledge sharing

It strikes me that, especially with the closure of APNET – which has deprived African publishers of a collective voice – there is now, more than ever, a need for *solidarity* among independent African publishers: to share experience and know-how, and leading to collaborative ventures and programmes. Many indigenous publishers in Africa share a great deal of common ground, and they all face the same formidable challenges to survive and prosper, and so more active collaboration and sharing of skills and expertise could be of mutual benefit.

There are many forms of collaborative ventures, for example co-publishing between African partners. At this time successful South-

---

[18] South African Booksellers Association publications available at: *http://www.sabooksellers.com/*
[19] BookData SAPnet address: *http://www.sapnet.co.za/*.

South co-publishing projects in Africa are perhaps still fairly limited.[20] Yet collaborative undertakings, co-publishing projects or partnerships, surely are the key: pooling editorial and management expertise, assisting editorial capacity building, sharing of production costs, or consolidating strength in production and technical skills, especially in the new digital printing and publishing environment. Co-publishing ventures can also extend print runs, thus reducing the unit costs for markets that might not otherwise be able to afford them.

There are other avenues for knowledge sharing, such as discussion forums and groups. There have been a number of attempts over the years to set up online discussion groups for the African book professions – for debate and comment, and to provide a platform for airing views and opinion – but, quite inexplicably to this writer at least, none of them ever really got off the ground.

A new attempt was made in 2013 with the launch of the Facebook 'Publishing in Africa' group (recently renamed as 'Book Publishing in Africa' group),[21] which is described as 'a group for book-publishing and bookselling professionals, as well as media professionals and authors with an interest in publishing and the book trade in Africa' and currently (October 2015) has over 2,400 members. This figure sounds impressive, but unfortunately, and despite the best efforts of the group's monitors, it continues to be heavily inundated with postings by self-published authors touting their books, or with posts that have nothing to do with book publishing. Meantime serious discussions and debate about publishing and the book industries in Africa still remain rather thin on the ground.

One interesting and positive development (as is reflected in the number of new records in the *Publishing, Books and Reading in Sub-Saharan Africa* database), is that there are now an increasing number of postings

---

20 For example, there has been a measure of collaboration, and publishing partnerships, between publishers in the East African region, while in the francophone countries of Africa there have been a number of successful co-publishing ventures, as well as a range of co-publishing projects initiated or supported by the Paris-based L'Alliance internationale des éditeurs indépendants/International Alliance of Independent Publishers *http://www.alliance-editeurs.org/?lang=en.*

21 See *https://www.facebook.com/groups/233568780016434/.*

on publishing and the book trade in Africa in a number of blogs, some of which have provided genuinely fresh perspectives and insights, for example on the topic of author-publisher interaction and (often strained!) relations; on self-publishing vs. conventional publishing, the print vs. digital debate and the erosion of print culture, book piracy, debilitating government taxation and import tariffs on books, and on the issues and challenges of publishing African creative writing within Africa.

Another welcome development is that the Oxford-based African Books Collective (ABC)[22] – the book marketing and distribution organisation founded, owned, and governed by African publishers, which is currently representing the lists of some 150 independent African publishers – has recently launched a new and greatly improved website which, as a sub-site, will shortly also include a blog or forum for debate and information sharing on a variety of topics. ABC hopes to attract posts and opinion pieces on a wide range of issues as they relate to African books and the publishing industries, and one of its principal objectives will be 'telling the African publishing story' to readers outside Africa, in order to generate greater awareness about the activities of the many independent African imprints which ABC now distributes. Additionally, the new sub-site will also be offering book reviews and book extracts for online reading.

A new e-journal or newsletter?

While it was still active, the African Publishers Network published a useful journal entitled *The African Publishing Review*. A total of 51 issues were published from 1992 to 2004, when it ceased publication. One more issue was subsequently published online in a 'New series vol. 1, no. 1', in 2011, but no further issues have appeared thereafter. This leaves only the quarterly *African Book Publishing Record* (ABPR), which, first published in 1975, is currently in its 41st year of publication. However, although ABPR does still publish occasional articles and includes some news items, it is largely a bibliographic and review journal, primarily for libraries, and with very limited circulation within Africa.

---

22 African Books Collective Ltd address is: *http://www.africanbookscollective.com/*

A new e-journal could provide an important repository of articles and wide-ranging analysis on the subject of African publishing and book development. A conventional academic journal published in both print and electronic formats would probably not be sustainable, and would require fairly substantial funding or institutional support, whereas an online open access journal would seem more appropriate and more manageable. It would require an energetic and dedicated editorial team, and led by an editorial board that is not merely 'decorative'.

An alternative might be a lively and informative online newsletter published three or four times a year, something like the *Bellagio Publishing Network Newsletter*[23] or *Partners in African Publishing*,[24] which both contained a wealth of useful information and analysis, but which ceased publication many years ago.

A Wikipedia page for African publishing?

Yet another joint effort that could assist to provide more visibility about the African book industries might be the creation of an up-to-date, fully documented, and authoritative Wikipedia page about indigenous African publishing and the book trade.

If anyone checks Wikipedia for sources of information about 'Publishing Africa', 'African publishing', 'Book publishing Africa' or 'Publishing sub-Saharan Africa', they will find that no pages on these topics exist. Wikipedia does have a very dated and patchy article about the now sadly dormant African Publishers Network (APNET),[25] but apart from entries about the (now discontinued) Noma Award for Publishing in Africa, the *African Book Publishing Record*, African Journals Online/AJOL, a small number of South African publishing houses, and

---

23 A total of 31 issues of the *Bellagio Publishing Network Newsletter* (Buffalo, NY, later Oxford), 1992-2002, were published. Its online archive is still accessible at *http://www.bellagiopublishingnetwork.com/newslett_index2.htm*.
24 A total of 20 issues of *Partners in African Publishing. Information Resource for African-European Publishing Cooperation* (Oxford, later London), 1995-2000 were published.
25 See https://en.wikipedia.org/wiki/African_Publishers_Network.

biographical profiles about one or two prominent African publishers, there is not a great deal else that is related to African publishing. So why not put this right, and create a set of Wiki pages as a collaborative undertaking?

Wikipedia's articles, pictures and data are created by a diverse community of people who volunteer to share their knowledge with the world, and the interactive process of Wikipedia would seem to make it particularly well-suited to developing a community in African publishing, while at the same time increasing global dissemination and visibility about the African book world.

Epilogue

As Henry Chakava has pointed out,[26] continental and regional organisations, or national bodies such as book development councils and book trade associations, are often still very weak in structure and management and have been unable to survive without continuing donor support, with the notable exception of the African Books Collective mentioned above, which is now self-financing and, having moved to a largely digital model, is still going strong and is currently celebrating its 25th year of trading.

In the new digital era, with its demand for skills and knowledge, and at a time of unprecedented change and promise, more informal collaboration between African publishers, as one-to-one relationships, or alliances of small independent publishers, may well achieve a greater measure of success and sustainability than Pan-African or regional organisations hampered by cumbersome constitutional and administrative management structures.

---

26 Henry Chakava, 'African Publishing: From Ile-Ife, Nigeria, to the Present,' in *Publishing, Books and Reading in Sub-Saharan Africa: A Critical Bibliography* by Hans M. Zell (Lochcarron: Hans Zell Publishing, 2008), p. xxxviii. This wide-ranging introductory essay, albeit now marginally dated, remains one of the most succinct and penetrating accounts of the African book industry today, exploring most of the key issues from a historical perspective, highlighting the most significant problems and constraints faced by the African book industries, and identifying the challenges and prospects that lie ahead.

11

Shared Visions and Challenges in Publishing in Africa: Henry Chakava and CODESRIA

By Francis B. Nyamnjoh

It is more than an honour for me to say a few words about Henry Chakava, retiring veteran Nairobi-based innovative, enterprising, indefatigable colossus of African publishing and publishing Africa. Chakava has influenced the Kenyan and African publishing landscape for nearly half a century in his tireless crusade to ensure the sustainable development of the book industry on the continent.

I first met him in 2004 at the African Books Collective (ABC) board meeting in Oxford. I had just been appointed Senior Programme Officer in charge of publications at the Council for the Development of Social Science Research (CODESRIA), headquartered in Dakar, Senegal. Chakava was on the ABC board in his capacity as a founding member and chairperson of East African Educational Publishers (EAEP), while I was representing CODESRIA, another founding member. It did not take more than an initial conversation for me to see that Chakava's vision and commitment to promoting African writers and publishing African scholarship dovetailed perfectly with CODESRIA's own vision, on which I come back below in some detail. During my six years on the board of ABC, it was an infinite pleasure and privilege to work with Henry Chakava, a man of great wisdom and experience, who inspired and spurred me on in my own dedication to help fulfill CODESRIA's ambition and mission as a leading scholarly publisher in Africa, and eventually as well, my enthusiasm and dedication to Langaa Research and Publishing Common Initiative Group, an institute I co-founded in 2004.

Chakava belongs with the generation of African scholars who created CODESRIA, and it is striking how similar their concerns have been through the years since the early 1970s. Just as Chakava has invested in promoting African voices and publishing especially in indigenous African languages, CODESRIA has sought to explore similar opportunities and overcome kindred challenges in the field of scholarly knowledge production in Africa.

CODESRIA was created in 1973 (around the same time that Chakava joined publishing) for the purpose of promoting multidisciplinary social research which derives from and is relevant to the experience of the African continent and its peoples. As a pan-African organisation, CODESRIA was and still is expected to fulfil this mission on a continent in which knowledge production, academic and scholarly activities was, and still is, very much conducted in what is generally termed colonial languages (mainly English, French and Portuguese[1]). With little success in the development of indigenous and endogenous languages despite early and repeated clarion postcolonial calls to this end, much scientific production, activity and collaboration among scholars across the continent continues to be mediated by these so-called colonial languages.

Headquartered in Dakar – the capital city of Senegal, a former French colony – and with a secretariat peopled by scholars and support staff speaking English or French or both, CODESRIA was faced with the imperative of operating in English and French from the outset. Conscious of the need to fulfil its pan-African mission with a constituency that draws from different linguistic repertoires, and to encourage greater communication and interchange among African scholars, CODESRIA embraced the 'early bilingualism/*un bilinguisme de bonne heure*'. Bernard Fonlon (2010[1964]) argued forcefully for with regard to Cameroon – a former German colony entrusted to Britain and France by the UN following the defeat of Germany in World War II. Thanks to its early recognition of the importance of multilingualism (albeit one highly dependent on colonial

---

1   Spanish was and still is limited to Equatorial Guinea and the Western (Spanish) Sahara, long contested by Morocco and Spain; and Germany, having been forced to give up its colonies after World War I and II, also lost its linguistic foothold in much of Africa, with the exception of Namibia, a resident colony.

languages), CODESRIA has over the years developed a framework for undertaking its research, training and publications activities in English, French, Portuguese and Arabic. It operates from a secretariat that is truly pan-African both linguistically and in terms of personnel, junior and senior, academic and administrative.

English, French and Portuguese languages are given status associating them with science, progress, civilisation and enlightenment, while every attempt is made to confine the relevance of African languages to rhetoric and porous claims on their critical importance to nation-building and development. In reality, African languages are reduced to gibberish and chased out of the mouths, ears and minds of African students and scholars born into these languages. This legacy has left an indelible mark on the continent. Writing about Kenya, Ngũgĩ wa Thiong'o shows just how widespread this practice was. The postcolonial instructors who inherited condescending English attitudes toward local languages, continued 'to ban African languages in schools and to elevate English as the medium of instruction from primary to secondary stages', and did not hesitate to mete out corporal punishment to and extort fines from students 'caught speaking their mother tongues' (wa Thiong'o, 1997: 620).

African intellectuals who want to take the valorisation of endogenous African languages seriously have found themselves swimming against the tides. Invited to address the OAU (Organisation of African Unity) [now AU (African Union)] at Addis Ababa, Ali Mazrui insisted on doing so in Kiswahili, but there was neither translator nor switch button envisaged for one of Africa's most widely-spoken languages. 'You needed to see how the Heads of States were bewildered, but I had passed my message across' (Mazrui, 1986). This situation has hardly changed since Mazrui published his *The Africans: A Triple Heritage* in 1986. Indeed, as if to demonstrate that a solution to this predicament is not, realistically, envisaged in the next generation or two, in January 2014, Dr Nkosazana Dlamini Zuma, Chairperson of the African Union Commission, delivered her statement to the Twenty-second Ordinary Session of the Heads of State and Government through an imaginative 'e-mail from the future, written from the year 2063', that contained the following passage on the language question in Africa:

> Our eldest daughter, the linguist, still lectures in Kiswahili in Cabo Verde, at the headquarters of the Pan African Virtual University. Kiswahili is now a major African working language, and a global language taught at most faculties across the world. Our grandchildren find it very funny how we used to struggle at AU meetings with English, French and Portuguese interpretations, how we used to fight that the English version is not in line with the French or Arabic text! Now we have a lingua franca, and multi-lingualism is the order of the day.[2]

Unlike Somalia, Ethiopia, Tanzania, Kenya, Mali, Burkina Faso, Botswana and South Africa, many an African country has yet to demonstrate in principle and in practice that literacy, even at primary school level, does not necessarily mean knowing how to read and write a European language.

Only a few African countries have bothered to adopt policies that encourage education in African languages. And even these countries tend to confine the importance of local languages to adult literacy training and to primary and secondary school education, thereby accentuating the remoteness and irrelevance of universities to the bulk of the population. With perhaps the exception of Tanzania and Ethiopia (and to some extent South Africa, if Afrikaans is considered an indigenous/endogenous African language), there is hardly a single sub-Saharan African university that 'offers a full diploma programme with an African language as principal medium of instruction' (Crossman and Devisch, 1999: 7; Chumbow, 2005, 2009).

In many countries, there are ongoing debates on use of mother tongue in the early years of schooling. In some where state policies already exist encouraging mother tongue education, these policies are yet to be effectively implemented. There is resistance from stakeholders who believe mother

---

2 *http://cpauc.au.int/en/content/statement-he-dr-nkosazana-dlamini-zuma-chairperson-african-union-commission-twenty-second-ordinary-session* accessed 12 February 2014.

tongue education will dilute education standards, as students are called to operate in a globalised world and may eventually proceed to universities where instruction is almost invariably in the colonial languages. This navigation within an increasingly interconnected world is, in and of itself, indicative of the hegemony that exists.

Language is the lifeblood through which we operate and its absence in any given configuration is just as significant as its presence. Cosmopolitanism, a common national citizenship and mobility have meant increasing spatial integration for peoples of different ethnic and linguistic backgrounds, thereby posing the question of whose mother tongue qualifies where, as well as whose mother tongue has top billing? Moreover, children of policymakers and many an elite group, like potted plants in greenhouses, attend private schools that follow not the national curriculum, but the so-called international curriculum of European and North American schools. Without a personal interest in mother tongue education and national curricula, it is hard to see how policies in favour of endogenisation can be implemented.

It is true that in many a context, Africans (students, scholars and in general) have succeeded in domesticating these colonial languages, such that – like the domestication of Dutch by Afrikaners and other Afrikaans-speaking South Africans – French, English or Portuguese Africans speak or write would send many a so-called native speaker back to school. Such domestication, however successful, is often at the expense of the development of the languages in which the cultural experiences and world views of the wider populations targeted by the scientific and scholarly curiosities of many a scholar have been expressed, documented, archived and transmitted. This, perhaps, translates as well into a profound and immeasurable loss within the economy of understanding.

CODESRIA's response to the language problem in Africa

The above is the context and background against which CODESRIA was created and has operated as a network of scholars and scholarship committed to African value-added in knowledge production and consumption. This paper looks at how CODESRIA has navigated, negotiated and sought to reconcile this challenging linguistic landscape in the interest of its mission.

Compelled to work almost exclusively in colonial languages (domesticated or otherwise), CODESRIA has invested resources and creative energy in promoting dialogue and collaboration across the different linguistic zones of the continent, namely:

- English Speaking (Anglophone) Africa (22 countries)
- French Speaking (Francophone) Africa (20 countries)
- Portuguese Speaking (Lusophone) Africa (5 countries)
- Arabic Speaking (Arabophone) Africa (12 countries)

Two or more of these languages are considered official languages in a handful of countries, such as French and English in Cameroon and Mauritius, and French and Arabic in North African countries such as Morocco, Mauritania, Tunisia, Algeria and Libya.

To address the challenge posed by linguistic or language barriers to the fulfilment of its pan-African ambitions, CODESRIA has sought to increase the percentage of its activities with participants coming from several linguistic zones, as well as the percentage of its bilingual activities. It has also sought to provide for translation of its documentation and interpretation at its meetings, workshops, seminars, conferences and general assemblies. As a pan-African organisation with a constituency that draws from different linguistic repertoires, and conscious of the need to encourage greater communication and interchange among African scholars ((Nyamnjoh and Shoro, 2011), CODESRIA publishes and encourages publications in Arabic, English, French and Portuguese.

Mechanisms used by the CODESRIA Publications and Dissemination Programme to realise its mission and objectives include, inter alia: publication of books, textbooks, monographs, working and discussion papers, and journals which are fed mainly by the various research programmes financed by the Council; an annual conference of editors of CODESRIA journals; the organisation of scholarly writing workshops for various CODESRIA institutes, research networks (Multinational Working Groups, National Working Groups, Comparative Research Networks), groups of scholars struggling to publish in CODESRIA journals, and laureates selected from universities across the continent; participation at book fairs and dissemination events; and, through the CODESRIA Documentation and Information Centre (CODICE) and the other scientific programmes of CODESRIA, feeding into and from the various networks and the scholarly debates which animate their existence and activities. A vigorous dissemination drive ensures that research produced by Africans in and on Africa is accessible in both electronic and non-electronic versions of CODESRIA journals, conference papers and reports.

The Council sends free copies of its major publications to African university libraries, subsidises the cost of its publications marketed in Africa, and offers free copies to review outlets. It also undertakes a regular dissemination exercise at which selected titles from its recent publications list are presented to a critical audience of scholars, policy makers, students, journalists and representatives of international organisations. While the various book, monograph, and working document series have served as outlets for CODESRIA-sponsored research, conferences, workshops and seminars, the journals, often published in collaboration with or on behalf of various professional scholarly associations on the continent, have facilitated debate and interchange more generally. In some cases, CODESRIA has assisted networks with the creation of and setting up of peer-review structures for their journals. This was the case with the Educational Research Network for West and Central Africa (ERNWACA), which launched its journal – *Journal of Educational Research in Africa / Revue africaine de la recherche en education* – in 2009 with funding from SIDA of Sweden, channelled through CODESRIA.[3] CODESRIA in this case was sharing expertise accumulated over many years with junior organisations on the continent in relation to the launch of scholarly publications.

The creation of CODESRIA was also partly motivated by a perceived need for greater recognition and representation for what Africa and African social scientists had to offer in debates where they were often reduced to passive observers whose role was to implement and not

---

3   See *www.ernwaca.org/web/spip.php?article334*, accessed 23 February 2014

to think. The prevalent high rejection rate for African scholarship in Northern journals and books, for example, meant that African scholars had basically to choose between bending over backwards to accommodate debates in colonial languages, whose origins and assumptions were at variance with the burning questions and concerns of their continent, or to create and sustain alternative outlets for their own research informed by greater relevance in theory and practice, and in tune with the diverse expectations and aspirations of Africans. This alarming incongruence between experience and mode of representation seeks further inquiry and contemplation (Nyamnjoh, 2004; 2012). Providing for a strong publications and dissemination component of CODESRIA was a clear indication that the founding fathers and mothers of this pan-African organisation had opted for independence of thought and scholarship – even if these continued to be articulated in colonial languages –, as well as a critical engagement with the African world.

CODESRIA has, over the past 40 years established itself as the leading scholarly publisher in the social sciences on the African continent, with 90 per cent of what it publishes fed directly by the research and activities it sponsors among various social research networks in universities and research institutes throughout the continent and increasingly in the diaspora. Since 2000, CODESRIA publishes – significantly in collaboration with scholarly professional associations in most cases – over six bilingual (usually in French and English) and a few multilingual journals covering various aspects of the social sciences and humanities.

CODESRIA also undertakes special programmes targeting marginal language communities, such as Portuguese or Lusophone Africa. CODESRIA launched its Lusophone Initiative in 2004, a year before its 11th General Assembly which took place in Maputo in December 2005. Until then, CODESRIA's main working languages were English and French. In 2008, for the first time in CODESRIA's history, 'the programme announcements were issued in three languages: English, French and Portuguese, with Portuguese being the new language added to the programme announcement strategy in order to ensure that researchers working in that language enjoy a more level playing ground for participation in all CODESRIA activities.'[4] This drop in the ocean is by no means enough, but indicative of the mammoth task ahead for mutual intelligibility and collaboration among African scholars. All CODESRIA programme announcements have, since this modest gesture, also been issued in the Portuguese language, to enhance participation of scholars from Lusophone African countries in CODESRIA research, training, grants, fellowships and publications programmes. This initiative aimed at providing greater inclusion for scholars from Portuguese speaking Africa, was meant to address the problem of poor scholarship and poor scholarly production in the countries involved. The lusophone initiative also involved a working visit by the Executive Secretary and the President of CODESRIA at the time, to Eduardo Mondlane University in Mozambique for the signing of the Memorandum of Understanding which provided, inter alia, for collaboration in the hosting and management of an annual methodological and writing workshop for postgraduate students and junior-to-mid-career teaching staff in lusophone Africa. On the back of that mission, agreements were also concluded with a local publisher and translator-editor for the processing of CODESRIA documents for production in the Portuguese language. This was followed by a contact, familiarisation and outreach visit to the University of Luanda and the Catholic University in Luanda as part of a long-standing institutional commitment to mobilise the participation of Angolan researchers in CODESRIA's work. Meetings were held with the vice-chancellors of both universities, the deans of faculties, senior academic staff and a selection of postgraduate students.

CODESRIA has occasionally (e.g. at the 66th Executive Committee meeting in Dakar in 2007) discussed incorporating African languages, but the challenge has always been that of choosing among the competing indigenous/endogenous African languages, as well as finite resources and the reality of ever dwindling donor funding. At one Executive Committee meeting, there was no such hesitation or indecision on the need to explore possibilities for translating African scholarly publications into Chinese and putting them online, especially as the Chinese government seems

---
4 Minutes of the 68th Executive Committee meeting of CODESRIA, Dakar, 21 – 22 July, 2008

to be willing to fund such an endeavour; universities in Senegal have announced their decisions to start Chinese language programmes, so translation should become more important and much easier to do.

Planning and preparing for a CODESRIA activity (General Assembly, conference, Seminar, workshop, institute, Executive Committee or Executive Committee meeting, etc.), must of necessity include budgeting for interpretation in two, three or four languages (English, French, Portuguese and Arabic) depending on the languages of participants, as well as for translation of documents into the appropriate languages. In some cases, key documents, however voluminous, have to be translated into all four languages. This was the case, for example, of the *CODESRIA Strategic Plan 2007-2011*, which was translated from its English original into French, Portuguese and Arabic – the first time in CODESRIA's history that its strategy document was issued in all of its four working languages.

Translation dilemmas

Investing in translation does not imply that these translations are going to be well done, because it is difficult to come by accomplished and competent translators. During my stay at CODESRIA, Executive Committee members often complained that translations into French and Portuguese of various documents originally written in English – the working language of the Executive Secretary at the time – were poorly done or inaccurate, and much time was spent correcting minutes and commenting on this aspect.[5] It was often observed that though there was need to seek to avoid disjuncture in documents, translation should seek more to reflect the spirit of a document than to be academically correct. To this concern, the Executive Secretary would apologise, sometimes adding that problems of translation are always delicate, even when done by expert translators. It should be added, however, that the documents were not often

---

5 On reading an earlier draft of this paper, Edith Félicité Koumtoudji, a doctoral student in Translation at the University of Witwatersrand, made the following pertinent remark, 'Quality translation requires sufficient time to translate, among other things. Are the translators given enough time or documents are sent to them at the last minute? It is also always important to indicate the brief for any translation project: who is the target audience and what purpose the translated document is going to serve.'

ready in time to ensure quality translation even by expert translators; and often translation of documents for meetings was done in-house under the coordination of an accredited translator employed by CODESRIA to head its translation service.[6]

Within the CODESRIA Publications Programme proper, work plans can at best only be indicative, as publishing a book has more imponderables than organising a conference, running an institute or following up on a research network. For one thing, a good translator CODESRIA regularly uses might not be available when CODESRIA comes knocking with an urgent manuscript, thereby forcing it to go shopping for expedient alternatives. It is true that CODESRIA needs to have, on its books, as many translators as possible for each of the language combinations so that when a translator is not available, he can easily be replaced. It is true that freelance translators are not always available when their clients need their services, but having long term contracts with translators is a very expensive arrangement for an organisation like CODESRIA, that depends almost exclusively on donor funding to run its activities and publication programme. Even when a translator indicates their availability, his or her workload might be such that they simply cannot meet CODESRIA deadlines. In this situation, the alternative is hardly one of cancelling the contract and starting afresh with someone else who might not exude the same competence or deliver in time either. Since translation is not everyone's expertise and because translators with good working knowledge of the social sciences and their jargons are not easy to come by, it is difficult to plan with certainty even with a pool of regular translators. CODESRIA is not their only client, and in some cases, not even their best paying. CODESRIA's work might be urgent, but it may not always be competitive for various reasons.

As the experience with the Africa Review of Books demonstrates, coordinating a collaborative endeavour between four institutions situated

---

6   Given the volume of translation CODESRIA regularly does, the need for such an in-house translation unit with someone to coordinate the work carried out by the various translators is clearly preferred rather than merely having to depend on freelance translators on an ad hoc basis. Over the years, the CODESRIA translation unit has compiled its own terminology database to assist translators working for the organisation.

in four different countries – CODESRIA in Dakar, FSS (Forum for Social Studies) in Addis Ababa, CRASC in Oran and the University of Southern Africa (UNISA) Press in Pretoria – and all expected to communicate effectively without necessarily evidence of mastery of both languages, can be most challenging. Thus, the very maiden issue of the review put together by FSS and printed by UNISA, had many glitches, including the omission of the French name *'Revue Africaine des Livres'*, thereby giving the misleading impression that Africa Review of Books was an English language publication only. Perhaps in anticipation of these problems, from the inception meeting in 2003 at Addis Ababa, the review was expected to have separate English and French editions after the first two issues. The relevant section of the minutes of that meeting read thus:

> This item was discussed in detail and it was agreed that, for the first two issues, a single *Review* will be published in English and French in a joint format to reflect the continent's linguistic diversity. In the long term, efforts will be made to explore the possibility of producing separate English and French versions of the *Review*, with FSS being responsible for the former and CRASC for the latter. In this particular case, Editorial messages and landmark articles will be translated interchangeably and featured in both versions to ensure a balanced coverage.

The problems and difficulties of translation, as well as possible solutions to them are well known to students and professionals of translation (Venuti, 2004; Ndi, 2008), who understand only too well the limitations of a decontextualised and dehistoricised word-for-word rendering of the original, and who advocate privileging the spirit over the letter of the text. Indeed, the concomitant issue of understanding context comes to the fore, as meaning is so composite that relaying information proves tricky when the understanding of concepts in one language cannot necessarily be transposed onto another. In his article 'Language Imperialism, Concepts and Civilization: China versus The West', Thorsten Pattberg uses his estimate of 'over 35,000 Chinese words or phrases that cannot properly be translated into the English language,' and the fact that the histories and traditions specific to European languages mean that 'they cannot sufficiently render Chinese concepts', and should therefore not seek to translate the most important foreign concepts at all'[7]. Instead, they should adopt them. Pattberg's point finds comfort in the argument that 'the idiosyncratic use of language makes it difficult for linguistic concepts to be universalised' (Ndi 2008:113).

Such caution notwithstanding, translation continues to take place, sometimes as a form of credentialism or crave for legitimation, that, as Pattberg argues in 'China: Lost in Translation', claiming a word such as 'philosophy' in a context where it does not quite apply, 'involuntarily supports Western sovereignty over the interpretation of Chinese thought'. Such efforts at translation by local Chinese scholars that caricature, mimic or reproduce in the image of the West, voluntarily or otherwise, often results in the legitimation of 'the Western onslaught on Chinese terminology and, without giving too much thought to it, enabling the Western hold for power over the history of thought.' Given the lesser of the two evils – bad translation for the sake of surface-level understanding as opposed to no translation at all – the power and stature of such local scholars desperately seeking to be relevant to the West and the debates it originates and oversees grows, and attention is often taken away from 'thousands of Chinese scholars who still fight for Chinese terminologies, but who will not be given a voice in Western mainstream media. Such Chinese are virtually unemployable globally, as they do not conform to Western standard.'[8]

A similar argument can be made of the myriad indigenous African languages, many of which, unlike Chinese, are yet to develop into written languages. In this regard, Munyaradzi Mawere, Associate Professor at Universidade Pedagogica in Mozambique, while recognising the important role played by CODESRIA in promoting African scholarship since 1973, is however frustrated by the failure by CODESRIA to adopt major

---

7   http://www.globalresearch.ca/language-imperialism-concepts-and-civilization-china-versus-the-west/28940

8   See Thorsten Pattberg, 'China: Lost in Translation' http://www.atimes.com/atimes/China/NG24Dj02.html, accessed 20 February 2014.

indigenous African languages for its activities, knowledge production and dissemination. He writes:

> Given such problems of translation as those highlighted by Thorsten Pattberg with regard to Chinese, what is the vision of CODESRIA in relation to African indigenous languages? Should Africa, forever, use colonial languages in research and dissemination of her own ideas? In fact, while CODESRIA is playing a pivotal role in fostering a spirit of research in and on Africa especially by African scholars, I think it still has a lot to do as far as African indigenous languages are concerned. For all these 40 years (since its establishment in 1973), I think by now it should have published or at least started publishing in some (of course not all as they are too many) of the African indigenous languages, such as Swahili, Shona, Hausa etc to show that it has a 'true' inclination towards the promotion of African indigenous languages. As the situation stands right now, one could say CODESRIA has an inclination towards colonial languages given that it only publishes in colonial languages (such as English, French, and Portuguese). My view is, if in the name of globalisation, those who speak African indigenous languages (indigenous Africans) are 'compelled' to feed in colonial languages, why cannot those who speak colonial languages (from Europe and America) feed in one or more of the African indigenous languages when they want to know, hear or read about Africa at least to show that we are TRULY in a global world? I, therefore, think that besides publishing in the four working languages (English, Portuguese, French and Arabic), CODESRIA should also publish in African indigenous languages such as Swahili, Zulu, Gĩkũyũ, Hausa, etc.

Mawere's concern echoes similar sentiments of those who have repeatedly critiqued the privileging of the English language in Kenya, where the educational system inherited condescending British attitudes towards local languages and continues 'to ban African languages in schools and to elevate English as the medium of instruction from primary to secondary stages' and do not hesitate to mete out corporal punishment to and extort fines from students 'caught speaking their mother tongues' (wa Thiong'o, 1997: 620). Leading by example, Ngũgĩ wa Thiong'o writes and publishes his novels in Gĩkũyũ, his mother tongue, and only then has them translated into English. He speaks metaphorically of colonial languages as a third leg and compares Africans' adoption of them as having to 'borrow a third leg' (wa Thiong'o, 2005). This concern is not to deny the fact that many Africans beyond the elite are like octopi in their facility with language and the cohabitation of the multiple worldviews they reflect.

Notwithstanding the challenges and shortcomings of translation, verbal communication between two linguistically different individuals and communities – or even different dialects within the same language – is absolutely necessary. Important though sign, body and other symbolic forms of communication are, they are not totally satisfactory to our communicative needs and aspirations. There might be much truth in the claim that to translate is to betray, misrepresent, distort or assimilate (*traduire c'est trahir*), few of us would want to give up entirely. We would rather be betrayed or misrepresented than give up entirely on developing our multilingual skills and on translation. As I prepared this paper, I stumbled on 'Found in Translation' by Hamid Dabashi[9] in which I found much comfort. Using philosophy and literature as examples, Dabashi argues that philosophical and literary works 'gain far more than they lose in translation'. He writes:

> Works of philosophy — and their readers — gain in translation not just because their authors begin to breathe in a new language but because the text signals a world alien to its initial composition. Above all they gain because these authors and their texts have to face a new audience.

---

9 Hamid Dabashi is the Hagop Kevorkian Professor of Iranian Studies and Comparative Literature at Columbia University in New York. See http://opinionator.blogs.nytimes.com/author/hamid-dabashi/ accessed 18 February 2014.

Dabashi argues that in some instances translations, however poorly done, bring a work, a philosopher or a literary figure, into the limelight, thereby saving it or him from the obscurity that would otherwise be it or his fate. By way of example, he writes:

> Consider Heidegger. Had it not been for his French translators and commentators, German philosophy of his time would have remained an obscure metaphysical thicket. And it was not until Derrida's own take on Heidegger found an English readership in the United States and Britain that the whole Heidegger-Derridian undermining of metaphysics began to shake the foundations of the Greek philosophical heritage. One can in fact argue that much of contemporary Continental philosophy originates in German with significant French and Italian glosses before it is globalized in the dominant American English and assumes a whole new global readership and reality. This has nothing to do with the philosophical wherewithal of German, French or English. It is entirely a function of the imperial power and reach of one language as opposed to others.

In this way, translation has a collaborate effect which could be seen as valuable for its own sake.

Drawing on this to understand African scholarship, and CODESRIA's investments in translation, what would our knowledge of the most misrepresented continent be without the capacity to access (mis)representations of our own, even if only in one colonial language or the other? Works by leading African scholars (Paulin Hountondji, Mahmood Mamdani, Achille Mbembe, etc.) and classics such as *The Meanings of Timbuktu* (Jeppie and Bachir 2008) have been translated into French or English, and in some instances into Arabic and Portuguese, thereby making it possible for students and scholars of Africa to access and claim knowledge of other parts of Africa than their own. Similarly, by encouraging research and publications in its four working languages, CODESRIA is able to promote intellectual networking, collaboration and conversation among Africans who would otherwise dramatise the hurdles of cross-language interaction in their research and scholarship.

Translation makes it possible to be truly pan-African in African scholarship, by enabling access to knowledge without the a priori consideration of whether or not one belongs in primary or primordial terms, to the linguistic community of origin of the text in question. Although peppered by unintended misinterpretation or mistranslation, the contribution of translated text should not be underestimated. The philosophical debate over understanding language leads one to accept that translation is always a process of negotiation, re-evaluation and revalorisation of meaning. Humans being fundamentally dissimilar in what informs their understanding, no translation is perfect even in its perfection. From this (albeit optimistic) perspective, translation does more good than harm. While still recognisably trapped in colonial geographies and languages, African scholars, as the CODESRIA experience suggests, are able at the same time to defy the confines of these languages and geographies.

Publishing and translating CODESRIA publications

Quality translation informs quality debate, but it takes quality research to yield both. The CODESRIA publications programme, as I have already alluded to, was created to support social research and knowledge production and consumption in Africa and by Africans, in line with the CODESRIA's vision and mission as articulated in its Charter in 1973.

CODESRIA publications have the formidable task of promoting greater visibility and accessibility of African scholarship in and outside Africa. But not just scholarship for the sake of scholarship, rather, scholarship in tune with African values, revelatory of social theory and practice in African contexts, and relevant to the developmental needs of the continent. What is needed is theoretically and methodologically creative and innovative scholarship, not unquestioning or unproblematised adoption and reproduction of conceptual and methodological outfits designed with scant regard for the lived experiences of Africans.

CODESRIA stresses the need for critical rethinking of development and related concepts and conceptualisation of social phenomena, thus emphasising thinking over doing, creative appropriation over mimicry and production over reproduction. The research projects supported by CODESRIA are meant to deliver scholarship that asserts African humanity and creativity while respecting the highest standards of scientific excellence and rigour. In turning to the wider social research community, beyond its immediate membership, the idea is to shop around for excellent scholarship that showcases the best from and on Africa and that is relevant to her peoples and their needs and aspirations.

Since journals are particularly adept at promoting and encouraging topical debates, CODESRIA has invested in publishing, often in association with professional scholarly associations on the continent, a significant number of journals. The current number of journals published by CODESRIA totals $$$$$: The role of CODESRIA journals, editors, and editorial advisory boards, for example, is detailed in CODESRIA's Publications and Dissemination Policy, last updated in 2005 and available in hard copy and from the web. They are expected to promote African scholarship relevant to African predicaments and aspirations. They also help CODESRIA orient the intellectual agenda on the basis of which Africa is studied. I invite us all to reread CODESRIA's 2007-11 strategic plan, anchored in how to promote rethinking of African development. Rethinking requires support for scholarship that deconstructs epistemological fallacies informed by ambitions of dominance that have sustained the caricaturing of African social realities. Such scholarship should legitimise African encounters and forms of knowing and knowledge construction.

What CODESRIA prescribes and expects of its journals is therefore quite clear. Because we are not here simply to rehash and re-enact those prescriptions and expectations, I would like us to dwell on the heart of the future: How to go about fulfilling the CODESRIA vision and mission beyond sterile rhetoric on the need for African scholarship and African voices in the marketplace of ideas. How do we translate our wishes into horses in real terms? For thirty-six years we have persevered in trying to create space for an alternative world through alternative research into alternative voices by alternative researchers. How will we fulfil CODESRIA's mission through its journals going forward? How alternatively will we ask the questions to ensure that we do not simply reproduce conventional wisdom and business as usual in the name of the African Alternative in scholarship and in the journals that communicate that scholarship?

There have been, and indeed, continue to be great debates in CODESRIA journals in the form of book reviews, review articles, thematic and special issues and reports on innovative research. We only need to flip through the pages of the *CODESRIA Bulletin*, *Africa Review of Books*, *Africa Development*, *Journal of Higher Education in Africa*, *African Sociological Review*, or any other CODESRIA journal to appraise some of these debates. Many of us would recall the Archie Mafeje/Ali Mazrui debate in the pages of the *CODESRIA Bulletin* (see No.3&4 2008), and are of course familiar with the attention and commentary received by Thandika Mkandawire's critical commentary on the intellectual itinerary of Jeffrey Sachs, published in the *Africa Review of Books* of March 2006. However, the quality of debate in CODESRIA journals and other publications depends on the quality of research and thought produced. For the research it sponsors, CODESRIA should provide quality assurance at each stage, from calls for proposals and abstracts, to methodology and writing workshops, fieldwork, and the submission of reports or articles for publication. Even before manuscripts are submitted for peer-review, coordinators of CODESRIA networks and journal editors play an important role in verifying that work rhymes with CODESRIA's strategic orientations, and that authors are sufficiently familiar with local and global debates that relate to African realities and that their scholarship is cognizant of the complex and nuanced nature of such realities.

This ensures that the peer-review process focuses more on how to enrich manuscripts than on having to eliminate scholarship running counter to the vision and mission which CODESRIA funds and supports and for which it receives core funding and other support. It is simply naive to presume that because someone looks or passes for African (by accident of phenotype or geography), their scholarship and intellectual habitus necessarily demonstrates deep understanding or meaningful representations of African realities. Similarly, it is not because someone espouses rhetoric about challenging paradigms that tend to caricature and misrepresent Africa that that person necessarily produces rigorous scholarship to help upset those paradigms.

A danger in preaching to the converted is that critical instincts are blunted by all the alleluias and amens that come in sharing the same basic faith, beliefs and assumptions. While there is a compelling need, both scientifically and politically, to continue to promote African voices articulating African predicaments, CODESRIA should augment attention to the scientific quality and social pertinence of research and scholarship. What is published should be in line with CODESRIA's mission. Every time we publish counter to it, we retard development and also jeopardise CODESRIA. CODESRIA must practice what it preaches. The quality and pertinence of the research questions we ask and encourage will determine the quality and pertinence of intellectual arguments and debates reflected and circulated in CODESRIA's publications and to some extent even in other social science journals on the continent.

Henry Chakava's legacy

Chakava has been unwavering in his zeal to promote African publishing and the rights and dignity of African writers in a global context where western models and values predominate and others are reduced to the status of hapless mimics of these. Through his East African Educational Publishers, Chakava has stressed the need for greater accommodation of African perspectives and outlooks in African education through African stories and African voices. He has argued without relent that African publishers have a responsibility to provide the type of books and stories that will inform and enlighten the younger generation of Africans often caught betwixt and between the imperatives of reviving dying African traditions and values systems on the one hand, and the lure and allure of a streamlined and aggressively globalised mass-mediated western consumer culture on the other. The story of his involvement with publishing since his days as representative of Heinemann Publishers in Africa can be compared a devoted struggle to confront and surmount a kilimanjaro of economic, cultural and political challenges to writing and publishing Africa in a manner relevant and sympathetic to the everyday experiences and predicaments of Africans.

Chakava's message, unfortunately, has often fallen on deaf ears, just as his efforts have been greeted by a myriad of cul-de-sacs. Forced to bend over backwards simply to survive, many an African publisher has chosen the often safer option to focus on publishing standardised and routinised textbooks with predictable content that what bring them profits, however modestly, without unsettling the waters, in a publishing industry where it is all too easy to perish economically even as a multinational publishing corporation. As a consequence Works of fiction well-tailored or predicament-oriented to African concerns or emphasising alternative voices to proliferated conventional accounts are overlooked because, to quote Chakava, editors 'do not have the time and patience to advise authors on how to revise and rewrite to an acceptable level.'[10]

Writing in 2008, Chakava argues that although some progress has been made, the general picture of African publishing since the 1973 Ile-Ife conference on the theme of the coming of age of African publishing is blurry. Growth in the 1970s was followed by decline in the 1980s, then by measured resurgence since the 1990s. While associational life among writers, publishers and book dealers has increased, as has the number of book fairs within countries and across regions, associations and organisations remain weakly structured and poorly managed, and the majority cannot survive without donor support. Notwithstanding the support and initiatives witnessed since the 1990s, Africa is yet to achieve its potential and remains at the bottom of the world book production chart. The problems that plagued publishing in the 1970s and 1980s – lack of capital, training, equipment and raw materials, an underdeveloped market, and competition from multinationals – may have diminished but have not disappeared.

Chakava has remained hopeful, despite factors that conspire against publishing in Africa, such as mediocrity of content and technical quality, language difficulties, invisibility, poor reputations of publishers, and insufficient marketing, distribution and readership. If these problems are universal, they are exacerbated in Africa. In addition to technical and financial difficulties, the publishing industry in Africa faces censorship and repression, limited investment in training, lack of incentives and conducive

---

10 According to Henry Chakava, Chairman of East African Educational Publishers, Nairobi, Kenya, on page xxxix in 'Introductory Essay to African Publishing: From Ile-Ife, Nigeria to the Present,' in Hans M. Zell (Ed.), *Publishing, Books & Reading in Sub-Saharan Africa: A Critical Bibliography*, Lochcarron, Scotland, United Kingdom: Hans Zell Publishing.

environments, as well as political bottlenecks. Governments are more concerned about, as Henry Chakava puts it, ensuring that children get books on their desks, regardless of their origin or content or language, than in ensuring development of local publishing industries. In many a country, the climate of repression since independence has meant a dearth of local publishing in general and of quality in particular. The few existing publishers have had to steer clear of controversial material, which, given the sensitivity of government to anything mildly critical, has forced them out of business or reduced them to printers of inoffensive but unprofitable literature.

All these factors militate to make the African publishing and book industry the underdeveloped underachiever that it is. It contributes a meagre three per cent to the total world publication output and is heavily dependent on school textbook publishing and donor-driven book procurement programmes. Well over 90 per cent of books published in Africa are school textbooks, and the majority of these are published by multinational companies. In South Africa for example, 60 per cent of educational publishing (i.e. 80 per cent of the entire publishing industry) is controlled by multinationals, and the remaining 40 per cent almost exclusively by local white-owned companies. Publishing of books of interest and relevance to the majority of Africans is rare. Multinational publishers target the elite few who can read and write European languages and – for economic, cultural or political reasons – reproduce work informed by a global hierarchy of creativity in which Africans are perceived to be at the very bottom. Most sub-Saharan African publishers north of the South African Limpopo River might have the will to promote alternative work, but they simply do not have the means to do so – or to survive doing so.

Created in the late 1980s and early 1990s to strengthen African writing, publishing and book distribution networks such as the African Writers Association (PAWA), African Publishers Network (APNET), African Booksellers Association (PABA), and African Books Collective (ABC) have certainly increased awareness and accessibility. The challenge remains, however, of ensuring the visibility and recognition of African publications as vehicles of African creativity and cultural content in Africa and beyond. This would require, among other things, creating space for ordinary people to contribute through the stories of their lives in shaping the book industry in Africa.

Writers suffer administrative censorship or high rejection rates at the hands of commercial multinational publishers. However, African publishers, through sheer resilience and commitment, have brought to the limelight books that otherwise would never have made it into print, though the quality of printing and binding leaves a lot to be desired. As Henry Chakava highlights in his introduction to this bibliography, many African writers of fiction and faction, from novelists to academics through poets, playwrights and journalists, seek visibility through publication yet perish, and not necessarily because of poor content. They perish because publishers simply do not have the capacity to guarantee quality and disseminate their publications. Things are particularly difficult for those writing and trying to publish in indigenous African languages.

In the social sciences, where objectivity is often distorted by obvious or subtle ideology, African scholars face a critical choice between sacrificing relevance for recognition or recognition for relevance. The politics of the cultural economy of publishing prevents them from achieving both recognition and relevance simultaneously. Yet Africa is suffering from famine – a famine of books grounded in and relevant to the cultures of Africa. Starved of their own culture, people have difficulty garnering confidence and strength. And like with every famine, Good Samaritans and enterprising opportunists are seldom too far away. Armed with good intentions or the rhetoric thereof, at least, the book famine in Africa has unleashed a tsunami of purported do-gooders all committed to curing Africans of cultural poverty by flooding them with books – most of which were conceived, written and published with scant regard to their or to their needs as defined and prioritised by themselves, and many of which were written to strip the continent of any sense of self-worth, pregnant as the books often are with unexamined assumptions and pretensions of a civilising mission targeted at Africans as the scum of the earth. In this regard, most of what comes to the continent in the form of book donations is the result of stiff prescriptiveness that is hardly amenable to the idea of a world that privileges creative cultural diversity.

Little wonder that some critically minded Africans have tended to relate to such book donations as an exercise at dumping or flooding Africa with cultural and intellectual toxic waste from Europe and North America, the main origins of such book donation programmes. Even those who would otherwise be supportive of book donations, if well-tailored, have had reason to criticise the lack of carefully thought out strategies in many of such endeavours.

Hans Zell, a foremost proponent of the development of the book industry and publishing in Africa, recently complained about the continued dependence on exogenously generated and coordinated book donations, instead of developing their own capacities in tune with locally engineered needs. How can African libraries remain eternally desperate for donated printed books (which usually come from outside the continent) despite over half a century of independence, and irrespective of the effort made by crusaders of African publishing such as Henry Chakava? Zell is right to worry if anyone is genuinely interested in an independent African library when he writes:

> ... I believe legitimate to ask why large scale book donation programmes should continue to be necessary today, after millions of books have been shipped and donated to African libraries, schools and other recipients every year, and over the last three decades or more. Just when can we expect African libraries to become independent of large scale foreign book aid and create their own sustainable library services? (Zell, 2015: 43)

Yet more and more commissioned studies seem to indicate that no one is in a hurry to rethink this sense of business as usual around book donations to Africa (Gray et al 2010), a practice that continues to exclude books by African publishers, despite what African Books Collective has done to market and distribute titles published by 155 publishers from 24 African countries with over 200 new titles being added every year.[11] This is all the more perplexing as even the World Bank has reported that locally published books are the cheapest and most suitable, and that the capacity is there in Africa to people the reading landscape on the continent with relevant books locally published (Fredriksen et al., 2015: 33). What could account for this stubborn resistance on the part of book donors to

---

11 See http://www.africanbookscollective.com/about-us, accessed 01 February 2016.

consider the possibility that something good or worthwhile could come out of Africa beyond famine and a predisposition to be assumed as fodder for those with ambitions of dominance? Why should donors assume, a priori, that African content is not there, or not easily available? This weakens local publishers and therefore the output of African publishing. The distribution solutions, especially with the advent of the technology of electronic publishing are there; what is missing are the budgets. This, unfortunately has gone backwards since Henry Chakava's heydays, where the Intra-African Book Support Scheme (IABSS), operated from 1991 to 2004, was running and there was a lot of co-publication happening with other African and international publishers. As Hans Zell explains:

> Established with the generous financial support from several donor organisations and foundations, the principle aims of this scheme were to help overcome shortages of culturally relevant African-published books in African libraries, to promote an intra-African trade in books, raise awareness of African-published material, and support autonomous African publishers through sales via African Books Collective, who operated the scheme from 1991 to 2004, in later years in cooperation with Book Aid International (see Profile). The scheme consisted of two components: (1) The supply of adult fiction and children's books/teenage fiction to African public, school and community libraries. (2) Provision of scholarly/tertiary level African published titles to university libraries in Africa. Both components of the scheme were completely recipient-request led, through provision of catalogues and other selection tools made available to recipient libraries. By the scheme's end, an average of some 12,000 literary and children's titles and 7,000 scholarly titles had been donated each year (Zell, 2015: 34).

This is definitely an initiative in the right direction, as it brings donors into conversation with Africa publishers and libraries around felt needs identified and articulated by African themselves, and supported or facilitated by donor funds in a manner that is not as prescriptive as the approach by donors who claim to know best and would engage Africa purely on their own terms.

With such stereotypes, prescriptiveness and general lack of encouragement vis-à-vis Africa and its creativity, it is hardly surprising that even the most non-commercial, 'progressive' or 'independent' publishers and university presses hesitate to promote diversity of content because they run the risk of putting themselves out of business by venturing away from the standardised, routinised and predictable menus the readership has been socialised to expect. Publishers uncritically recruit reviewers – who are arbitrators of taste, standards and knowledge – regardless of ideological leanings or cultural backgrounds. This implies that publishing is about policing ideas to ensure plurality without diversity in national, regional and global book markets. The future of African publishing must go beyond the market in its fundamentalist sense. Scholarly and other traditions are invented and reinvented. It is the place and duty of scholarly publishers, in and outside Africa, to populate a global marketplace with multiple identities and cultural conviviality and provide space for unique and powerful voices.

Current investments in knowledge and cultural production by Africans are insufficient to ensure production informed by the lived and dynamic realities of Africans. Outside Africa, knowledge of Africa beyond popular stereotypes is poor. Given that perceptions are shaped and reshaped over time and given the importance of cultural diversity in a fast globalising world, conscious efforts should be made to develop policies aimed at eradicating 'cultural poverty' in and on Africa. Such policies should encourage the production and consumption – in Africa and the rest of the world – of cultural products created by Africans who are crying out for the space and means to tell the story of African creativity in dignity. This mission is not achievable in a context where the global cultural industries are driven by the desire for profit with few incentives for ensuring representation for the world's cultural diversity. Publishers could contribute to the eradication of cultural poverty through publication and dissemination of African books as cultural products. African publishers have a long way to go to provide for a rainbow continent.

Harnessing e-publishing and print-on-demand technology will make it possible to publish books that would otherwise be too costly to print in large quantities where markets are not assured. With African Books Collective, a brain child of Henry Chakava and his peers growing from strength to strengthen, distribution is no longer the weakest link in African publishing. What Chakava would like to see in his retirement, I venture to guess, is the day those who genuinely want to see African writing and publishing flourish, begin to put their money where they have so far put their rhetoric: ensuring that Africans do not publish and perish, and that African children eager for education and self-cultivation are not eternally fed books with scant relevant to their lived experiences.

References

Chumbow, B. S. 2005. "The Language Question and National Development in Africa." In *African Intellectuals: Rethinking Politics, Language, Gender and Development*, pp. 165-192, edited by Thandika Mkandawire. Dakar: CODESRIA/Zed.

_____. 2009. "Linguistic Diversity, Pluralism and National Development in Africa." *Africa Development* 34(2): 21–45.

Devisch, René. 2002. "Endogenous Knowledge Practices, Cultures and Sciences: Some Anthropological Perspectives." Paper presented at the conference on Science and Tradition at Brussels, April 2001.

_____. 2007. "The University of Kinshasa: From Lovanium to Unikin". In *Higher Education in Postcolonial Africa: Paradigms of Development, Decline and Dilemmas,* pp. 17-38, edited by Michael Afolayan. Trenton, NJ: Africa World Press.

Fonlon, B.N. 2012 [1964) "A Case for Early Bilingualism/Pour un Bilinguisme de bonne heure". In *The Task of Today and Other Seminal Essays*, pp. 193-269, edited by Bernard Nsokika Fonlon. Bamenda, CAmerron: Langaa.

Fredriksen, B., S. Brar and M. Trucano. 2015. *Getting Textbooks to Every Child in Sub-Saharan Africa Strategies for Addressing the High Cost and Low Availability Problem*, Washington DC: World Bank.

Gray, E., A. Rens, and K. Bruns. 2010. *Publishing and Alternative Licensing Models in Africa: Comparative Analysis of the South African and Ugandan PALM Studies*. Ottawa: IDRC.

Jeppie, S. and S.B. Diagne. eds. 2008. *The Meanings of Timbuktu*. Pretoria: HSRC & CODESRIA.

Mazrui, A. 1986. *The Africans: A Triple Heritage*. London: BBC.

Ndi, William. 2008. "The Translation Studies Reader." *Australian Review of Applied Linguistics* 31(1):111-114.

wa Thiong'o, Ngugi. 1986. *Decolonising the Mind: The Politics of Language in African Literature*. London: James Currey.

_____. 1997. "Detained: A Writer's Prison Diary." In *Perspectives on Africa: A Reader in Culture, History, and Representation*, pp. 613–622, edited by R. R. Grinker and C.B. Steiner. Oxford: Blackwell.

_____. 2005. "Europhone or African Memory: The Challenge of the Pan-Africanist Intellectual in the Era of Globalization." In: *African Intellectuals: Rethinking Politics, Language, Gender and Development*, pp. 155–164, edited by Thandika Mkandawire. Dakar: CODESRIA/Zed.

Nyamnjoh, Francis B. 2004. "A Relevant Education for African Development – Some Epistemological Considerations." *African Development* 23(1): 161-184.

_____. 2012. "Potted Plants in Greenhouses: A Critical Re-flection on the Resilience of Colonial Education in Africa." *Journal of Asian and African Studies*, 47(2): 129-154.

Nyamnjoh, Francis B. and Shoro Katleho. 2011. "Language, Mobility, African Writers and Pan-Africanism." *African Communication Research*, 4(1): 35-62.

Venuti, Lawrence. ed. 2004. *The Translation Studies Reader*. New York: Routledge.

Zell, Hans M. and R. Thierry. 2015. *Book Donation Programmes for Africa: Time for a Reappraisal? Two Perspectives*. Lochcarron, Scotland: Hans Zell Publishing.

12

African Publishing in the Digital Age

By Roger Stringer

Doing the research for this contribution, I became very conscious of changes that have occurred in 'African publishing' since the development of what were dubbed 'Information and Communication Technologies' (ICTs), when their use became widespread in the 1990s. I was also very aware that the sources I was consulting about the situation twenty-five or thirty years ago were largely in print form: those I was looking at for more recent information were nearly all in a digital format or online. I think it would be fair to say that in those days we had expected that these 'new technologies' would offer both opportunities and 'challenges' to African publishers, but I'm not sure that we expected that they would have such a significant effect on the nature of publishing on the continent.

Publishing began in Africa, particularly in the former British colonies, largely through arms of British and then multinational companies, as well as with a degree of state publishing that appeared along with the need to expand educational opportunities as countries obtained their independence. Gradually, locally owned publishing companies were formed, in some cases by buying out the local branch of a multinational publisher and being able to develop their own lists while at the same time representing the established publisher. Those publishers that have survived are now the 'grand old men' of African publishing, and, like the multinational publishers, they find themselves faced with challenges arising from a changing world, albeit in a different way.

Things were initially not easy for the new African indigenous publishers, particularly when it came to accessing large sums of money that started to become available from institutions such as the World Bank to support the supply of educational books in Africa in the 1980s. The 1990s became perhaps a 'golden age' for African publishers, when, partly in response to this situation, the African Publishers Network (APNET) was founded on 17 February 1992, almost simultaneously with the Bellagio Publishing Network – 'an informal association of donors, African publishers, and others committed to working for the advancement of indigenous publishing and book development in Africa'.[1]

During the same decade, the Zimbabwe International Book Fair (ZIBF) became established as the most important book fair on the continent, and publishers from twenty African countries were represented among the nearly three hundred exhibitors at the ZIBF in 1999. A physical presence was essential then in order for publishers to negotiate distribution, co-publishing and rights agreements, and that led to around 250 individuals, many from Africa, being registered among the ZIBF's Trade and Professional Visitors that year.

It was also at this time that we saw the beginning of what would become 'the digital age', though we didn't know then how it would develop. The first major technology to prove a benefit to publishers was 'desktop publishing'. Suddenly, with the arrival of the Apple Macintosh computer in the late 1980s, publishers could typeset and make up their own publications in-house, printing out 'camera-ready copy' on a laser printer to take to commercial printers for reproduction. At that stage, we still expected the output of publishing activities to be in print form, and desktop publishing offered publishers both cost savings and better control over elements of the production process.

At a very low and slow level, the Internet was developing at the same time. From about 1988, e-mail messages to and from Zimbabwe,

---

1 'Bellagio Group statement of aims and scope', *Bellagio Publishing Network Newsletter* (March 1996), 19: 3. For more information about the Bellagio Publishing Network, see <http://www.bellagiopublishingnetwork.com>, where it says: 'Although the Network has closed and the site is no longer updated, the archive is being maintained by volunteers to support publishing development and to attest to the important work the Network had achieved in this area.'

for example, were being sent through telephone lines using a 'store and forward' method, linking nodes within the Association of Progressive Communications.[2] By 1991, e-mail from the University of Zimbabwe was going through a different system of dial-up links via Rhodes University in Grahamstown, South Africa,[3] but it would still be a few years before the World Wide Web would take over the stage.

With hindsight, it is interesting to look back at what we thought was necessary to develop African publishing in those days. In mid-1993, Henry Chakava summarised the 'key issues' that needed to be tackled in order to develop indigenous African book Publishing:[4]

> *Ownership:* firstly, the industry has to be wrested from foreign publishers and state parastatals ... Secondly, the state must step out of publishing and must dismantle all its publishing monopolies.
>
> *Manpower:* for a publishing industry to succeed, it requires trained managers, editors, readers, artists, designers, illustrators, etc. It also requires the services of trained writers, printers, booksellers and librarians in getting books to the user.
>
> *Capital:* as a business, publishing is unique and risky. ... Publishers entering the market for the first time would need to launch at least five books to make an impact. ... One needs a lot of money to venture into publishing.
>
> *Manufacturing:* ... Our new policy here should be to import machinery and raw materials.
>
> *Distribution:* many African publishers have complained that they are unable to get their books to places where the would-be buyer can see them. They say that there are too few bookshops and libraries in Africa.

---

2 Brian Murphy, *Mike Jensen and the Code that Stitched together the APC: The Pre-Internet Days and Early Efforts at Linking APC Nodes*, available at: <https://www.apc.org/about/history/mike-jensen-pre-internet-days>. Accessed 15 Oct. 2015.

3 John G. Sheppard, *Electronic Mail in Zimbabwe*, available at: <http://www.africa.upenn.edu/E_Mail/E_Mail_11700.html>. Accessed 15 Oct. 2015.

4 Henry Chakava, 'An Indigenous African Book Publishing Industry: In Search of a New Beginning', *African Publishing Review* (1993), 2(5): 9-11.

> *Market:* the book-user constitutes the publishers' market [which] is adversely affected by diminishing national budgets ... and small home markets characterised by declining purchasing power.

Gillian Nyambura, APNET's Executive Secretary, speaking about the organisation's Five-Year Strategic Plan for the years 1999 to 2004, noted that the problems affecting indigenous publishers in 1999 remained unchanged since the establishment of APNET in 1992:

> Indigenous publishers are still grappling with lack of skilled human resource, lack of capital, the absence of enabling political environment, the underdevelopment of book markets, the lack of infrastructure to enable communication among publishers at local, regional and international levels and the lack of information.[5]

Technology issues began to dominate discussions about publishing in the early 21st century. The 26th IPA congress held in Buenos Aires, Argentina, in May 2000 focused on the 'new technologies' that were now significantly influencing the book industry.[6]

> The third revolution of books is now underway, said Roger Chartier, former chairman of the Science Council of the Library of France. The first revolution was when the papyrus roll was abandoned for the codex -bound volumes made of paper. ...
>
> The printing press brought the second book revolution, leading to wider dissemination of knowledge. Now we have the electronic book, both through the Internet and through the personal reading devices that will come. Electronic books are organized differently and they will profoundly change reading and study habits. ... Readers will be able to make their own book out of the many books

---

5 'Strengthening indigenous publishing in Africa – APNET's Five-Year Strategic Plan 1999–2004', *African Publishing Review* (1999), 8(6): 9–10.

6 H. Daniel Calabia, 'Tech concerns dominate global publishers event', *Computerworld*, 2 May, 2000, <http://www.computerworld.com.au/article/100004/tech_concerns_ dominate_global_publishers_event>

they can browse through hyperlink connections. 'It is the very notion of 'book' that is being challenged by the new technology,' Chartier said.

Brian Wafawarowa, one of only three delegates from Africa among the 700 attending, said that the conference 'left [him] thinking seriously about the place of African publishing on the world arena' and wondering whether the voice of African publishing will ever be audible enough at world fora like the IPA Congress or whether Africa will continue to be discussed and suggestions made for its improvement as a market of international book and information products.[7]

There were major concerns about copyright and the respect for intellectual property, and Microsoft was predicting that an eBook would become the only form of book and that the last paper book would be published in 2017. Others noted the disadvantages of eBooks, which included the weight of computers, their screens being difficult to read, and their being subject to memory loss and viruses.[8]

Chief Victor Nwankwo saw immediate opportunities in Africa for the printed book. The late Managing Director of Fourth Dimension Publishing in Nigeria and the first Chairman of APNET was a great proponent of Print-on-Demand and had predicted in 1999 that 'the book as we know it will stay with us in Africa for some time to come'.[9] Print-on-Demand (POD) enabled publishers to use their in-house desktop-publishing systems to create PDF files that could be sent electronically to a printer anywhere (though not exactly everywhere!) in the world where a hard copy could be produced locally when required, thereby avoiding high warehousing and shipping costs.

In his last presentation at the Zimbabwe International Book Fair in 2002,[10] he reported on his experience in using print-on-demand

---

7 Brian Wafawarowa, 'The 26th IPA congress: The new digital era', *African Publishing Review* (2000), 9(3): 12.
8 Alan Ross, 'The impact of technology on the publishing trade', *African Publishing Review* (2000), 9(3): 2–4.
9 Victor Nwankwo, 'Print-on-Demand for an African publisher', *African Publishing Review* (2001), 10(5): 1–4.
10 Victor Nwankwo, 'Print-on-Demand: An African publisher's experience', *African Publishing Review* (2002), 11(5): 28–39.

technologies in a pilot project and concluded that 'the revolutionary advances of information and communications technology ... create a pressing agenda to seize [extraordinary] opportunities to address specific needs in the publishing process'.

By 2003, Mamadou Aliou Sow, then Chairman of APNET, described the African publishing industry as being 'still halfway between the traditional and new publishing techniques' and saw a number of 'daunting' challenges facing the African publisher.[11] Although recognising that opportunities had increased, and particularly that 'a wider market has been opened up for books through e-commerce' and 'new cost-saving methods (e.g. POD) being introduced', he still bemoaned the domination of the textbook sector by 'publishers from the north', and the 'limited or total absence of access to capital for publishers'. The same issues were still there.

Publishing in Africa, as in other parts of the world, was still largely following established structures and processes. Traditional publishing companies were still expected to dominate, and Internet start-ups such as Amazon.com, taking advantage of print-on-demand technology, were regarded as 'online bookshops' that provided just another, albeit different, retail outlet for publishers.

But in the early 21st century, everything changed for African publishers. To start with, the interests of funding agencies changed, and the Bellagio Publishing Network closed at the end of 2002. This had a significant influence on APNET's sources of funds, and the organisation had to trim its activities. In addition, the uncertain political and economic situation in Zimbabwe had led APNET to relocate its secretariat to Ghana, and the associated costs had been a drain on its funds. Publishing of the *African Publishing Review* became erratic and had ceased by 2004. For a variety of reasons, APNET was not the force it had been in the 1990s, and was not able to provide the guidance and support to African publishers that was perhaps needed for the adoption of new technologies as that decade went on.

---

11 M. Aliou Sow, 'Current opportunities and challenges facing African publishers', *African Publishing Review* (2003), 12(4–6): 4–5.

The World Wide Web, 'search engines' and e-commerce, with secure online payment systems, had changed everything. From around 2002, we saw the development of 'Web 2.0' which enabled 'user-generated content'. Information on Websites could be edited by users; immediate interaction, not just e-mail, between parties was possible, and over the rest of the decade 'social media' sites appeared. We are now all familiar with Wikipedia, Facebook, YouTube, Twitter, and the like. But do African publishers make use of them and take advantage of the opportunities they offer?

In 2002, I co-ordinated the compilation of a directory of the 'book chain' in anglophone Africa.[12] I randomly 'Googled' some of the publishers listed in that book from various African countries to see if they had Websites or other forms of Internet presence today. Most of the 'established' African publishers had Websites, but almost none of the lesser-known ones did. Very few had active Facebook pages or Twitter accounts. The best one could find about the lesser-known publishers was their listing in commercial business directories of countries or cities – and then all that appeared were physical and postal addresses and telephone numbers. Are they still trading, or is it just that they have not moved into the digital age?

Justin Cox, CEO of the African Book Collective (ABC) that was founded in 1989 largely to market and distribute African-published books in Europe and North America, has reported that ABC has seen an increase in the number of publishers they represent but that they are 'dealing with more publishers/organizations with a few books here or there rather than publishers with big lists'.[13] He also noted that not many publishers have Websites, and, of those that do, most don't work. The number of 'clickable links' on the ABC's page of 'Participating Publishers' is very few.[14]

In the meantime, with the arrival of Amazon's Kindle (in 2007) and Apple's iPod (2010), the 'digital age' had truly arrived for the book. All the disadvantages of the eBook (reported above) vanished, as the

---

12 Roger Stringer, *The Book Chain in Anglophone Africa: A Survey and Directory* (Oxford: INASP, 2002).
13 Personal communication, Oct. 2015.
14 See <http://www.africanbookscollective.com/about-us>.

new eBook readers were portable, lightweight, easy to read from, and relatively inexpensive. Amazon was transformed from being simply an online bookshop to becoming a publishing-services provider. Authors can publish their books directly with them – in either eBook or print form or both – through Kindle Direct Publishing and CreateSpace.[15] Similar services are now also offered by a large number of other companies, and recently even Penguin/Random House have joined in through their Author Solutions service.[16] So where does this leave African publishers? Are they using these continuously evolving technologies to maintain or improve their position in the publishing world?

In May 2015, Emma Shercliff reported responses from Nigerian publishers about 'the key issues currently facing their businesses':

> ... three issues surfaced repeatedly: the cost of doing business in Nigeria (high price of paper, high price of ink, tariffs & import duties); the failure of government to understand what publishers do (as exemplified by the recent book import tax debacle, little distinction is made between the role of the publisher and that of the printer), and difficulties with the distribution of books (poor transport systems, weak bookselling networks, lack of decent bookstores).[17]

These issues sound little different from those identified by Henry Chakava more than twenty years earlier. Is African publishing really no different in 'the digital age'?

Walter Bgoya and Mary Jay had commented in 2013 that 'Education and language policies, weak infrastructure, and lack of purchasing power continue to present hurdles to African publishers, with textbook and language policies creating probably the most significant brake to

---

15 See <https://kdp.amazon.com> and <https://www.createspace.com>, respectively.
16 See <http://www.authorsolutions.com>.
17 Emma Shercliff, 'The possibilities and challenges of digital African publishing', *Publishing Perspectives*, 12 May 2015, <http://publishingperspectives.com/2015/05/the-possibilities-and-challenges-of-digital-african-publishing>.

progress.'[18] Once again, issues similar to those cited twenty years earlier were being given, though they did recognise that 'the digital age is empowering African publishers', but qualified this with 'a caveat ... about infrastructure':

> the cost of an Internet connection, the reliability of electricity, as well as the affordability of computers and software for populations that are living in grinding poverty and staggering levels of unemployment necessarily slows its affects. The widespread use and relative expense of mobile phones is well known, but that technology is limited in terms of the receipt of manuscripts, editing, etc. Tablets, such as the iPad, may assist, but are available only to a small elite portion of the population.[19]

Not all African publishers are the same, however. Emma Shercliff contrasted these two types of publisher in Nigeria:

> UPL, a publicly listed company, founded as a branch of Oxford University Press in 1949, today has a staff of 305, 20 branch offices and revenues of 2.3 billion naira (£7.5 million). By contrast, even some of the best-known non-educational publishers have no more than two or three permanent members of staff, a minimal sales and marketing function and slim revenues. And whilst this new generation of African publishers do, of course, face significant challenges of limited capacity and reach, their lean structures also mean that they are amongst the most nimble, creative and experimental publishers operating anywhere in the world.

These 'nimble, creative and experimental publishers' are breathing new life into African publishing as a younger generation, fully comfortable with the technologies, begins to move on to the stage. The new, small

---

18 Walter Bgoya and Mary Jay, 'Publishing in Africa from independence to the present day', *Research in African Literatures* (2013), 44(2), 17–34.
19 Walter Bgoya and Mary Jay, 'Publishing in Africa from independence to the present day', *Research in African Literatures* (2013), 44(2), 17–34.

publishers on the continent are adapting their approaches to publishing to take advantage of the opportunities that are available in the digital age. Many of them are publishing 'genre fiction' – moving away from 'literature' and towards a focus on thrillers, crime, romance and science fiction.[20]

One such company in Nigeria is Cassava Republic Press, founded in 2006, who describe their mission as follows:

> Our mission is to change the way we all think about African writing. We think that contemporary African prose should be rooted in African experience in all its diversity, whether set in filthy-yet-sexy megacities such as Lagos or Kinshasa, in little-known rural communities, in the recent past or indeed the near future. We also think the time has come to build a new body of African writing that links writers across different times and spaces.[21]

In 2014, Cassava established the imprint Ankara Press:

> Our mission is to publish a new kind of romance, in which the thrill of fantasy is alive but realised in a healthier and more grounded way. Our stories feature young, self-assured and independent women who work, play and, of course, fall madly in love in vibrant African cities from Lagos to Cape Town. Ankara men are confident, emotionally expressive and not afraid of independent and sexually assertive women.[22]

Their titles are available as eBooks, downloadable directly from their Website in either mobi format (for use on Kindles) or ePub (for most other e-readers): 'Our books are for the moment not available anywhere else (for instance on Amazon). We are keen to build our own platform, rather

---

20 Emma Shercliff, *Digital Futures: The Changing Landscape of African Publishing – Review & Response* <http://africainwords.com/2013/10/31/digital-futures-the-changing-landscape-of-african-publishing-review-response>,

21 <http://www.cassavarepublic.biz/pages/about-us>. Accessed 20 Oct. 2015.

22 <http://www.ankarapress.com/pages/about-us>. Accessed 20 Oct. 2015.

than rely on other companies to make our books available.'²³ They are matching their output with their market and their readers' use of digital technologies.

Cover2Cover Books in South Africa is another innovative publisher that is targeting the mass youth market:

> The narratives are gripping and pacy; the messages positive without being preachy. The books read like soap-opera paperbacks, dealing with teenage angst in a highly readable and accessible way. The language is easy to understand, the chapters are short and the plots – built on tension and excitement – aim to keep readers hooked and interested in turning the page.²⁴

Cover2Cover also founded the FunDza Literacy Trust, through which they 'publish' short stories on mobile phones aimed at young people. Each story comprises seven 'chapters', and each chapter contains no more than 500 words. One chapter is sent out every day to cellphone 'subscribers' using Mxit – 'a mobile social network that lets you connect with friends and apps using any mobile phone'. They reach 'around 50,000 readers monthly, with an average visit duration of over 12 minutes'.²⁵

Africa is also beginning to develop its own online book stores, though they are few and far between at the moment. South Africa and Nigeria, of course, have several. Some online bookselling initiatives are also supporting content creation. In Kenya, for example, there is eKitabu:

> Operating under the banner – Tunaenda Digital – eKitabu is East Africa's premier eBook store, selling and distributing eBooks and interactive content to schools and individuals at ekitabu.com. The platform works with all leading publishers in Kenya and internationally

---

23 Ankara Press, *A Guide to Downloading and Reading Ankara Press E-books*, <https://cdn.shopify.com/s/files/1/0554/2553/files/Ankara_Press_full_download_guide.pdf>. Accessed 20 Oct. 2015.
24 <http://cover2cover.co.za/about-us/the-need>. Accessed 20 Oct. 2015.
25 <http://www.fundza.co.za/our-programmes/growing-communities-of-readers-programme>. Accessed 20 Oct. 2015.

in content provision. It also carries books approved by relevant authorities like Kenya Institute of Curriculum Development (KICD).[26]

As the Kenyan poet Njeri Wangari has noted, 'the challenge for most publishers has been a reliable payment system and ensuring that the digital books are not pirated'.[27] eKitabu enables payments through the M-Pesa, a mobile-phone money-transfer service used in Kenya as well as in other countries. In Zimbabwe, Mazwi, a recent start-up, is similarly attempting to address the payment and piracy problems.[28]

On the multinational front, of particular note has been the growth of Worldreader, an NGO based in the USA, who are 'on a mission to bring digital books to every child and her family, so that they can improve their lives'. With financial support from the likes of UNESCO and the Bill and Melinda Gates Foundation, Worldreader reaches 'readers in 69 countries, providing them with 28,514 book titles in 43 languages'.[29]

> Wordreader strives to work with our publisher partners in a way that matches our mutual ambitions. We understand the important role that the publishing industry plays in the ecosystem of literacy and know that the success of our readers is tied to the success of publishers.
>
> Our partnerships are therefore varied and dynamic: we've conducted practical digital workshops in Zambia, forged close partnerships with American publishers looking to make a positive impact and contributed to the Ghanaian and Kenyan publisher associations as members.[30]

---

26 'Kenya: EKITABU Transforms Learning within East African Schools', *MyInforms*, Sept. 2014 <http://myinforms.com/en/a/16437256-kenya-ekitabu-transforms-learning-within-east-african-schools>. Accessed 4 Jan. 2015.

27 'E-Kitabu; Kenya's first EBook Store launches at the Nairobi International Book Fair', *Kenyanpoet.com*, 30 Sept. 2012 <http://www.kenyanpoet.com/2012/09/30/e-kitabu-digital-book-store-launches-at-the-nairobi-book-fair>

28 'Techzim Podcast: Interview with Mazwi – Could it be Zimbabwe's Amazon?', *TechZim*, 1 Dec. 2014, <http://www.techzim.co.zw/2014/12/techzim-podcast-interview-mazwi-zimbabwes-amazon>. Accessed 4 Jan. 2015.

29 Worldreader, <http://www.worldreader.org/what-we-do>. Accessed 4 Jan. 2015.

30 Worldreader, <http://www.worldreader.org/thank-you/publishers>. Accessed 4 Jan. 2015.

In addition to the new, innovative African publishers described above, we should not forget that the digital age has provided an opportunity for self-publishers to produce their own books. This has meant that many novels and short stories that may have not made it past the editors in a publishing company – for quality as well as commercial reasons – have appeared. Some may be of dubious value in a literary sense, but on the positive side they have helped create an interest in 'reading for pleasure'. This, in turn, has led to the emergence of 'literary festivals' on the continent, which are replacing the 'book fairs' of the past. The digital age has made it less necessary for publishers and distributors to meet, so there is greater focus on authors and their readers and the overall expansion of the book-buying and -reading market.

Even though they have perhaps been initially driven by overseas interests, literary festivals have gradually started to become a regular occurrence on the African continent. In January 2015, the Kenyan blogger, James Murua, listed nearly thirty literary festivals in Africa that were coming up in 2015.[31] Ake, Storymoja, Port Harcourt, Writivism and Franschoek are already becoming familiar names. African publishers need to participate in these festivals and take advantage of them in promoting reading and the use of books, thereby expanding the overall market.

Finally, what does all this mean for the 'traditional' resources and methods involved in promoting and marketing African publisher's output? Bibliographic tools such as *African Books in Print* are ceasing to be relevant. The last edition was published in 2006, and we may not see another. Even though there may be no hard copies left of a particular title, if it is available in POD format it will never really be 'out of print', so such listings are not needed.

Publications such as the *African Book Publishing Record* (*APBR*) will surely continue to have a value in listing new titles from African publishers and in providing reviews, but who, other than libraries, will pay 93 euros for a single issue? And how will they keep up with what is being published on the continent? The established publishers will no doubt continue to

---

31 *African Literary Festivals You Can Attend in 2015*, <http://www.jamesmurua.com/african-literary-festivals-you-can-attend-in-2015>. Accessed 20 Oct. 2015.

submit details of their new titles, but what about the new publishers and self-publishers? The *APBR*'s Facebook page has only 18 'likes' at the time of writing and has posted nothing on it for three years, so it is not using Facebook to get publishers to inform them of their new titles, or to tell its community about new titles. Innovative publishers will rely on reviews on social media, on Amazon, in book-review sites such as GoodReads,[32] and on direct interaction with their target audience.

The 'nimble, creative and experimental publishers' represent the future of African publishing, particularly in the general publishing and literary arena. They are building on the foundations laid by the now-established African indigenous publishers, but are better placed to use the technologies and approaches required by in the digital age. Hans Zell commented in 2013 that:

> What is clear is that the new digital technologies and the e-revolution have radically changed the whole publishing landscape and many publishers in Africa, as indeed elsewhere, are grappling with a move to a digital environment.[33]

It is perhaps the older publishers that are 'grappling' rather than the younger ones.

I will end with a quotation from another doyen of African publishing, Chief Victor Nwankwo, who noted that 'people are more comfortable to live with what they know, no matter how imperfect, rather than seek new solutions.[34] This is as applicable today as it was thirteen years ago, and African publishers must not be afraid to seek new solutions if they are to survive in the digital age.

---

32 Links to over 240 book-review sites appears here: <http://www.complete-review.com/links/links.html>. Accessed 20 Oct. 2015.
33 Hans M. Zell, *Print vs electronic, and the 'digital revolution' in Africa* (Last updated and expanded: 28 January 2013), <https://www.academia.edu/2514725/Print_vs_Electronic_and_the_Digital_Revolution_in_Africa>. Accessed 19 Oct. 2015.
34 Victor Nwankwo, 'Print-on-Demand: An African publisher's experience', *African Publishing Review* (2002), 11(5): 38.

13

Internationalising the African Book

By Mary Jay

Background

The development of publishing in Africa is integral to the wider development of the continent: social, economic and cultural. The publication of books from the indigenous culture both contributes to national identity, and is the driver of educational development without which no country or continent can develop. In the words of Paul Tiyambe Zeleza, the Malawian historian:

> Books constitute crucial repositories of social memories and imaginations, containing the accumulated cultural capacity of society, of its accomplishments, agonies, and aspirations. Books, therefore, are not and cannot be a luxury, a dispensable dessert on the menu of development, nationhood, or human progress. They are an essential component of these processes – indeed their intellectual salt, spice, and starch.[1]

The arrival of the European missionaries, heralding the advent of colonialism, spread the book for the purposes of conversion to Christianity. The erroneous belief that this was how the book was introduced to Africa is belied by the fact that there was a long indigenous history of written scripts from the early civilisations of the Nile Valley and western and eastern

---

1 James Gibbs and Jack Mapanje, eds. *The African Writers' Handbook* (Oxford: African Books Collective, 1999), p.5.

coastal regions of Africa. Religious centres had spread the written word: Christian monasteries in Ethiopia, and the great centres of Islamic learning which housed the oldest libraries and universities in sub-Saharan Africa.

With the 'scramble for Africa' by the European powers, all but two African countries – Liberia and Ethiopia – were under occupation by 1914. In sub-Saharan Africa, the majority of countries had gained their independence in 1960 from Britain and France, albeit it is salutary to note that this trickled on for a minority of countries: the last French colony to become independent was in 1997, the last British colony in 1980, and the Portuguese colonies were not freed until the 1970s.

Taking 1960 as the dawn of independence, the average rate of African literacy was then 9 per cent.[2] African leaders met in Addis Ababa in 1961, and resolved that:

> African educational authorities should revise and reform the content of education in the areas of the curricular, textbooks, and methods, so as to take account of the African environment, child development, cultural heritage, and the demands of technological progress and economic development, especially industrialisation.[3]

As governments invested in national development, particularly education, the literacy rate is estimated to have risen to 27.8 per cent in 1970, and by 2004 to 59.7 per cent overall and 72 per cent for the Youth rate.[4] The Youth rate has continued to increase with a number of countries achieving rates in the 80-90 per cent range.[5] Primary school enrolment, impacting on literacy rates, increased between 1965 to the mid-1980s from 41 per cent to 68 per cent of the eligible population. The Association of African Universities was established in 1967 with a membership of 34, and now has 340 members.

---

2   Ibid. p.6.
3   UNESCO report quoted in *UNESCO General History of Africa Volume VIII*.
4   'Mapping the Global Literacy Challenge' in *Education for All Global Monitoring Report 2006*.
5   The World Bank data *http://data.worldbank.org/indicator/SE.ADT.1524.LT.ZS*

Thus the environment was set fair for publishing to develop in independent Africa, producing books from within the local culture, whether scholarly, literary or children's books.

Post-independence

Indigenous publishers seized the opportunity of the contribution necessary for cultural and economic development. Overseas publishers seized the opportunities for economic enrichment, and quickly dominated the lucrative educational books market. With limited success in accessing that market, indigenous publishers were not earning the funds needed to subsidise and develop general publishing. Government policies and the judicial framework were not helpful to local publishers, including taxes on import of book manufacturing materials, and lack of training for the publishing and printing industries. Many countries established parastatals as the way to counter foreign publishers.

Kenya well illustrates the point. By 1968, many British publishers had offices in Kenya, the content not being drawn from the local culture. For example, the international publishers, Longman and Oxford University Press (OUP) had established local offices, but did not publish locally: rather, in the words of Henry Chakava:

> ... neither company published locally; rather their function was to collect good manuscripts and forward them to London for vetting and publishing.[6]

An academic study of the creation of post-colonial literature illustrates how commercial decisions by an imprint of OUP outweighed its cultural mission, and how ... persistent and cultural inequalities became entrenched in the global literary marketplace in the twentieth century.[7] The textbooks developed by the East African Literature Bureau were placed for publication with foreign publishers. Heinemann's African Writers Series in the UK largely licensed titles to their subsidiary Heinemann Kenya.

---

6   Chakava, Henry. *Publishing in Africa. One Man's Perspective* (Oxford: Bellagio Publishing Network, and Nairobi: East African Educational Publishers Ltd., 1996) p.6.
7   Davis, Caroline. *Creating Postcolonial Literature. African Writers and British Publishers* (Basingstoke: Palgrave Macmillan, 2013) pp. 194-196

The gains nonetheless made by indigenous publishers were negatively impacted upon by the economic structural adjustment policies imposed in the 1980s. This compounded the weaknesses of the sector which publishers were seeking to overcome. In addition to the textbook issue, there was undercapitalisation, lack of access to funding, lack of purchasing power, weak distribution, low literacy levels particularly in English as the main language of publication, and the collapse of the few public libraries.

It was against this background that the foresighted and enterprising publisher of Heinemann Kenya, Henry Chakava, achieved the feat of organising the full local buyout of Heinemann Kenya in 1992, establishing it as East African Educational Publishers (EAEP), the leading Kenyan publisher. Despite this gain, the general publishing infrastructure remained weak, exchange controls still pertained and access to capital was limited. Foreign publishers were in Kenya, but Kenyan publishers had little or no presence internationally; and individual publishers' capacities to make the investment necessary to have a presence in the North, and have access to relevant marketing and distribution know-how, did not exist. The few publishers who had made distribution agreements with companies specialising in what was then called Third World books had encountered less than encouraging results, and indeed some publishers had lost money. In addition, dealers visited Africa, buying books at discounted local prices and selling them in the North in foreign exchange at marked up market prices. Thus the dealer benefitted rather than the publisher.

The publishers' capacity for underpinning their primary purpose of publishing for their own markets was not bolstered by earnings from overseas sales. The Dag Hammarskjöld Foundation had organised a key conference in 1984 in Arusha, Tanzania, on 'The Development of Autonomous Publishing in Africa',[8] which identified weak distribution as an important development brake. This was a foundation for the next stage of tackling the major obstacles faced by the publishers.

---

8   Conference papers in *Development Dialogue*, 1-2, 1984 (Uppsala: Dag Hammarskjöld Foundation, 1984) pp.73-140

African Books Collective (ABC)

Establishment

So a great adventure got under way, in which three of the leading lights of post-independence publishing were the key drivers: Walter Bgoya of Mkuki na Nyota Publishers, Tanzania (then at Tanzania Publishing House), Henry Chakava of East African Educational Publishers, Kenya, and the late Victor Nwankwo of Fourth Dimension Publishing, Nigeria. With a small group of like-minded publishers from other African countries, they brainstormed in 1985 to examine how best to showcase their titles outside Africa, both for sales revenue and for the wider aim of establishing Africa's own voice in scholarly and development research and debate in the North.

There was evidence that US libraries in particular found acquisition of African books very difficult, and conversely if a publisher was willing to supply, the hurdles of infrastructure and expensive and not necessarily efficient postal services were largely prohibitive. It was decided to strengthen indigenous African publishing by establishing African Books Collective (ABC) as the publishers own collective UK company. The company is not capitalised, but is constituted so that the original founders own and govern the company. As legally required, there are two UK Directors of the Limited Company, and they bear the financial responsibility; not least they would be responsible for any debts in the unlikely event of liquidation. ABC headquarters were established in the UK, since it was a main centre of English-language publishing in the North. Thus, as European and American publishers establish branch companies worldwide, or appoint distributors in the relevant territories, so African publishers would establish their own company in the UK, initially primarily to access Europe and the US.

ABC had two part-time UK based staff tasked with its establishment: seeking seed finance, setting up international marketing and distribution, and more widely promoting the cause of African publishing in international counsels. Twelve publishers attended the 1985 meeting in London, being the active leading publishers from all the regions of sub-Saharan Africa. Thereafter a large number of publishers known to have scholarly, literary or children's titles suitable for promotion in the North were mailed. Whilst work ensued on the establishment of the company, a total of 17 publishers confirmed their wish to be founder publishers; and signed exclusive distribution agreements with ABC for sales outside Africa. Africa was left as an open market, except that ABC would not sell into a publisher's own domestic market.

Mission

The mission at foundation was:

> African Books Collective, being an African founded, owned and governed organisation, seeks to promote, market and distribute African-published materials worldwide outside publishers' domestic markets, through collective action: to strengthen indigenous African publishers; to increase the visibility and accessibility of the wealth of African scholarship and culture, while at the same time meeting demand for these materials by educational, cultural and other institutions, particularly in the North.

This was later simplified to:

> 25 Years of the best of African Publishing from a Single Source of Supply. African Books Collective, founded, owned and governed by African publishers, seeks to strengthen indigenous African publishing through collective action and to increase the visibility and accessibility of the wealth of African scholarship and culture.

Finance

The legal constitution of the company and operational organisation were time-consuming but not unduly onerous. The main challenge was raising funds to get the company off the ground until such time as sufficient sales revenue would lead to it becoming self-financing. A business plan could not be formulated until financing and funds available were clear. At that time, donor organisations in the North had funds for development support and ABC's pitch was for cultural and economic development through publishing. It was decided that the publishers themselves would contribute finance to the start-up, both underpinning the nature of ownership and demonstrating to donors that publishers themselves were investing in the company and the funds sought were supplemental to the publishers own efforts. It was decided therefore that ABC would be a membership organisation: founder publishers would pay £1000 and receive 64⅔ per cent of net proceeds from sales; thereafter, after the start of trading, full members would pay £500 and received 60 per cent; and associate members would not pay, and would receive 55 per cent. Any full member unable to pay upfront could have the fee gradually deducted from sales remittances.

The objectives of membership were to raise initial and early stages finance, and to allow any publisher to participate without necessarily paying up front. The payment requirement was however essentially applied to the founders. The projected £17,000 from their fees was crucial to eliciting donor funds. This was at a time when exchange controls were in place in Africa and £1,000 remittance was a huge hurdle for many, both the amount and the hard currency. Gradually the funds trickled in, not unusually through ingenious albeit legal means. For example, a non-grant making development organisation paid for one publisher – maybe on extended loan; another by money being due to them for consultancy work being paid to ABC on their behalf. There is no doubt that this considerable self-help was a positive factor with donors. The donor funds were projected to meet the shortfall between ABC's net share of retained income from sales, and actual expenditure to fulfil the mission. The objective was for sales income to build until such time as ABC was self-sufficient.

The 1985 meeting and preliminary research had been funded by the Swedish International Development Agency (SIDA). Thereafter, together with the £17,000 from publishers, seed funding for the start-up was granted by SIDA, the Ford Foundation, and the Norwegian Agency for Development Cooperation (Norad). Other donors from time to time made grants, notably the Rockefeller Foundation. A dynamic head of Arts and Humanities at the Foundation was receptive to ABC's pitch for funding; subsequently ABC made the introductions for her fact-finding tour in Africa, and the Foundation then organised a seminal conference at the Bellagio Centre in Italy in 1991 on 'third world' publishing at which ABC had a strong presence. An edited book of the papers from the conference was published,[9] and Rockefeller took the lead in planning a new body of the main donors to African publishing together with the main recipients, notably ABC. This became the Bellagio Publishing Group, which was an important vehicle to maintain, inform and explain issues to the donors; and likewise, for donors to keep ABC abreast of their policies and thinking.

Governance

African Books Collective Ltd. was incorporated in September 1989 as a UK company limited by guarantee. The founder publishers elected from amongst their number a 6-member Council of Management, subsequently increased to 7 members, with responsibility for strategic direction, policy and overview of operations. The constitution provided for elections every three years. The Council was elected with regard to regional and gender balance, different types of publishers – large, small, and commercial, University presses, non-profits, and the experience which could be brought to bear. Henry Chakava was one of those publishers, and has remained on the Council to date. The internationally famous Blackwell Bookshop in Oxford hosted a welcome reception at the bookshop for the first meeting of the Council of Management, with a splendid full window display. A sure sign that Africa was turning the tables!

First meeting of ABC Council of Management in June 1998.

Left to right: Hans Zell, Senior Consultant; the late Victor Nwankwo, Fourth Dimension Publishers, Nigeria; Ayo Bamgbose, Ibadan University Press, Nigeria; Mamadou Diouf, CODESRIA, Senegal; Mothobi Mutloatse, Skotaville Publishers, South Africa; Henry Chakava, Heinemann Kenya (later East African Educational Publishers), Walter Bgoya, Tanzania Publishing House (later Mkuki na Nyota Publishers), Mary Jay, Consultant

9   Philip Albatch, ed. *Publishing and Development in the Third World* (Oxford: Hans Zell Publishers, Nairobi: East African Educational Publishers, New Delhi: Vistaar Publications, 1992).

International trading

Trading started in May 1990. When new title samples were received, orders were placed for publishers to send stocks to the ABC warehouse in the UK. Marketing included listing of titles on the major international bibliographic databases, catalogue mailings, and exhibits attendance in Europe and the US, and at the then thriving Zimbabwe International Book Fair. There were expenses from wastages of stocks when quantities ordered were over-optimistic in the light of actual sales, taking up warehouse space. In that case, either ABC or the publisher paid for the stocks to be returned to publishers, or they were wasted.

However, sales built slowly, and feedback was given to publishers as to the categories of books which sold best, their formats and design. Whilst the titles were primarily published for the local markets, some titles were published with the Northern market specifically in mind: not to distort publishers' own programmes, but rather to earn sales income to underpin their local market publishing. Scholarly books sold best, and occasionally literature titles if they were adopted for courses in the US. Children's books did not fare well, partly because of the very high production standards and low price points in the North. There was too a disconnection in the US as to African content, when the market was primarily interested in African-American content.

Trading in the US

The US has always been an important market, given its size, the number of African Studies programmes in numerous universities, and the many libraries. Since ABC shipped from its UK warehouse, sales were limited by customer resistance to shipping costs. More importantly, many institutions were required to order from within the US, not from overseas publishers or distributors. Titles either had to be listed in the American books in print publication, obviously impossible, or to have a physical distribution site in the US. ABC had unsuccessfully sought funding from 1994 to establish a US distribution point and stock-holding operation. By 1999, the UK and Europe were a bigger market than the US because of this handicap. Happily, an evaluation by Sida recommended in 2000 that 'ABC and its donors should actively pursue setting up a North American distribution point as soon as possible', finding that sales were seriously hampered by the lack of a distribution point and the organisation's potential was limited by this.

ABC commissioned a study in 2001, to inform the five year Strategic Plan 2002-2006. The study was undertaken by an experienced US publisher who was sympathetic to ABC's mission. He examined three main options: whether ABC should establish its own a branch office and warehouse in the US, contract a US distributor to stock titles, or to contract with a publisher for marketing and distribution in the US. He recommended the latter, and in 2002 agreement was entered into with Michigan State University Press (MSUP), active from 2003. Thereafter, as the difficulties of coordinating activities became clear, ABC appointed a member of staff as manager of the list to be based at MSUP to effect joined up activities and liaise with ABC. He undertook energetic direct marketing.

There were however considerable disadvantages given the almost standard demand of US customers for 50 per cent discounts or more, and the pretty unique system in the US whereby returns can be made up to one year from fulfilment. That had negative implications both for publisher remittances which had already been paid, and for stock levels. The partnership did however expand ABC's reach into the US, from where Canada was also supplied; and it established a stronger ABC profile. It lasted until the end of 2006, when the need to move to the digital environment overtook the need for a stocking arrangement; and ABC could thus better manage the market itself.

There remains an impediment to genuine international exchange in publishing with the US. Much has been written about the dilemma for African scholars as to where they publish. For example, articles in African journals are little cited in the North, and there remains prestige for scholars and literary writers about the perceived superiority of first publishing in the North. It may have career merit, but it should not be so. Why should the many lauded literary diaspora writers not be co-publishing with African publishers? Conversely, committed scholars do publish in Africa, but very few since it does not count for example as a plus on their CV for tenure, and citations are fewer in the North than for Northern publishers. And yet scholars want their works to be distributed in Africa, and maybe unintentionally contribute to the weakness of genuine international exchange. The prices are too high in Africa, there is no continent-wide distribution, they study Africa, yet Africa is dominated by the discourse of Northern scholars.[10]

Intra-African Book Support Scheme

A major factor of survival in ABC's early years was the operation of the Intra-African Book Support Scheme (IABSS), not least big sales earnings for many publishers. Donor supported, it enabled 33 higher education institutions to order books from ABC, and literature and children's books were also sent to public, school and other libraries in Africa. All titles were selected by the recipients, which should be a *sine qua non* in donated schemes. Whilst the scheme was not directly relevant to 'internationalising' the African book, it was important in disseminating information within Africa about what was available from different African countries. It addressed the problems of intra-African book trade through African institutions receiving books from different African countries and from within the African cultures; and it was a counter to the overwhelming content of book donation schemes of European and American published books. It was too a material contribution to the viability of ABC itself, increasing its own earnings from sales as well as those of the publishers.

'Internationalising' has been one-way in book donations to Africa, rather than Africa receiving books from its own cultures. The broad thrust of these foreign donations is another aspect of the cultural dominance of the North. An exhaustive study has recently been made about book donation schemes in Africa, both in the English language and French language speaking countries. It makes a powerful case about the negative effect Northern organisations, no doubt well-meaning, sending container loads of foreign books to Africa, largely not specifically requested; those negative effects concern the weakening of the viability of African publishers through limiting their reach into their own markets for which they are publishing.[11]

---

10 Paul Tiyambe Zeleza, *Manufacturing African Studies and Crises* (Dakar: CODESRIA, 1997).

11 Hans Zell and Raphaël Thierry, 'Book Donation Programme for Africa', *African Research & Documentation,* No, 125 (2015); and online:

Language

At the outset, it was decided that English language books would be stocked, since the aim was to access the Northern markets. It became clear however that there might be demand for titles in the African languages, particularly requests for Kiswahili titles from the US. Titles were then stocked and marketed, and the response was disappointing. Currently, ABC stocks a small number of titles in the African languages; and can do so without loss to publisher or ABC given the digital age, detailed below. The other European languages of Africa, French and Portuguese, are also handled. Nonetheless, the preponderance of titles received are in the English language.

Furtherance of the cultural mission

ABC's evolution has benefitted from three major evaluations commissioned by donors; all the reports supported the imperative of ABC's wider cultural mission, as well as its trading work: re-affirming that internationalising the African book was both about sales and income support for publishers, but also the wider mission of knowledge, research and dissemination of information about the African publishing industry, and seeking to 'brand' publishers and ABC as their own organisation. Many activities were undertaken with donor support: author tours, book launches, resource publications, and training exchanges with African publishers, sponsorship of publishers to attend book fairs, seminars and partnerships.

Notably, the Dag Hammarskjöld Foundation seminar series continued. In 1998, ABC co-organised the African Writers-Publishers Seminar in Arusha. The headline publishers and writers attended and hammered out a 'New Deal', still little implemented. ABC subsequently published *The*

Zell, Hans. 'Book Donation Programmes for Africa: Time for a Reappraisal? Part 1
https://www.academia.edu/13165497/Book_Donation_Programmes_for_Africa_Time_for_a_Reappraisal_Part_I

Thierry, Raphaël. 'Le don de livre, mai à quel prix, et en échange de quoi?' /Book donations for Africa part 2.
https://www.academia.edu/13166294/Le_don_de_livre_mais_%C3%A0_quel_prix_et_en_%C3%A9change_de_quoi_Book_donation_programmes_for_Africa_part_2_

African Writers Handbook[12] distributed free widely in Africa, including the text of the 'New Deal'.[13]

The next joint seminar was in 2002 on the theme of scholarly publishing, including looking at the digital age. The resulting publication was *African Scholarly Publishing. Essays*[14] again distributed free within Africa. ABC published other titles from time to time, as resources for African publishers, and to disseminate information outside Africa.[15] From an early stage, ABC also took on distribution of a small number of non-profits, specifically publishing within the context of furthering ABC's mission and with whom partnerships had been formed: the Bellagio Publishing Network, INASP, the international global development charity, and ADEA (Association for the Development of Education in Africa), Books and Learning Materials Working Group. These publishers were associated rather than integral, and received 50 per cent of net sales proceeds. Key research publications from the senior consultant, resources for African publishers, were distributed to publishers with donor funding.

The dawn of the digital age

Print-on-Demand

The digital revolution offered possibilities both for print and for eBooks. In 1998, ABC saw the possibilities of Print-on-Demand (POD), and held a workshop for publishers about the possibilities. Rather than send stocks to ABC, publishers could electronically send files to ABC for upload to its designated digital printer. Thereafter, whilst titles could still be

---
12 James Gibbs and Jack Mapanje, eds. *The African Writers' Handbook* (Oxford: African Books Collective, 1999), published in association with the Dag Hammarskjöld Foundation.
13 Ibid. pp. 131-134.
14 Alois Mlambo, ed. *African Scholarly Publishing. Essays* (Oxford: African Books Collective, 2006, Stockholm: Dag Hammarsjköld Foundation, Oxford: INASP).
15 ABC. *Women in Publishing and the Book Trade in Africa. An Annotated Directory.* 2nd rev. ed. (Oxford: African Books Collective, 1997); Hans Zell, *The Electronic African Bookworm: A Web Navigator* (Oxford: African Books Collective, 1998); Mary Jay, and Susan Kelly, eds. *Courage and Consequence. Women Publishing in Africa* (Oxford: African Books Collective, 2002).

marketed in the conventional ways, there were two major advantages. First, customer orders could be fulfilled direct from the printer, without recourse to warehouse stocks. That saved on much, though not all, direct invoicing. ABC entered into 3-way partnerships whereby the printer could supply direct to the third parties: mainly wholesalers. The printer, under legal agreement, simply reports sales, deducts print costs and discount, and pays ABC monthly. This results in big savings for both publisher and ABC on importing stocks, warehousing and wastage.

Secondly, availability by POD unleashes a marketing bonanza of listings, by the printer and ABC, of the titles on multiple internet selling sites; all such sales can only be fulfilled via the printer or ABC. A digital workshop was held for publishers in 1998, but it was slow to catch on: partly lack of resources at ABC to pay title set-up costs, and partly publisher nervousness about copyright. Nonetheless a first title had been available since 1999 by a far-sighted publisher. In 2001, another publisher took it further and pioneered 100 titles with the POD printer. It was clear that it would be a revolution in cost savings for publishers and for ABC; and would unleash greatly enhanced marketing activities. By 2007, ABC had been able to afford to set-up some 400 titles, unable to afford anything more.

Internet selling has led to the demise of bricks-and-mortar bookshops. African books always had a profile problem in any case in bookshops. Unless the bookshop was extremely specialist, books were unlikely to be stocked unless particularly notable – authorship, topicality – but even then they were likely to be a small number in a basement corner. If a bookshop could be persuaded to stock, they would de-stock as soon as it was clear that books were not selling in the time and quantities they required. With the advent of selling via the internet, many bookshops in the UK and US have sadly demised. They are no longer the important sales outlet for the kind of books which ABC handles. So the internet has effectively become the 'bookshop', circumventing (alas, maybe in some ways) the ways in which it became clear well before 2007 that it was the route for ABC.

At the end of the last funded Strategic Plan 2002-2006, it was clear that donor funding was not going to continue. Funding under the Millennium Development Goals had moved to government to government funding for poverty reduction, in which culture or publishing did not feature. ABC entered into a commercial partnership whereby all the then 1500 titles were digitised, the partner envisaging the development of African books with no ownership stake for itself. This was a take-off. Since that time, publishers simply send ABC digital files of new titles; ABC does any necessary pre-press and uploads to the printer, free to publishers. A few titles which are not suitable for POD are warehoused (e.g. illustrated Art books, or occasionally a title for which a donor has funded a print-run to a publisher). ABC very rapidly became self-sufficient. Whilst publishers remain appreciative of those early years of support, the Council of Management has greatly welcomed the freedom of being completely their own masters.

eBooks

Most titles are also set up as eBooks, as well as POD. When publishers send files of titles, they can either send in the necessary eBook format, or otherwise ABC will convert for sales worldwide on multiple platforms. Titles are uploaded to key library platforms, and also to the main retail outlets. Since eBooks don't have territorial restrictions, the opportunities are both within Africa and internationally. The library sales outside Africa can be considerable, but retail sales remain a plateau. Indeed, industry analysis in the US and UK shows that, after the rapid growth of eBooks to the retail trade – largely individuals buying fiction on readers – the market has become static. There are welcome separate eBook retail platforms in Africa, but also initiatives offering 'free' books which undercut the opportunities for publishers own direct sales. How eBook sales in Africa become truly productive for African publishers remains an open question.

Conclusion

Internationalising the African book remains a huge challenge. The needs remain to engage with Northern scholars, to counter negative perceptions, and to stand on an equal footing with publishers worldwide. Problems may still be faced by indigenous publishers in Africa with enduring unconducive policies; but they are not constrained in internationalising their books. The digital age has greatly enhanced the opportunities, and that remains ABC's mission.

Throughout the 25 years of trading, the Council of Management has embodied the solidarity of the publishers' collective working for the benefit of individual publishers, and the overall health of their organisation. Twenty-five years of trading have not all been plain sailing. It took endurance to build up to the self-sufficiency of the last eight years, with times of financial strain, and anxiety as to ABC being able to pay its way month to month. Following a donor evaluation, the publishers' remittance terms had reduced in 2000 from 50-60 per cent, with no membership fees payable. In 2007, when the organisation re-modelled for the digital age, publishers' agreed that all remittances should be reduced to 35 per cent to enable ABC to survive. This was a remarkable commitment to keeping control of their own trading, and happily it was soon possible to increase to 40 per cent – with a 'bonus' being paid in more recent years when sales revenues were sufficient. The aim remains to increase the percentage further as growth in sales allows. The joint enterprise has brought many publishers together; and the annual meetings of the Council of Management, and in earlier years with donors, have given rise to much camaraderie and friendship, signifying the enduring joy in the common endeavour. Hard work, tough times, but control is still being held by African publishers, and an upholding of cultural pride.

Since ABC's inception in 1989, Henry Chakava has served on the governing body as a founder member; and has contributed to its growth as the outlet for now 155 publishers from 24 African countries. Together with his key founder publishers, notably Walter Bgoya of Tanzania, and the late lamented Victor Nwankwo of Nigeria, Henry has overseen all the vicissitudes encountered, always providing both great publishing expertise, knowledge of the international scene, and unflagging commitment of his time and concerns. His key contribution to the development of African publishing and cultural pride, and internationalising the African book, as well as to ABC itself, is an enduring salutation to a great publisher.

Lobby for the Book: The Politics of African Publishing and the Growth of Professional and Trade Organisations

By Lily Nyariki

Preamble

The book is not going anywhere any soon. Dr Theodor Seuss Geisel (Dr Seuss) wrote, 'The more that you read, the more things you will know. The more that you learn the more places you'll go.'[1] Research suggests that reading on a screen can slow you down by as much as 20-30 per cent.[2] In the wake of popular media of communication, there is nothing which has yet replaced the book as the simplest, easiest and most versatile tool in the transfer of information and knowledge. The book then remains the most versatile and accessible learning device available to man and will continue to be so for generations to come. Among the many benefits given for reading a book include: it boosts your brain power; makes you more empathetic; flipping pages can help you understand what you're reading; it helps fight Alzheimer's disease; it helps you relax; and also it helps you sleep. If the foregoing is anything to go by, then, the book is worth lobbying for and must therefore be harnessed to meet the needs for which it is meant.

Hans Zell (2008) wrote about a major conference on publishing and book development in Africa, consisting of publishers, booksellers,

---

1   *https://www.goodreads.com/quotes/*. Quotes by Dr Seuss.
2   *http://www.ibtimes.com.au/top-5-reasons-why-reading-real-book-better-perusing-e-book* 1413191

librarians, writers, and scholars from many countries, who reaffirmed their belief, 'That books are an indispensable cornerstone in education and that a nation's book industry must be considered an essential industry in terms of national development planning'.[3] Hans further argues that the reality of the book sector anywhere in the world is closely related to government policies or the lack of them. He also observed that the main reason why the African book sector has not yet realised its full potential is that very few governments have provided positive support for their book industries, or created environments conducive to writing, reading, and publishing. In addition, it is our belief that many people even those in high offices and especially within the academic circles, do not understand the nature of the book industry, neither its intrinsic value to socio-economic and cultural development of nations.

Introduction

Books embody the world's knowledge. For generations now the book has been associated with the acquisition of knowledge and skills. At the lowest level, data leads to information; information leads to knowledge and skills; knowledge leads to higher level of understanding that leads to wisdom. Wisdom is seen as the state of highest level of processed data that is then used to enable proper decision making for sound management of programmes, projects and nations which lead to development, both at personal and national levels. It is for these reasons that the book becomes a critical element in the development agenda. As a result, the book industry is commonly referred to as 'strategic and at the centre of every development effort in each nation state'. It is easy to see why some countries have recognised its strategic nature and have therefore ensured that their book industries and attendant sectors are well managed to gather and record all books written not only within their borders but worldwide. The United States is in the forefront of this trend followed by the UK and other developed nations.

---

3   Hans Zell, 'Publishing in Africa: Where are We Now? Part One: Some Spurious Claims Debunked', LOGOS 19/4 2008.

Unfortunately, African leadership has not quite understood the strategic nature of their book industries. Consequently, the industries have continued to lack support and proper nurturing due to the absence of suitable policies to help them grow. Darko-Ampen (2000) asserts, 'Most developing countries have not conceived a clear policy regarding the development of a publishing industry, and in many cases government policies have actually hindered the creation of a viable publishing community.'[4] Faye (1998), observed that, 'Government neglect of the industry continues to be a significant reason for the very slow progress of its development in Africa.'[5] He continues to say, 'Support for the infrastructure is generally negligible and very little is given in terms of incentives such as tax concessions, book studies and subsidies.'[6] This is true for most of Africa including Ghana, Kenya, Nigeria, South Africa, Zambia and Zimbabwe, who although the book policy was enacted and/or is in the stage of being implemented, government support is still negligible. This is the state of African publishing that has given rise to a number of lobbyists who believe in the power of the book and have offered their resources, time and effort in order to help sustain efforts to keep the book alive.

African book publishing

The African book industry is young compared to those in the other continents. It dates back to about six decades, and only started growing soon after independence. Early publishing is associated with missionaries who introduced books for purposes of evangelising and educating Africans who were expected to serve the local administration and to support the spread of Christianity. Political leadership was of course the preserve of the white settlers. However, this trend is truer of anglophone countries than it is for francophone countries. The English speaking countries have by far attempted to develop their book industries that are more indigenous

---

[4] Kwasi Darko-Ampen, 'Indigenous Publishing in Africa: An Overview of Accelerated Training and Research, and African Self-help Efforts.' s, no. 13 (April 2000): 10. Available at: http://www.arts.uwa.edu.au/MotsPluriels/MP1300koda.html

[5] Djibril Faye, 'Evaluating Publishing for Children in Africa,' BPN Newsletter Issue No 23 (October 1998). Available at: http://www.bc.edu/bellagio.

[6] Ibid

than the French speaking countries which until today heavily depend on France for their book imports.

Darko-Ampem (2000) observes that, 'In the face of countless problems facing the industry there has been significant growth during the last two decades.'[7] The growth has been most significant beginning in the late 1980s to mid-2000s when the African book industries saw marked expansion in various aspects, including increase in number of publishers, number of titles published, number of training institutions, and also the intensity of lobbying institutions and organizations in support of the book. This fact is attested by Hans Zell who wrote,

> Happily, by the early 1990s, African publishing entered a period of recovery, transformation and innovation. In many countries economic liberalisation, deregulation and privatization led to sweeping improvements in the book business.[8]

Faye (1998) argued for the progress made in African publishing saying that reasons included: the creativity of African publishers; increase in state purchase of books for schools and libraries; and support to both publishing and book acquisition by development agencies.[9] However, he also asserted that there are numerous problems that militate against the growth of African publishing. These problems are not peculiar to Africa as they are also experienced in Asian and Latin American countries. These countries had to start their publishing industries from scratch. It is therefore important that Africa exploits the many opportunities presented by illiteracy, book scarcity, suppressive environments, and poor reading habits to give impetus to the struggling industry.

Unfortunately, the development of publishing in Africa has been very slow and has largely been influenced by various political, economic, social, technological and educational changes. Few of these changes can be said to have had a positive impact on the development of publishing. On the contrary, they have created, and continue to create, major problems that

---

7 Darko-Ampen, 'Indigenous Publishing in Africa', op cit.
8 Zell, 'Publishing in Africa', op cit.
9 Faye, 'Evaluating Publishing for Children in Africa,' op cit.

hinder the growth of the industry. Although Africa has a deep reservoir of human resources and intellectual capacity, it still lags behind in publishing development, and relies heavily on the North for its book needs.

Why lobby for the book?

Makotsi and Nyariki (1997) wrote,

> The book industry is seen as the heartbeat of every nation and although it claims only a small portion of the national budget, its benefits to a nation have far-reaching effects. These benefits manifest themselves at every level of society: People become knowledgeable about topical issues and ideas, aware of their rights and obligations, enlightened about their various vocations, adept at taking advantage of opportunities in socio-economic activities, and thus become an asset to the country.[10]

The two authors further observed, 'The world economy is changing rapidly and the richer Northern countries are beginning to experience economic pressures that will lead to the side-lining of Africa in terms of economic support. Donor countries are beginning to tire of feeding Africa, while Africa shows very little signs of freeing itself from the quagmire of poverty. Donor fatigue has become real, and donor conditions on funding are increasingly becoming impossible for developing nations to meet.'

For these reasons, African leaders need to awaken to the things that are important for the purposive growth of their people and the continent. Reading is regarded as a foundational skill upon which every other skill is obtained. We argue here and submit that unless and until the African leaders recognise and support the publishing industry, their efforts at nation building and economic growth will continue to be an uphill task. It follows that in the age of knowledge based economies, Africa cannot afford to continue depending on knowledge that is not home grown. Neither can it continue to be a consumer of other people's knowledge and hope to be

---

10 Ruth Makotsi and Lily Nyariki, *Publishing and Book Trade in Kenya* (Nairobi: EAEP. 1997).

truly independent and free from domination of their ideas. With the rapid increase of African intellectuals and academicians there should be no real excuse for Africa to continue to consume information and knowledge from other countries. What we must realise is that the knowledge industry is worth billions of dollars and the question is: who is benefiting? For example, there are hardly any textbooks written by African professors, what then are the African students in universities across Africa reading? And who is the loser in this scenario?

Politics in book publishing

The general statistics in sub-Saharan Africa tell an interesting and revealing story: more than 1 in 3 adults cannot read; 182 million adults are unable to read and write; 48 million youths (ages 15-24) are illiterate; 22% of primary aged children are not in school and that makes 30 million primary aged children who are not in school. Life expectancy is 58 years; 44 per cent of people live below the international poverty line of $1.25/day. While 63 per cent of people have access to 'improved' (adequate) water sources, 25 million people are living with HIV/AIDS. Further, in 1990 the adult illiteracy rate in all of Africa was 53 per cent, but in 2015 it is estimated to be 63 per cent. Similarly, in 1990 there were 133 million illiterate adults in sub-Saharan Africa, but by 2011 there were 182 million.[11] These statistics are depressing and should call for immediate action by African leaders who lead a continent rich in natural resources which if utilised could create a conducive environment for the book to thrive.

The above statistics notwithstanding, the climate for African book development has mostly deteriorated and the gains of the mid-1980s to mid-2000s have slipped through the fingers. One hardly hears of any forums to discuss important issues like the need for national book policies which are prerequisite for proper development of the book industry. Hans Zell asserts,

> Many of the initiatives started with high hopes in the late 1980s and early 1990s have been withheld or are dormant.

---

11 http://www.africanlibraryproject.org/book-drives/start-a-book-drive

The wave of enthusiasm has largely passed. There does not seem to be a great deal of energy left. The conviction and hope of the early 1990s seem to have fizzled out. World aid agencies have backed away. Donor policies and priorities have shifted. The climate for funding of book programs is becoming increasingly difficult.[12]

In addition, he writes,

Social, cultural and infrastructure problems abound. Low literacy levels, the multiplicity of languages, limited access to books and library services, poor transport and communications networks, severely under-funded educational systems, and shortages of capital and skills – are some of the obstacles that have always been cited as hindrances to the development of African publishing. They still are.[13]

What is interesting is that Africa has not been short of coming up with great initiatives for accelerating development. The New Partnership for Africa's Development (NEPAD), for instance has failed to live up to its expectations and to date it is not clear what its achievements are. The African Union is not without exception as it has failed to guide African countries in recognising areas of priority in education and the attendant sectors like publishing and library development which can accelerate knowledge and skills acquisition to ensure the masses are freed from ignorance and illiteracy.

The fact is that with these two evils that have continued to plague Africa and without tackling them, Africa will always remain in the negative statistics. The African Union and individual governments must tackle tribalism, poor leadership, endemic corruption, stem out ill-gotten gains of an elite few and flight capital stashed away in foreign bank accounts. They also must formulate and implement policies that support quality education to enable skills and knowledge acquisition beginning

---
12 Zell, 'Publishing in Africa', op cit.
13 Ibid.

at the lowest to the highest level of the education system. South Korea, Singapore and Malaysia managed to make the right decisions and are now counted among the first world. Surely, Africa too can do the same but with concerted effort and political will. Think tanks are needed comprising all professionals who must guide on priority areas to jumpstart African economies.

Walter Bgoya wrote,

> Behind the backwardness of the publishing industry is a history of inappropriate educational and cultural policies, absence of national book policies including ineffective copyright laws, high duties and taxes on paper and other printing inputs, and underfunding of libraries.[14]

He concludes, 'Book production and distribution cannot prosper in societies where reading is limited to functionality – passing school and professional examinations.'[15]

Professional and trade organisations

This section highlights some of the formidable efforts that have been made over several decades to ensure the book industry in Africa remains alive despite the odds.

Noma Award for Publishing in Africa

The Noma Award for Publishing in Africa was an annual prize for outstanding African writers and scholars who published in Africa. The Award was initiated in 1980 and ceased in 2010 for lack of funding. It had a prize of $US10, 000 and within four years of its establishment, the prize became the major book award in Africa in honour of sponsor – Shoichi Noma of Japan who died in 1984. The purpose of the award was

---

14 Walter Bgoya, 'Scholarly Publishing in Africa: An Overview'. In *African Scholarly Publishing Essays*, edited by Alois Mlambo (Oxford: (African Books Collective, 2006), pp. 2-3.
15 Ibid.

to encourage the publication of works by African authors. The award was annual and given to any new book published in three categories: literature, juvenile and scholarly. It was administered by the quarterly journal – *African Book Publishing Record*, and presented under the umbrella of UNESCO. Entries were admissible in any of the languages of Africa.

Zimbabwe International Book Fair (ZIBF)

The first Zimbabwe International Book Fair (ZIBF)[16], whose vision is to be the most viable market place for books and information on and about Africa and the ultimate meeting place of the literary cultures of the North and South, was held in 1983 and has continued to feature to date. Its headquarters is in Harare, Zimbabwe, and in its heyday it had representative offices in the UK, India, Ghana and Kenya. These were closed due to the financial crises suffered in early 2000. Its mission statement was to create a marketplace for the exhibition and promotion of books, periodicals and publishing technologies while facilitating intra-African and international trade in these and to provide a meeting place for the exchange of ideas and information for all stakeholders in the literary industry.

African Books Collective (ABC)

African Books Collective[17] was founded, and is owned and governed by African publishers, who seek to strengthen African publishing through collective action in order to increase the visibility and accessibility of the wealth of African scholarship and culture and seeks to grow the market for African books worldwide. A group of African publishers met in 1985 and founded ABC as a collective self-help initiative to strengthen the economic base of independent African publishers and to meet the needs of Northern libraries and other book buyers. With initial support from funding agencies, trading began in 1989. It is now self-financing, and largely operates a digital model leading to profitability with publishers seeing bonuses paid out.

---

16 http://www.zibfa.org.zw/
17 http://www.africanbookscollective.com/

Bellagio Publishing Network

The Bellagio Publishing Network[18] was an informal association of organisations and individuals committed to strengthening indigenous publishing and book development in the South, particularly Africa. The Network included publishers, government and private donor organisations concerned with books and publishing, providing a forum for discussion and collaboration on publishing and book development activities. The Network evolved out of an international conference on publishing and development in the south held at the Rockefeller Center in Bellagio, Italy, in 1991. Apart from organising meetings, seminars and workshops it also published the *Bellagio Publishing Network Newsletter* under the Bellagio Studies in Publishing Series, whose aim was to provide a base of practical information, knowledge, and theory about publishing and book development. This network however seems to have died a natural death because there are no records beyond 2005.

African Publishers Network (APNET)

The African Publishers Network (APNET) was formed in 1992 as a Pan African organisation to connect African publishing associations in order to exchange information and promote and strengthen indigenous publishing. Prior to its formation, publishers in Africa had difficulty sharing information and learning from one another's experiences, as there was no database containing the addresses of libraries, bookshops or fellow publishers and also there was no networking structure connecting the agencies. Between 1992 and now the secretariat has moved from Harare in Zimbabwe to Abidjan, Ivory Coast, to Ghana and then back to Zimbabwe – due to political unrest. The vision of APNET was, 'The transformation of African peoples through access to books'. The mission was to 'strengthen African publishers through networking, training and trade promotion in order to fully meet Africa's need for quality books relevant to African social, political, economic and cultural reality'. Unfortunately, APNET's former glory has sadly faded away from the limelight due to lack of financing as donors abandoned it.

---

18 http://www.africanbookscollective.com/

African Book Publishing Record (ABPR)

The African Book Publishing Record[19] (ABPR) is the only bibliographical tool which offers systematic and comprehensive coverage of new and forthcoming African publications in a single source, providing full bibliographic and acquisitions data. In addition to its bibliographic coverage, ABPR also includes an extensive book review section, reviews of new journals, and features a variety of news, reports, and articles about African book trade activities and developments. The titles included in the bibliographical section are arranged according to subject area, country and author. It also has indexes of publishers and their currencies. The ABPR is available online.

African Journals Online (AJOL)

African Journals Online (AJOL) is the world's largest and prestigious collection of peer-reviewed, African-published scholarly journals. In partnership with hundreds of journals from all over the continent, AJOL works to address the difficulty faced by African researchers to access the works of other African academics, so that research of African-origin output is available to Africans and to the rest of the world. AJOL is a non-profit organisation based in South Africa.

Association for the Development of Education in Africa (ADEA): The Working Group on Books and Learning Materials (WGBLM)

ADEA[20] is a dialogue on education for leadership and change in Africa and offers a forum for policy dialogue on education in Africa. Its Working Group on Books and Learning Materials (WGBLM) is committed to supporting processes conducive to formulating adequate national book policies that improve the provision of good quality educational materials, effective schooling, and literacy across sub-Saharan Africa. It strives to

---

19 *The African Book Publishing Record (ABPR)* 1975 — Quarterly. Edited by Hans M. Zell & Cécile Lomer; from vol. 28, no. 3, 2002 — edited by Cécile Lomer. Munich: K.G. Saur. http://www.degruyter.de/journals/abpr/detail.cfm Online: (as from vol. 27, 2001) http://www.atypon-link.com/WDG/loi/abpr (online access requires subscription).

20 http://www.adeanet.org/portalv2/en/working-group/books-and-learning-materials

accomplish this by calling on governments, the private sector, development agencies, and Civil Society Organisations (CSOs) to consider a holistic approach that includes substantial input from African partners to achieve viable book policies. The WGBLM seeks to broaden its impact by creating a forum of policy makers, teachers, curriculum planners, publishers, materials designers, book distributors, booksellers, librarians, authors and illustrators with a professional interest in book content and book delivery strategies.

United Nations Educational and Scientific Organisation (UNESCO)

UNESCO[21] is noted for contributions towards the establishment of National Book Development Councils in many countries, some of which have successfully organised book fairs, run training programmes, and sponsored book prizes. UNESCO sponsored the now 'moribund' Regional Book Centre for Africa with headquarters in Yaoundé, Cameroon; and has sponsored, organised or co-organised training programs for African publishers.

Dag Hammarskjöld Foundation

Also at the forefront of assisting local publishing efforts in Africa is the Dag Hammarskjöld Foundation who organised three major seminars on the development of autonomous publishing in 1984, 1989 and 1996; and co-sponsored several others including the African Writers-Publishers Seminar held in Arusha, Tanzania in 1998. The Foundation is noted for its loan-guaranteed scheme started in Kenya in the 1980s in support of indigenous publishing.

Book Aid International

In 1954, Book Aid International (BAI) recognised the power of books to change lives. Since that time BAI has sent over 31 million books to libraries in Africa and trained hundreds of librarians. This support has transformed hundreds of libraries and reached millions of people. They work closely with the book and publishing trade in the UK who donate

---

21 Darko-Ampen, 'Indigenous Publishing in Africa', op cit.

nearly all of the high quality, relevant books sent to Cameroon, Eritrea, Ethiopia, Kenya, Malawi, Somali Federal Government, Somaliland and Puntland, Tanzania, Uganda, Zambia and Zimbabwe.

International Literacy Association (ILA)

The ILA[22] believes that the ability to read, write, and communicate connects people and empowers them to achieve things they never thought possible. It does this by: Honing the skills of thousands of literacy educators through practical research journals, publications, professional development, conferences, and advocacy efforts, publishing over 900 books on issues in literacy education and developing and managing dozens of global literacy projects across the developing world, among others. For a number of years the ILA sponsored the Pan African Reading conference now in its 9th Edition, the first having been held in Pretoria South Africa in 1999. The 10th edition will be held in August 2017 in Lagos Nigeria. Its National Affiliates are in Botswana, Egypt, Kenya, Liberia, Liberia, Mali, Nigeria, South Africa, Swaziland, Tanzania and Uganda.

Pan African Writers Association (PAWA)

PAWA's Secretariat is located in Accra, Ghana. In 1991, the Government of Ghana granted full diplomatic status to the Secretariat of PAWA thus enabling it to relate with African governments, the AU and various institutions across the world in ways that would facilitate the ideas in its founding declaration and vision. PAWA has engaged in a variety of activities within and outside Africa including conferences, readings, lectures, performances and visits. PAWA has also organised specific programmes that target issues of major concern to Africa and humanity as a whole. PAWA has been especially active in honouring African writers and encouraging/providing training to younger generations of writers to build upon and extend the best literary achievements of African and other writers in the world. Africa's most prominent thinkers and writers including the Nobel laureates – Wole Soyinka and Nadine Gordimer, have played prominent roles in the activities of PAWA.

---

22   http://www.literacyworldwide.org/about-us

The Pan Africa Booksellers Association (PABA)

The Pan African Booksellers Association[23] (PABA) was formed in 1997 to promote the interests and welfare of Booksellers and booksellers' associations across Africa. Its main objectives are: to encourage closer co-operation between the members of PABA; to collect data, statistics and information for dissemination amongst members, on all matters affecting the trade and for the interests of the members among others. In its heyday, PABA had 24 countries in its membership and it conducted capacity building workshops in several member countries to empower booksellers and their associations giving them a voice to be heard. However, just like APNET, PABA has remained inactive during the past 10 years due to financial constraints. Together with its member, Booksellers Association of Tanzania (BSAT) and other book trade stakeholders in Tanzania, it organised for a conference dubbed 'The Africa Book Conference' in November 2015 in Dar es salaam, Tanzania at the Mwalimu Julius Nyerere International Conference Centre.

Librarians regional and national associations

There are several professional groups which support indigenous publishing. These include the Africana Librarians Council of African Studies in the US. The Standing Conference on Library Materials on Africa (SCOLMA); the Standing Conference of Eastern, Central and South African Librarians (SCECSAL); the West African Library Association (WALA), Individual country Library Associations across Africa, that have remained active over the past 30 decades and have all continued to provide synergy for the book industry through book purchases and holding of conferences in support of the book industry.

On the international scene, the Carnegie Corporation of New York has given support for collection development, automation, staff training, public Internet access, access to global databases and networks, e-resources, digitisation projects, model libraries, and community services. Other donors and foundations assisting the library and information sector include

---

23 Constitution and Regulations of the Pan African Booksellers' Association (2005)

Canadian CODE, the Bill and Melinda Gates Foundation, the Sabre Foundation, UNESCO, NGOs such as the International Network for the Availability of Scientific Publications (INASP), and a variety of French government support schemes and initiatives. *BookPower* provides relevant textbooks to university and vocational students in low-income countries in English-speaking Africa and elsewhere at prices which students and their institutions' libraries can afford, by subsidising publishers' production costs in these countries

Council for the Development of Social Science Research (CODESRIA)

CODESRIA[24] is based in Dakar-Senegal and has over the years published a most impressive array of scholarly work, in book and journal formats, attracting authors from all over Africa and the Diaspora. CODESRIA has made a major contribution to academic publishing on the continent, and has played a vital role in the dissemination of African scholarship. CODESRIA is a not-for-profit NGO and, like many NGOs with publishing activities, is heavily donor-supported. Unfortunately, despite various proposals and attempts to encourage cooperation between scholarly presses in Africa – nationally, regionally, or continent-wide – there is still little evidence of collaborative ventures.

Observations

We observe that the African book industry has not received recognition neither support by African governments. Instead it has heavily relied on development agencies and or donors who, depending on their own interests shift gears as and when they wish. A National Book Policy (NBP) which is a plan directed at a sound approach towards the development of books and the promotion of a healthy national book industry is long overdue. It is a prerequisite as it provides the basis for the development of a self-sustaining indigenous book industry and sets the scene for awareness about a country's book industry.

---

24 Darko-Ampen, 'Indigenous Publishing in Africa', op cit.

We also observe that countries like Australia, Canada, and India have built substantial publishing industries from scratch. At various stages in the development of Australian publishing, for example, printing was subsidised and there were tariff barriers against imported books. In addition, it has been observed that private publishing operates in the context of governmental policy.

Due to lack of adequate support by governments the African book industries have continued to operate below par while causing a great challenge to the stakeholders who despite spirited efforts always seem to be talking to themselves – because issues they raise are never discussed at the highest levels of their governments.

Conclusions

At the recent 2015 UN General assembly, the US President Barrack Obama said, 'The strength of the nations is defined by its people's success.'[25] We wish to add that success heavily depends on the amount of information, knowledge and skills one has. Information, knowledge and skills are predominantly found in books, and they contain the world's knowledge, notwithstanding the advent of the internet and search engines currently available. Africa needs to awaken to the reality that the modern world is heavily dependent on knowledge. Therefore, strategies in support of authors, publishers, printers, booksellers, librarians and readers must be put in place so Africa is able to reclaim its image given that several of its countries have some of the fastest growing economies.

After all, a sustainable book industry that continues to flourish is only possible with deliberate government support that recognises the strategic importance of publishing and demonstrates this in its official commitment through policies and budgets.

Recommendations

Authors are especially significant in the book chain because without them, we cannot really talk of a book industry. They have been unrepresented,

---

25 US President Barrack Obama addressing the UN General Assembly in New York. 28th September 2015. Aljazeera TV.

unrecognised and unsupported by African governments. We recommend that the Africa Union institute an Africa Book Award for African writers and the individual member countries do the same to spur writing and creativity.

Publishers are the investors in the book industry because they take the initial financial burden to make the manuscripts consumable. They have since independence worked at ensuring the education sector is supported with relevant reading materials especially at the lower levels of education. We recommend that individual governments take the responsibility of enacting a National Book Policy that will support book development and publishing activities.

Printers ensure the edited book is mass produced for the market with specifications for quality products. The equipment they use is capital intensive. We recommend that subsidised loans and waiver of taxes on imported raw materials be made available in support of educational printing.

Booksellers have been singled out as the least recognised, understood and supported despite the fact that without them the book chain will not function well. We recommend that booksellers are supported in capacity building of their management skills and recognition of their associations by governments to empower them to distribute books across their countries.

Librarians are the biggest consumers of books and need to be helped to organise themselves and given sufficient funding to support regular book purchases. We recommend that librarians be empowered to understand the various roles of each book chain stakeholder so that they help develop the chain efficiently – they are adept to thinking that they have the right to buy directly from publishers which is rather unhealthy.

Readers are the reason the book industry exists and they need to have at their disposal products that resonate with their needs and interests for personal development. We recommend that African governments provide opportunity for reading promotion campaigns especially among the young so they can grow with a natural love for books and reading.

Governments are the overall regulators of the book industry through relevant laws and policies that are critical for the sustainable development of the book industry. We recommend that the African Union takes the lead in ensuring that each African country enacts a National Book Policy and establishes a National Book Development Council (NBDC) fully funded by the exchequer charged with the responsibility of developing the book industry across Africa. Further, the African Union should consider reviving the Regional Centre for Book Promotion in Africa (CREPLA) once hosted by the government of Cameroon and sponsored by UNESCO.

References

AABC. 1993. *Formulating the National Book Policy: Need and Guidelines*. New Delhi: Afro Asian Book Council.

Albatch, Philip G. ed. 1998. *Knowledge Dissemination: The Role of Scholarly Journals*. Oxford: Bellagio Studies in Publishing.

_____. ed. 1999. *Publishing in African Languages: Challenges and Prospects*. Oxford: Bellagio Studies in Publishing.

Albatch, Philip G. and Damtew Teferna. 1998. *A Book of Readings. Bellagio Studies in Publishing*. Oxford: Bellagio Studies in Publishing and Obor.

Chakava, H. 1996. *Publishing in Africa: One Man's Perspective*. Oxford: Bellagio Publishing Network.

Dag Hammarskjöld. 1997. *The Future of Indigenous Publishing in Africa*, Development Dialogue no.1997:1-2. Uppsala: The dag Hammarskjöld Foundation.

Garzon, Alvaro. 1997. *National Book Policy: A Guide for All Users in the Field*. Paris: UNESCO.

Hamelink, Cees J. 1983. *Cultural Autonomy in global communications: Planning National Information Policy*. London: Centre for the Study of Communication and Culture.

Indaba97. 1997. *Access to Information*. Harare: Zimbabwe International Book Fair Trust.

Indaba2000. 2000. *Millennium Marketplace*. Harare: Zimbabwe International Book Fair Trust.

Makotsi, Ruth. 2000. *Expanding the Book Trade across Africa: A Study of Current Barriers and Future Potential.* London: ADEA)/APNET.

Makotsi, Ruth and Lily Nyariki. 1997. *Publishing and Book Trade in Kenya.* Nairobi: EAEP.

Montagnes, Ian. 1998. *An Introduction to Publishing Management. Perspectives on African Book Development, 5.* London: ADEA.

Priestly, Carol. 2000. *Book and Publishing Assistance Programs: A Review and Inventory.* Oxford: Bellagio Studies in Publishing.

ZBDC. 1994. *Book Power. No.2.* Harare: Zimbabwe Book Development Council.

15

Training Opportunities for African Publishers

By Richard A. B. Crabbe

Introduction

This paper focuses on the publishing industry rather than publishers, to emphasise the synergy that should exist among all players that are needed: writers, editors, illustrators, designers, publishers, printers, distributors, and booksellers. It is the failure to think in such terms that has led to book provision programmes side-lining one group or other, but especially distributors and booksellers. To strengthen one part of what is often referred to as the book chain, and neglect other parts makes for an overall weak chain.

Also, the paper does not offer an analysis or a critique of what has happened or training opportunities that are available. Overall, the intent has been to present what has been done, what is being done, and how the African publishing industry and interested parties might prepare to equip a new generation of publishing professionals for the continent.

Why do we need training?

In 2010, Henry Chakava (2010), contributing to a collection of essays published in the book, *Scholarly Publishing in Africa*, posed the question, 'Can Africa make the technological 'leap' by harnessing the new technologies to exploit its knowledge potential?' Six years on, we can revisit his question in the light of current developments and how Africa is preparing qualified professionals to lead this effort. The simple truth is that there could be 54 different answers – as varied as the number of countries on the continent; such is the complexity of the issue for Africa – functionality of the publishing industry is at different levels. In fact, in some countries, particularly in francophone Africa, a national publishing industry is non-existent. Yes, more than 50 years after independence, there are countries that almost completely rely on external publishers to supply textbooks and other reading materials for their people!

Past training efforts

What type of training has been delivered in the past? What training efforts have been made at university level?

Zell and Lomer (1996) reported seven post-graduate degrees in African publishing between 1975 and 1991, with Nigeria producing four, and Kenya, South Africa, and Zimbabwe sharing one each.

The African Publishing Institute (API)

The founding of the African Publishers Network (APNET) in 1992 brought with it a concerted effort to professionalise the African publishing industry. The flagship of APNET's efforts was its training programme, the African Publishing Institute (API). Based on the curriculum (available in English and French) that was developed for the API, APNET conducted over 30 workshops in 18 countries in the first four years of the programme. The main areas of training include management, editorial and other professional skills, design and production, sales and marketing and electronic publishing (Christensen et al., 1999). An evaluation carried out in 1999 noted, 'Training has played an important role in the recurrent upgrading of skills of employees at various levels in publishing firms in Africa.'

Henry Chakava served as the first Board member responsible for the African Publishing Institute, when it was established in 1992. His vision for a professional cadre of Africans capable of running publishing houses and contributing to increasing the knowledge and voice of Africa on the international market has borne good fruit and continues to do so. Today, several beneficiaries are in key executive positions in publishing houses in every country where a publishing house participated in a training programme.

Box 1: API Training Programme

Objectives

- To empower African publishers with relevant and constantly updated skills.
- To support African publishers in the production of quality books.
- To familiarise African publishers with advanced marketing techniques likely to enhance their competitiveness and facilitate their positioning on the international book market.
- To create a body of African publishing trainers and develop a database of APNET resource persons.

Who could attend?

Any professional member of a National Publishers Association (NPA) could attend. Training was generally free, with a nominal administrative charged by NPAs.

Curriculum

The curriculum covered every facet of the profession, from the publishing process, through book marketing, the legal aspects of publishing, and up to the application of new technologies in the production of books.

Forms of training

National seminars (workshops) are aimed at intermediate executives. They focus on basics and the whole publishing process, including the marketing of books. They are usually national in scope and depend on the needs expressed by the local Publishers Association

Regional seminars are intended for top publishing executives, and preferably decision-makers. The workshops tackle general issues, such as inter-African and intra-African book trade, copyrights, co-publication, international bidding procedures, lobbying or advocacy.

The Certificate course is organised in collaboration with African universities whose curricula include publishing. It is intended for active publishing executives willing to enhance their knowledge in their speciality or earn a degree with a view to a promotion. This training offers a thorough study of 4 options: Management of a Publishing Concern; Editorial Functions; Book Design and Production; Book Marketing, Sales and Distribution. Participants can gain new professional knowledge of university standard, share on crucial issues relating to the African book industry and consolidate the foundations of inter-African cooperation in the book sector.

Four institutions supported the Network in the implementation of that programme:

- Kwame Nkrumah University of Science and Technology in Kumasi, Ghana
- Moi University Eldoret, Kenya
- University of Yaoundé II, Cameroon
- University of Pretoria, South Africa

Training manuals

APNET prepared and published a series of manuals based on the API curriculum in order to provide African book professionals with reference tools. The first titles of the series include Book Marketing Sales and Distribution; Communication Skills Manual and Editorial Functions. French translations of some titles were produced.

Source: http://web.archive.org/web/20100801234114/http://www.african-publishers.net/index.php/apnet-training

Other industry-led activities

These consisted mainly of workshops through APNET at national levels through publishers associations (NPAs). Topics ranged from editorial, marketing to copyright and piracy. The Pan African Booksellers Association (PABA) did the same for its members. Occasional joint workshops or seminars, which sometimes involved the Pan African Writers Association (PAWA) attempted to foster better cooperation among all concerned, especially in their dealings with governments. Sometimes, training at regional level took place in association with international bodies such as the World Intellectual Property Organisation (WIPO).

A point worth noting here is that much of the training was donor-funded. This trend has continued with the East African Book Development Association (EABDA), funded largely by the Swedish International Development Agency (SIDA). A notable exception was Publishing Training Project (PTP) established in mid-1994 by the Independent Publishers' Association of South Africa (IPASA) to provide work-related training to publishers and NGOs. After the Project started, IPASA merged with the Publishers Association of South Africa (PASA) and the Project operated under the auspices of PASA, with the proviso that it retained its developmental emphasis and remained accountable to the original committee appointed by IPASA. Within the first four years of its existence, the PTP assisted a wide range of organisations and publishing companies, mounting courses on various aspects of book publishing, and providing specialised advice and assistance.

By the end of 1997, more than 1200 trainees had attended some 22 different short courses mounted in various centres in South Africa. The courses were attended by staff from the commercial publishing sector as well as freelancers, people from NGOs, and small publishing initiatives and some educational institutions. The courses attracted participation from publishing staff from Botswana, Lesotho, Namibia, Zimbabwe, Zambia and Malawi (Ralphs 1998).

Training resources

In addition to the manuals that APNET produced for the API, the following offered materials that supported training efforts:

1. Book Aid International

    Through the Publishers' Resource Pack project (Nicholson, 1998), BAI supplied professional resource materials – training and reference books – to publishers, national publishers' associations and other organisations producing and disseminating written materials throughout Africa. At its peak in 1998, over fifty organisations participated, ranging from national publishers' associations to independent commercial publishers and also included small NGOs actively involved in publishing.

2. Hans Zell Collection

    In 1995, Hans Zell, arguably one of the foremost researchers and bibliographers regarding African publishing, donated his archives of books, articles, reports, complete runs of African book trade journals, ephemera, and more, to APNET, covering 35 years of publishing and book development in Africa, from 1960-1995, as well as providing APNET with software containing the database of all records. However, APNET's Research and Documentation Centre never really took off in earnest, and failed to offer the services it was intended to provide. The collection was never properly catalogued, there was no systematic collection development in any shape or form, and APNET has failed to build up a corpus of reliable data on the African book sector. Zell has made a second donation in 2015, the collection covering 1996 to 2014, and this time going to Kwara State University in Nigeria. Accompanying the collection will be a rich online database containing over 3,000 fully annotated records, making it the most comprehensive documentation, and ongoing analysis, of the state of the book sector and the 'book chain' in Africa.[1]

---

1   Press release received from Hans Zell, April 16, 2015.

3. World Bank

In 1997, the Office of the Publisher at the World Bank launched its African Publishing Initiative[2] with two objectives: expand local publishing capacity of sub-Saharan publishers, and strengthen distribution networks. The activities included:

(a) *Staff exchange*: Every year, EXTOP hosts a mid-level staff member from an African publishing house for a 3-month formal and on-the-job training, and reciprocated by placing suitable staff for a similar period with the African publisher. In addition to 'being on the staff' the WB personnel conducted a needs assessment. The programme allowed for important skill transfer and training of trainers.

(b) *Internship prize programme:* EXTOP annually offered a 3-month attachment to a student competitively selected from publishing programmes at African universities (currently Cameroon, Ghana, South Africa, and Kenya). The programme was later expanded to include universities in Europe that had several international students in their post-graduate publishing programmes.

(c) *Regional seminars/workshops:* These dealt with cutting edge issues and acquiring good business practices in areas such as electronic publishing, print-on-demand, and fostering cross-border trade.

(d) *Development of distance learning tools for the book sector:* The pilot of these learning tools was Editing Educational Materials. A Course for Editors in Sub-Saharan Africa. Developed in association with the Commonwealth of Learning,[3] and with the support of APNET and some African universities offering degree courses in publishing, this is a very useful resource for all those keen to acquire editorial skills.

This initiative has now ended.

---

2 http://go.worldbank.org/MPLH6G3200
3 www.col.org

Along with more training opportunities came the fear that staff who undertake courses are likely to be poached by other companies that entice them with better pay and benefits. As a result, some companies were loath to send their staff for courses, even when these were heavily-subsidised. But this argument is like a double-edged sword: I know that without opportunities for training, some staff actually left their employers to join establishments that offered opportunity for capacity building. At the time APNET's training programme was targeted to middle level staff, senior executives began to talk about being neglected; they felt their juniors were becoming more knowledgeable, and were benefiting from travel to courses and building a network of contacts. They wanted in, and pushed hard for courses at their level.

What training is being delivered today, and how?

Current training opportunities

Academic/university

Twenty years after it was reported that Africans had earned only seven postgraduate degrees in 16 years, the story is vastly different. The following university programmes have catered over the years to a steady stream of Africans interested in pursuing publishing as a career.

1. *Kwame Nkrumah University of Science and Technology* (KNUST) in Ghana: BA Publishing Studies, a four year programme.

2. *Moi University* (Kenya): Master of Philosophy in Information Sciences (Publishing Studies)

3. *Oxford Brookes University* (United Kingdom): The Oxford International Centre for Publishing Studies is one of the leading institutes for publishing education in the world, with a reputation for innovation and excellence in teaching and research. The Centre offers a range of postgraduate and undergraduate awards in book, magazine and digital publishing, and carries out academic research, professional development programmes and consultancy.

4. *University of Buea* (Cameroon): The only English-speaking institution of its kind in predominantly French-speaking Central Africa, the university offers publishing courses through its department of journalism and Mass Communication.

5. *University of Ibadan* (Nigeria): Master in Publishing and Copyright Studies (MPCS) is offered through the Faculty of Education.

6. *University of Pretoria* (South Africa): The Department of Information Science offers three main programmes with courses relevant to the trends of the information and knowledge age and economy, being Information Science, Multimedia and Publishing Studies at both undergraduate and graduate levels.

7. *University of Stirling* (Scotland): The Stirling Centre for International Publishing and Communication offers students an exceptional opportunity to study publishing at Masters level or to undertake postgraduate research leading to a PhD. Their taught postgraduate courses are the MLitt in Publishing Studies and the MRes in Publishing Studies. These programmes provide a comprehensive and coherent approach to all forms of publishing: book, journals, magazines, and digital.

8. *University of the Witwatersrand* (South Africa): BA Honours Publishing Studies and MA Publishing Studies courses are offered on an attendance basis at Wits. There is no distance option for any of these courses.

Sponsored programmes

These consist of programmes funded or sponsored by international development agencies. Notable ones in recent times include:

1. Reading CODE programmes in Liberia and Sierra Leone.[4] While not directly training publishers, the programmes have assisted in training a solid core of writers and illustrators that can provide

---

4   *http://www.codecan.org/reading-code*

a conduit for publishing-worthy manuscripts on children's books. Reading CODE is the comprehensive readership initiative at the heart of CODE's programmes in developing countries, currently being implemented in eight African countries. The programme works with local teachers, librarians, writers, and publishers to support and sustain the development of literacy learning in from kindergarten through the 12th year of formal schooling. The result of CODE's 55 years' experience supporting local children's book production in Africa and Latin America, it adds best practices in teaching reading, writing, and critical thinking, along with a proven model of successful collaboration with in-country partners

2. Burt Award for African Literature:[5] It incorporates a workshop for writers and sessions with publishers as part of activities held in conjunction with the award. 'The Award is supported in part by IBBY Canada, the Canadian National Section of the International Board on Books for Young People. Members of IBBY are nominated to act as jurors in the Award process. IBBY's role has recently been expanded to include workshop facilitation for emerging and experienced writers and publishers of youth fiction in Africa.'

3. USAID: Currently, the Enabling Writers, Bloom Software developed by SIL-LEAD is being piloted in the field.[6] Bloom aims to make it easy for authors to create grade-level appropriate reading stories with the optimised wordlists.

Workshops organised by NBAs

Whether for booksellers, printers or publishers, the practice of organising workshops by the national book trade associations is generally *ad hoc*. Also, since APNET's API folded, such training is not linked to any professional curriculum or standards.

---

5 *http://www.codecan.org/burt-award-africa*
6 *http://bloomlibrary.org/landing*

Internships

Training without employment opportunities is sheer wastage of academic and human resources. Here are two examples of good practice about ensuring a strong linkage between academia and the industry.

1. AISA (South Africa):[7] Every year the Publications Division of the Africa Institute of South Africa (AISA) recruits a publishing intern from either the University of Pretoria or the University of the Witwatersrand – the only two universities in South Africa that offer degrees in publishing studies. The position is advertised through the Publishers' Association of South Africa (PASA) and, after an intense recruitment process, a candidate is identified and placed in the division for a period of 12 months during which they undergo experiential learning.

2. KNUST/GBPA (Ghana): A partnership established between Ghana's KNUST and the Book Publishers Association (GPBA) in the late 1990s offers internships to students of the KNUST's Book Industry degree programme as part of their professional development. Annually, this provides a pipeline of academically trained and industry-ready professionals in the Ghanaian book industry.

The role of government

Where are African governments in all this? Largely absent. It is well-known that some African countries do not have a well-developed publishing industry, so to think of a cadre of professionals is out of the question. But for how long should this persist, allowing external suppliers to sometimes hold Ministries of Education to ransom when it comes to book provision for schools? Hans Zell has written that,

> Publishing and book development in Africa have always been, and will continue to be, closely influenced by development in general. The book sector is inescapably tied to government policies or, in many countries, the lack of policies.[8]

---

7 *http://www.ai.org.za/*
8 Hans Zell, 'Publishing in Africa: Where are We Now? Part One: Some Spurious Claims Debunked.' LOGOS 19/4 (2008): 187-195.

Box 2 highlights an excellent example from South Africa of a collaboration bringing together government policy, industry ownership and implementer.

Box 2: Industry Skills Development & Training PASA/FP&M SETA Internship Programme

The Fibre Processing and Manufacturing (FP&M) SETA was established by the South Africa's Minister of Higher Education and Training on 1 April 2011 after government took a decision to cluster sectors in order to strengthen value-chain linkages between related industries.

Goals and objectives of the programme

The publishing industry recognised the need to expand its current employment profile and committed itself to introducing new blood and perspectives through the implementation of a black empowerment internship programme for graduates.

The Publishers Association of South Africa (PASA) Internship Programme aimed at unemployed black graduates wishing to gain entry into the book publishing industry. It included a practical workplace experiential learning component and a theoretical learning component integrated to provide interns with a solid foundation of skills for employment in the book publishing industry. The internship primarily focused on the development of key skills needed within the publishing industry and is structured in such a way so as to maximise learning opportunities for interns.

In the long term it is hoped that such a transfer of skills will also improve the quality of books published in South Africa, contributing to transforming South Africa's reading culture and developing our multi lingual society in the academic, economic, scientific and cultural spheres. A particular contribution can be made to increasing and developing

> publishing in African languages.
>
> As the industry body, PASA acted as the custodian of the project and undertook co-ordination of the necessary components of the programme to ensure the successful completion of the project.
>
> Source:http://www.publishsa.co.za/skills-development-and-training/internship-programme

What else does Africa need to do?

Seeding the future

1. *Industry leadership:* Primarily, those in the industry should take charge of matters pertaining to the strengthening of their profession, not only to equip its members to deliver quality service, but also to ensure that it garners the respect it has long craved, especially in developing economies. Every country must establish its needs. National African book trade associations need to step up to the challenge and strengthen professional quality among members. Training should feature on their list of ongoing activities for which members should be prepared to pay. This is also one way of ensuring that their members keep abreast with trends in the industry worldwide. It takes a few dedicated individuals, with the support of their companies, to come together to brainstorm on how to map their training needs and how to handle them. Companies should also be prepared to pay for such training. After all, they will be the first beneficiaries if their staff become better skilled at what they do.

2. *Government policy framework:* Training of professionals should be systematic and backed by national policy. It is easy and relatively inexpensive – often free to government – when training is provided by international bodies. But as Hans Zell stated rightly,

   > A sustainable system of book provision and book

development, and a flourishing book industry, are possible only with government support that recognises the strategic importance of publishing, and demonstrates this in official commitment in policies and budgets.[9]

Writing on 'The State of African Publishing' in 2009, one year before Chakava's question, Francis Nyamnjoh also pointed out that,

> Given that perceptions are shaped and reshaped over time and given the importance of cultural diversity in a fast globalising world, conscious efforts should be made to develop policies aimed at eradicating 'cultural poverty' in and on Africa. Such policies should encourage the production and consumption – in Africa and the rest of the world – of cultural products created by Africans who are crying out for the space and means to tell the story of African creativity in dignity.[10]

Much of this statement is still valid today. We need the leadership of governments – they make policies. For example, South Africa's FP&M SETA (Media, Advertising, Publishing, Printing and Packaging Sector Education Training Authority, is an Authority established in terms of section 9(1) of the Skills Development Act 1988.[11] The prescribed core business of the FP&M SETA is the development and implementation of a Sector Skills Plan by identifying and developing Leaderships and Skills Programmes by which Discretionary Grants are allocated to fund the Internship Programme. It is integrated into a national skills development and training framework.

3. *Public-private collaboration:* This also focuses on national

---

[9] *Ibid.*
[10] Francis B. Nyamnjoh, 'The State of African Publishing.' Langaa Research and Publishing Common Initiative Group. July 31, 2009. Available at: http://www.langaa-rpcig.net/+The- State-of-African-Publishing-by+.html. Accessed on 21 February, 2016.
[11] http://www.fpmseta.org.za

ownership. Courses can be developed and delivered with external expertise, if necessary. World Bank projects for textbooks may have a capacity building component, which could provide resources for capacity building for professionals involved in textbook development, production, and distribution. In some countries, capacity building has been left to national or international NGOs. Box 3 sets out some ideas.

Box 3: A Sample Capacity Building Programme for Textbook Development			
Participants	Training Required	Primary Responsibility	
		Vibrant book industry	Weak or No book industry
Curriculum designers	• Understanding goals of the national education programme. • Academic integrity. • Pedagogy.	Ministry of Education (MoE)	MoE
Book reviewers / Evaluators	• Understanding curricula goals. • How to determine if content is pedagogically and academically sound.	MoE	MoE

Authors/ Writers	• Curriculum: Help authors understand the curriculum, deductive thinking, methodology, and core competencies – skills and knowledge to be achieved for each grade. • Gender: Ensure balanced portrayal of gender. Particularly, girls and women should have positive roles. • Cultural diversity: How to write inclusive content. Consider positively representing tribes, ethnic groups or cultures in the country. • Writing mother-tongue content: It should not be assumed that an author who writes well in English or French, for example, can write equally well in local languages. • Criteria for book selection.	Industry (publisher)	MoE/Industry
Editors	Same content for authors, plus • Evaluating a manuscript for suitability. • How to edit for a grade level.	Industry (publisher)	MoE/Industry

Book illustrators and designers	• Appropriate illustrations, font, and layout.	Industry (Publisher)	MoE/Industry
Printers (Printing house)	• Approved technical specifications for textbooks and supplementary readers. • Desired packaging, including labelling for deliveries,	Industry (Printing house)	MoE
Distributors and Booksellers	• Effective promotion • Bookstore management/ record-keeping	Industry professionals	Industry professionals
Teachers and teacher trainees	• How to use books to achieve learning objectives. • Teaching children to read.	MoE	MoE
Librarians	• How to select suitable books. • How to teach reading skills and encourage reading	MoE	MoE

Distance learning options: Generally, African publishing houses tend to be of small and medium size. As such, they find it difficult to release staff to pursue resident or full-time degree courses. This is where e-learning can find a niche. And companies can offer part or full scholarships to their staff for the purpose. Apart from seminars the World Bank's API hosted in the early 200s, there has been little training offered to those who work in book publishing. As a result, for a good proportion of African book professionals their interest in the Internet, and more specifically the World Wide Web, has been limited and remains largely underutilised (Zell, 2009).

Conclusion

Much has been done in the past; quite a bit is being done now, but we need to do more and better. So, to answer Henry Chakava's question: 'Can Africa make the technological 'leap' by harnessing the new technologies to exploit its knowledge potential?' we can say, Yes, if . . . those interested in recording, packaging and disseminating Africa's knowledge to equip its populations and to make its voice heard and read in the literary world, understand the need, arise to the task and;

1. We are better able to project Africa's future publishing needs and identify the human resources that will be required to meet such needs;
2. We stop working in a fragmented manner and collaborate more effectively, bringing together government, private sector, non-governmental organisations (national and international), and the publishing industry;
3. We are determined to ensure that Africa contributes a continuous pipeline of quality content to the body of knowledge in circulation worldwide not only for this generation, but for the future as well.

In his acceptance speech for the 1st ZIBF Award for Life-Long Contribution to the African Book Industry in Harare on 2nd August 2004, Henry Chakava made these comments, succinctly encapsulating a confident and optimistic view of a future direction for African publishing:

> African publishing has come of age, and the challenge facing us now is to democratize the book so as to make it available, accessible and affordable to all our people. These are the challenges I must now place before our new generation of publishers. You must build on the foundations we have established, take advantage of the liberalized marketplace, and harness the emerging technologies to put African publishing squarely on the world map (Smith 2006).

Africa can proudly hold up Henry Chakava as one of those who blazed the trail, taking leadership in an industry once the preserve of non-African multi-nationals. He himself can look back with satisfaction over decades of training and providing opportunities for other Africans in his country Kenya and other parts of Africa. It is now our collective challenge to work on and prepare subsequent generations of publishing professionals by building upon this rich heritage.

References

Chakava, Henry. 2010. "The Challenges of Book Distribution in Africa." In *Scholarly Publishing in Africa: Opportunities & Impediments*, pp. 117-127, edited by Solani Ngobeni. Pretoria: Africa Institute of South Africa.

Christensen, Lars P., et al. 1999. *Strengthening Publishing in Africa: An Evaluation of APNET.* Stockholm: SIDA.

Darko-Ampem, K.O. 2000. "Indigenous Publishing in Africa: An Overview of Accelerated Training and Research, and African Self-help Efforts." *Mots Pluriel* no. 13 (2000).

Ngobeni, Solani ed. 2010. *Scholarly Publishing in Africa.* Pretoria: Africa Institute of South Africa.

Nicholson, Catherine. 1998. "Book Aid Expands Publishing Support." *Bellagio Publishing Network Newsletter,* Issue No 24 (December, 1998).

Nyamnjoh, Francis B. "The State of African Publishing." Langaa Research and Publishing Common Initiative Group. July 31, 2009. Available at: http://www.langaa-rpcig.net/+The- State-of-African-Publishing-by+.html. Accessed on 21 February, 2016.

Ralphs, Mary. 1998. "South African publishing training initiative." *Bellagio Publishing Network Newsletter,* Issue No 22 (July 1998).

Smith, Kelvin. 2006. "African Publishing from the Outside." *African Research & Documentation,* Volume No. 100 (April, 2006).

Zell, Hans. 2008. "Publishing in Africa: Where are We Now? Part One: Some Spurious Claims Debunked." *LOGOS 19/4* (2008): 187-195.

_____.2009. "Publishing in Africa: Where Are We Now? Part Two: Accomplishments and Failures." *LOGOS 20/*1(2008): 169-179.

Zell, H.M. and C. Lomer. 1996. *Publishing and Book Development in Sub-Saharan Africa: An Annotated Bibliography.*

16

Copyright and Copyright Infringement: The Legal and Institutional Framework in East Africa

By Marisella Ouma

Introduction

In the recent past, we have seen an exponential growth in various sectors of the copyright industry within East Africa. The copyright industry, which is key part of the knowledge economy, play an important role in growth and development of the economy, preservation and dissemination of culture and are source of income especially for the youth. The industry, which covers books, software, music, film, photography, sculptures, painting, fashion and design, and architectural drawings, is part of the knowledge economy that needs to be nurtured within the region.

Copyright is part of the intellectual property rights and refers to the protection of the creations of the mind. Intellectual property is divided into two main areas; Industrial Property which includes patents, trademarks, utility models, industrial designs, and geographical indications. Plant varieties may be covered under industrial property or have a separate legal regime as is the case in Kenya. The second category of intellectual property is copyright and related rights which covers books, software, music, film, photography, sculptures, painting, fashion and design, and architectural drawings. There are other rights, which do not necessarily fall within the traditional intellectual property but are considered within the framework under *sui generis* protection namely; traditional knowledge, traditional cultural expressions and genetic resources.

Copyright grants exclusive rights to the authors/owners of copyright to prohibit or allow the use of their works subject to specific exceptions and limitations for a limited period of time. It provides an incentive for authors to create their works as it offers them protection and returns for their intellectual efforts.

International legal framework

Copyright, like other intellectual property has become part and parcel of international trade hence the need to have an international regime to ensure its protection and enforcement. The first international treaty to address copyright and related rights was the Berne Convention of 1886 – last revised in the Paris Act of 1971. The Berne Convention, sets out the minimum standards of protection for copyright and related rights at the international level and for the World Intellectual Property Organisation (WIPO) Member States. The World Trade Organisation (WTO) administered Trade Related Aspects of Intellectual Property (TRIPs) agreement makes its compulsory for all WTO member states to ensure that they adhere to the minimum standards of protection set out under the Berne Convention. The TRIPs Agreement also has extensive provisions for enforcement of intellectual property rights that include; administrative actions, civil procedures and remedies as well as criminal liability in the case of copyright infringement.

There are other WIPO administered treaties such as the WIPO Copyright and WIPO Performances and Phonograms Treaty (known as the WIPO Copyright Treaties) adopted in 1996 to address what is known as the 'digital agenda' as this had not been covered by the TRIPs Agreement which was concluded before the issues arose and considered within the context of copyright and related rights. These treaties build upon the provisions of the Berne Convention and the TRIPs Agreement. In addition, they ensure provisions of limitations and exceptions within the three-step test, introduce provisions on the right of making available, protection of technological protection measures and rights management information in the digital environment.

Two other important treaties were adopted by WIPO Member States namely; the Beijing Treaty for the Protection of Audio-visual Performances in 2012 and the Marrakesh Treaty to Facilitate Access to Published Works by Persons who are Blind, Visually Impaired or Print Disabled, 2013. These two are yet to come into force and none of the countries in East Africa have ratified or acceded to them. There are other treaties in the field of copyright but the above are the most significant. All countries are members of the World Trade Organisation and therefore members of the Berne Convention.[1] In East Africa only Burundi has acceded to the WIPO Copyright Treaty. None has ratified or acceded to the WPPT, Beijing Treaty and the Marrakesh Treaty.

Legal and institutional framework in East Africa

Copyright in East Africa dates back to the colonial period, and can therefore be considered a recent development. There are two systems of copyright: the common law system and the civil law system. The latter influenced copyright law in Rwanda and Burundi while the former formed the basis of copyright law in Kenya, Tanzania and Uganda. The distinction in the two systems lies in their different philosophical foundations. After independence, the countries passed and ratified copyright laws that were amended over the years to what we have today.

The legal framework

Recently, the East African Community passed the Creative Economy Act, which covers the regulation of creative industries within the region. However, national laws provide protection of copyright and related rights in all the countries within East Africa. All the five East African

---

1   Burundi, Kenya, Rwanda and Tanzania all acceded to the Berne Convention and Uganda became a member due to its status as a Member of WTO. Under the Article 9 of the TRIPs Agreement, all WTO member states are bound by the provisions of the Berne Convention save for Article 6 *bis*.

countries have legislation for protection of copyright and related rights which are amended when necessary taking into account developments at local, regional and international level. In some countries such as Kenya, protection of intellectual property is entrenched in the Constitution. Constitutional protection ensures that copyright and other intellectual property rights are recognised and well protected. The Constitution of Burundi does not expressly protect intellectual property but the Charter on fundamental rights and duties of an individual guarantees the protection of the right to property.[2] The Constitution of Kenya guarantees the protection of intellectual property as a fundamental right. It recognises intellectual property as a property like any other.[3]

The main legal instruments dealing with copyright and related rights are the Copyright and Neighbouring Rights Act 2006 and Regulation 2010, in Uganda, the Copyright Act Cap 130 of the Laws of Kenya and Regulations, The Copyright and Neighbouring Act of 1999, in Tanzania, The Copyright Act of 2003, Zanzibar, Act No 1/021 of December 30 2005 on the Protection of Copyright and Related Rights, in Burundi and Law No. 31/2009 of 2009 on Protection of Intellectual Property, in Rwanda. Other significant laws relating to copyright and related rights include Anti Counterfeit Act of 2008, in Kenya and the Cybercrimes Act 2005, in Tanzania.

Rwanda has had an Intellectual Property Policy in place since 2009 which not only recognises the role of copyright and related rights but also lays out the relevant framework for administration and enforcement of copyright and related rights. It takes cognisance of the need to balance the rights of the authors and access by users especially in the case of libraries, archive, educational and research institutions and facilitation of access to published works by visually impaired persons. From the policy, the role of the copyright office within the Ministry of Culture and Sports is very clear. It is notable that the other East African countries are yet to adopt intellectual property law policies and this affects the management of intellectual property.

---

2   Article 6 of Chapter 1 of the Constitution of Burundi 2005
3   Article 40(5). Article 11(2) (c) obliges the government to protect intellectual property rights in Kenya

Copyright laws provide for the legal framework of copyright protection as discussed below.

Under the law, copyright is a statutory right that is granted to the author to control the use or otherwise of his creative works which as stated earlier include literary works such as books, computer software, poems, lyrics, anthologies among others, musical works, artistic works such as sculptures and paintings and also protects audio-visual works such as films, television programmes and documentaries. Protection of copyright is automatic after the idea has been reduced into any tangible format and is original. However, it does not protect ideas and concepts.

Copyright law grants two types of rights: exclusive rights and moral rights. Moral rights are the inalienable rights granted to the author, and are independent of the economic rights. They cannot be transferred to a third party under the laws within the East African countries. The rights are recognised in the case of authors and performers in both audio and audio-visual performances. Moral rights include the right to be acknowledged as the author of the work, the right to object to any distortion or mutilation of one's works or use of the works in a manner that may be prejudicial to the interests of the author. The author also has the right to decide whether or not to have the works published.

Economic rights granted under the copyright laws in East African countries include the right of reproduction, right to disseminate/distribute the work, right to sell, right to hire, right to import, right to adaptation and translation of the work, right to broadcast or right to make the work available to the public. These rights are subject to specific exceptions and limitations. The exceptions include what is known as fair dealing for the purposes of quotation and reporting of news, use of works for educational purposes, research, archiving and use by public libraries. In Uganda, for instance the law provides for exceptions under fair use, fair dealing and also the application of the three-step test. The laws also take cognisance of exceptions as they apply to computer programmes.

The law also grants rights to performers, producers of sound recordings and broadcasting organisations and these are known as related rights. Initial ownership of copyright vests in the creator of the work. However, if the work such as a book or computer software is made during one's employment or under commission, unless there is a contract to the contrary, ownership shall be deemed to vest in the employer or the person who commissioned the work.

Protection granted lasts for the life of the author plus fifty years. This allows the rights holders and heir in title to enjoy the benefits of copyright and related rights. However, in case of anonymous works, copyright will only last fifty years from the date of publication. The limitation granted by law ensures that works are not held in perpetuity and provides an opportunity for further creativity. Works whose copyright time has expired, or the author has waived his/her copyright fall into public domain and third parties are free to use the works.[4]

Like any other moveable property, the economic rights in copyright can be transferred by licensing, sale and or may be inherited. This makes it a valuable tool in the economy. The licence may include all the rights or some of the rights for a limited period of time in consideration. Assignments may also be in whole or in part. Assignments form the basis of collective management of rights as specific rights are assigned to the Collective Management Organisation (CMO) by the rights holders for them to manage on the latter's behalf. In the book publishing industry, there are CMOs known as reprographic rights organisations that collect royalties on behalf of the rights holders.

Infringement

Infringement of copyright has become a major problem in East Africa especially with increased Internet speed, affordable Internet connectivity and proliferation of mobile phones. Infringement occurs when a third party exploits the exclusive rights without the authorisation of the rights holders. Primary infringement occurs where the third party reproduces, sells, offers for sale, communicates to the public, adapts or translates copyright protected works without the authority of the rights holder. For instance, any person who reproduces a literary work by way of photocopying, infringes on copyright. The rights holder has the right to take civil action

---

[4] Although the works fall into public domain, some laws make provisions for anyone wishing to exploit the works to seek authority form the Minister in charge of copyright.

against the alleged infringer through the courts where he will be entitled to civil remedies such as damages, accounts for profit and delivery up. Once an infringement is reported and investigated, criminal proceedings may be instituted and where the case is determined in favour of the rights holder, the alleged infringer is liable to pay a fine or a jail term, or both.

Where a person provides or manufactures equipment that is primarily used for copyright infringement, such person shall be liable for secondary infringement of copyright. All copyright laws provide for both primary and secondary infringement and create both civil and criminal liability. Where infringement is done for commercial purposes (piracy), it has adverse effects on copyright industries. Where broadcasting organisations broadcasts content without the consent of the authors in the case of collective management, they are liable for copyright infringement.

All cases of unauthorised commercial use of copyright and related rights are infringements but not all acts of infringement amount to piracy. There are cases where one may for instance make a copy of a book and distribute it to others through digital channels as social media. This amounts to infringement of the right of distribution and making available. On the other hand, where a person reproduces works and offers them for sale without the rights holder's authority, they are engaged in acts of piracy and these often lead to criminal prosecution.

Institutional framework

For an effective copyright protection system to be realised, it is important to have the relevant institutional framework. The main institutions responsible for management, administration and enforcement of copyright and related rights are the copyright offices, collective management organisations, industry organisations and law enforcement agencies. Copyright offices are in charge of the policy and legal issues, training and awareness creation, registration of copyright where applicable, investigation and prosecution of copyright cases. In Kenya, the Kenya Copyright Board (KECOBO) was established under section 3 of the Copyright Act to administer and enforce copyright and related rights in Kenya. It among other things deals with licensing and regulation of collective management organisations, investigation and prosecution of copyright infringement cases and advising the government on matters of copyright and related rights.[5]

In Tanzania, copyright administration is through the Copyright Society of Tanzania (COSOTA) whose duties include among other things, advising the minister on matters that fall under the Copyright Act.[6] COSOTA has a department that deals with legal and dispute resolutions and deals with copyright infringement cases. It also carries out awareness creation activities, anti-piracy campaigns and enforcement of copyright and related rights. So in a way it acts as both the collective management organisation and the copyright office. This applies in the case of Zanzibar which also has a separate collective management organisation known as the Copyright Society of Zanzibar (COSOZA), and is governed by the Copyright Act of Zanzibar.

Management of Copyright and related rights in Uganda falls under the Uganda Registration Services Bureau. The office, like the Kenya Copyright Board has the mandate to administer and enforce copyright and related rights including registration of copyright, training and awareness creation and regulation of collective management organisations. In Rwanda, management of copyright and related rights falls within the copyright office under the Ministry of Sports and Culture. A division within the Rwanda Development Board however, deals with registration of copyright and related rights. It is important to note that registration is voluntary and does not in any way contravene Article 5(2) of the Berne Convention, which requires that copyright protection shall not be subject to any formality.

Collective management organisations also play an important role in administration of rights in the music, film, book publishing and visual arts sectors. In most of these cases, individual licensing and collection of royalties can be quite difficult taking into account the multiple uses and users, and more so in the digital environment. The collective management organisations can be statutory bodies such as COSOTA, and COSOZA

---

5   Section 5 of Cap 130 of the Laws of Kenya
6   Section 47 of the Copyright and Neighbouring Rights Act No. 7 of 1999 (CAP 218 RE 2002)

or private organisations but under government supervision such as the Reprographic Rights Organisations of Kenya (KOPIKEN), the Music Copyright Society of Kenya (MCSK), the Rwanda Society of Authors (RSAU), Uganda Reprographic Rights Organisation (URRO) to name a few. In Kenya and Uganda, although these are private organisations. The law makes provisions for their regulation: from registration, licensing and overall supervision to ensure that they effectively and efficiently fulfil their mandate which is collection and distribution of royalties.

Copyright, like other intellectual property rights are private rights and the onus of ensuring that third parties do not use the works without their authority rests with the rights holders. The government comes in by providing the legal framework and necessary infrastructure for enforcement of these rights. Enforcement agencies such as the judiciary, police, customs and standards organisations and copyright offices play a crucial role. The police investigate reported cases of infringement and take cases to court where appropriate. The courts have to determine the cases, whether criminal or civil based on the evidence provided. Customs help through use of border measures to prevent importation of illegal copyright works. The internet has also made it possible to access and download works thus the need to come up with innovative ways to ensure enforcement online. This includes use of technological protection measures and Rights Management Information Systems (RMIS).

The Kenya Copyright Board has an enforcement unit consisting of police officers, investigators and prosecutors. Apart from the KECOBO, Kenya also has an Anti-Counterfeit Agency whose mandate is to fight counterfeit and pirated products in Kenya. In Uganda, enforcement is done through the Uganda Business Registration Bureau in collaboration with the police. COSOTA and COSOZA in Tanzania also engage in anti-piracy activities such as anti-piracy campaigns, raids, and confiscation of copyright infringing works. The use of the anti-piracy security device such as a hologram helps in the fight against piracy. This is currently only applicable for the physical works and does not cover works that are reproduced and distributed online.

Other industry organisations that may be relevant in enforcement of copyright and related right are industry organisations, trade unions and associations. The Recording Industry Association of Kenya (RIAK) is an example of an industry organisation that was formed by producers of sound recordings to help in the fight against piracy in Kenya. It works with the Kenya Copyright Board and police by providing information and helping identification of pirates and also provides evidence in court as the rights holders or on behalf of their members.

Challenges

Having looked at the legal and institutional framework, it is important to discuss various challenges within the copyright industries in East Africa. The first is the lack of a policy framework both at regional and national levels. As discussed above, only Rwanda has an intellectual property policy. It is important to have a clear policy framework for an effective system as it provides the blue print as well as the road map for management and enforcement of intellectual property.

Second is limited knowledge on copyright and related rights among the rights holders, users, policy makers and law enforcement agencies. This may be attributed to the general societal attitude towards copyright and related rights. The intangible nature of copyright makes it possible for several people to use the work while the author still has the original. Most people do not seem to have a problem downloading films, music and other digital content online without paying for it. Indeed, there are proponents of free access of content online on the premise that copyright is no longer relevant in the digital environment. However, we need to appreciate that copyright is a property like any other and should be treated as such. Law enforcement agencies tend to treat copyright cases as minor offences and fail to understand the negative impact of copyright infringement. This may also be attributed to lack of policies in the area of copyright and intellectual property in general.

Third is the issue of ever-changing technology and increased internet bandwidth and more affordable access to the internet. It is possible to download content in real time at a nominal cost and disseminate the same through various networks. This makes infringement easier and management and enforcement of rights more difficult. Use of anti-piracy security devices are currently limited to physical copies. Technological Protection Measures (TPM) provide solutions but sometimes for a limited period as people come up with ways to circumvent the technologies which allow them by by-pass passwords, scramble encrypted signals and remove any TPM employed. They also use technology to facilitate dissemination of content through file sharing. It is interesting to note that when these sites are pulled down, they end up being set up again. One may therefore argue that the law enforcement agencies within East Africa lack the capacity to enforce copyright and related rights online.

Fourth is the issue of unauthorised commercial use of copyright and related rights otherwise known as copyright piracy. This has been exacerbated by increased Internet access. Lack or limited distribution channels contribute to the growth of piracy in East Africa. In several cases, works are released but they are not made available to the users and pirates come in to fill the gap. There is also the issue of lack of appreciation of copyright, especially as contributor to the national and regional economy. This may also be attributed to lack or limited awareness of copyright and related rights.

Fifth is failure by users to take out licences for use of copyright works. This affects the reprographic rights organisations where educational institutions and other users fail to pay for use reproductions of works. Others are the broadcasting organisations and mobile phone operators who use works and fail to take out licences with collective management organisations. This seems to be endemic in the region and needs to be addressed urgently.

Need for policy/paradigm shift

Infringement of copyright and related rights continues to be a plague in the industry and needs to be tackled from a policy and practical perspective. From the above, we can see that there is a legal framework in place and several institutions set up to manage and enforce copyright and related rights. It is important to have a sound policy framework both at the national and regional level, which may help in harmonisation of laws. It is also crucial to embrace technology and look for ways in which we can have the balance between the rights of the author and access by users without prejudicing the interests of the rights holders. It is also necessary to look at the new business methods for content over digital networks.

Education and awareness creation are necessary and should start at an early age so that people can grow to appreciate copyright and related rights as an important aspect of our daily lives and a major contributor to the economy. This is likely to reduce the levels of copyright infringement. Several commentators have argued that the digital era has ushered in the end of copyright industries and book publishing in particular. Such arguments notwithstanding, it is important to note that the Internet is not the end but provides endless opportunities for copyright industries to grow, and creative authors need to take advantage of these opportunities.

References

Ficsor, Mihaly. 2002. *Collective Management of Copyright and Related Rights*. Geneva: WIPO.

Ouma, Marisella. 2004. "Copyright and the Music Industry in Africa", *The Journal of World Intellectual Property,* Volume 7, Issue 6 (November 2004): 919-932.

Sihanya, Ben. 2001. "Intellectual Property Confronts Counterfeiting in Africa: Protecting Innovators and Consumers in the Cyber Society," in *Consumer Law in the Information Society,* edited by Thomas Wilhelmsson, Salla Tuominen and Heli Tuomola. Cambridge, Massachusetts: Kluwer Law International.

Stokes, S. 2014. *Digital Copyright Law and Practice, 4th Edition.* Oxford and Portland: Hart Publishing.

Tom Fleming Creative Consultancy. 2015. "Scoping the Creative Economy in East Africa", Available at: *www.britishcouncil.org/sites/ default/files/scoping-creative-economy-east-africa.pdf/* Accessed on 31 January 2015.

Legislation

Act No 1/021 of 2005 on Protection of copyright and Related Rights, Burundi

Anti-Counterfeit Act, Chapter 130A of the Laws of Kenya

Copyright Act of 2003, Zanzibar

Copyright Act, Chapter 130 of the Laws of Kenya

Copyright and Neighbouring Rights Act 1999 Tanzania

Copyright and Neighbouring Rights Act 2006, Uganda

Law No 31/2009 of 2009 on Protection of Intellectual Property, Rwanda

Appendix

University Institutions in Africa with Departments of Book and Publishing Studies

Ghana

Department of Publishing Studies, Kwame Nkrumah University of Science and Technology, Kumasi Web: http://publishing.knust.edu.gh/

Principal contact:

Dr. Kwasi Opoku Amankwa, Head, Department of Publishing Studies, and Dean, Faculty of Arts kopokuamankwa@googlemail.com

Mount Crest University, School of Publishing and Communication Studies, Accra http://www.mountcrestuniversity.com/ (new university, established in 2011; offers a BA in Publishing Studies)

Principal contact: n/a info@mountcrestuniversity.com

Kenya

Department of Publishing and Media Studies, School of Information Science, Moi University, Eldoret http://www.mu.ac.ke/informationscience/index.php/departments/publishing-and-media-studies

Principal contacts:

Dr Duncan Omanga, Head, Department of Publishing and Media Studies ankodani@yahoo.com

Professor Daniel C. Rotich, Associate Professor dcrotich@hotmail.com

Professor Justus Wamukoya, Dean, School of Information Sciences info@mu.ac.ke

Nigeria

Centre of the Book – Nigeria (proposed, *not* operational as yet), Kwara State University, Malete, Kwara State *http://www.kwasu.edu.ng/*

Principal contacts:

Professor Abiola Irele, Provost, College of Humanities, Kwara State University, and Director, Kwara State University Press *abiola.irele@kwasu.edu.ng* or *abiolairele@gmail.com*

or David Dorman, Visiting Principal Librarian and Acting Director, Centre for Innovation in Teaching and Research, Kwara State University david.dorman@kwasu.edu.ng or ddorman@marlboro.edu

Department of Library Archival and Information Studies, Faculty of Education, University of Ibadan (offers a Master in Publishing and Copyright Studies) *http://educ.ui.edu.ng/welcomelib*

Principal contact:

Professor (Mrs.) Iyabo M. Mabawonku, Head of Department [email: n/a]

South Africa

Department of Information Science, University of Pretoria, Hatfield, Pretoria *http://www.up.ac.za/information-science*

Principal contacts:

Professor T J D Bothma, Head, Department of Information Science *infosci@up.ac.za*

Dr Beth le Roux, Senior Lecturer, Department of Information Science (and coordinator Publishing Studies) *beth.leroux@up.ac.za*

School of Literature, Language and Media, Publishing Studies, University of the Witwatersrand, Wits *http://www.wits.ac.za/sllm/publishingstudies/7719/publishingstudies.html*

Principal contact:

Colleen Dawson, Lecturer, and Course Coordinator and Administrator, Publishing Studies Programmes *Colleen.Dawson@wits.ac.za*

Zimbabwe

National University of Science and Technology, Faculty of Communication and Information Science, Department of Publishing Studies, Bulawayo *http://www.nust.ac.zw/index.php/medicine/communication-information-science/publishing*

Principal contact:

Dr Ndabezinhle Luke Dlodlo, Chair, Department of Publishing Studies *nldlodlo@gmail.com*

INDEX

Academy of Science of South Africa (ASSAf) 122
Academy Science Publishers 118
Achebe, Chinua 3, 4, 6, 8, 16, 28, 29, 37
A Comparative Study of Religions 116
A Course for Editors in Sub-Saharan Africa 241
Act No 1/021 of December 30 2005 on the Protection of Copyright and Related Rights [Burundi] 258
Adagala, Kavetsa 66
Adam, Michael 112
ADEA 148, 212. *See also* Association for the Development of Education in Africa
ADEA Working Group on Books and Learning Materials 148
Adelekan, A.I. 71
Adesina, Segun 76
Africa Development 176
Africa Institute of South Africa 244
'African Orature: Back to the Roots' 58
'African Publishing' 71
Africana-First Publishers 73
Africana Librarians Council of African Studies 229
African Book Publishing Record (ABPR) 155, 156, 198, 224, 226
African Books Collective (ABC) 11, 42, 88, 125, 155, 157, 158, 179, 181, 182, 184, 192, 200, 204, 205, 207, 212, 224
   Council of Management 207
   cultural mission 211
   establishment 204
   founder publishers 206
   international trading 208
   trading in the US 208

African Booksellers Association (PABA) 179
African Books in Print 198
African Classics Series (ACS) 5
African Crop Science Journal 120
African Film: Re-imagining a Continent 116
'Africanisation' of knowledge 113
African Journal of Peace and Human Rights 120
African Journals Online (AJOL) 120, 156, 226
African Literature in English 101
African Philosophy 98
African Philosophy in Search of Identity 117
African Popular Theatre 116
African Publishers Network (APNET) 11, 87, 133, 141, 145, 151, 155, 156, 179, 187, 225, 236
African Publishing Initiative 240
African Publishing Institute (API) 236
African Publishing Review 191
African Religions and Philosophy 117
African Religions in Western Scholarship 116
African Scholarly Publishing. Essays 212
African Sociological Review 176
African Theatre in Development 116
African Union 91, 160, 222
African Writers Association (PAWA) 179
African Writers-Publishers Seminar 211, 227
African Writers Series (AWS) 3, 5, 14, 16, 24, 25, 27, 28, 38, 40, 41, 42, 46, 50, 56, 74, 89, 102, 105, 202
Africa Review of Books 168, 176
Africa Writes Back 30, 48, 55

After 4.30 100
A Grain of Wheat 3, 16
A History of Kigezi in South-West Uganda 111
A History of Tanzania 110
A History of the Kipsigis 112
Aidoo, Ama Ata 59
AISA 244. *See also* Africa Institute of South Africa
Ajeluorou, Anote 90
Akare, Thomas 34
Ake 198
Akokhan 9
Alice Lakwena & the Holy Spirits 116
Alidhani Kapata na Hadithi Nyingine 8
Allied Sciences (Tanzania) 121
A Love Affair with the Sun 9
Alpers, E. A. 111
Altbach, Philip 76
Amazon.com 103, 191, 192, 193, 195, 197, 199
Amazon Kindle 192
A Methodology to Collect International Book Statistics 147
Amin, President Idi 111, 129
Ankara Press 195
A Nose for Money 5
An Outline History of the Babukusu 112
Anti Counterfeit Act of 2008 [Kenya] 258
Anti-Counterfeit Agency [Kenya] 263
Anyumba, Henry Owuor 124
API 239, 244, 251. *See also* African Publishing Institute
APNET 141, 153, 189, 190, 191, 238, 239, 240, 244. *See also* African Publishers Network
APNET Research and Documentation Centre 240
A Political History of the Pare of Tanzania, ca 1500-1900 110
A Political History of Uganda 113
Apple Macintosh computer 187
Aromolaran [Publishers] 72
Arusha Declaration in 1967 vi
Asali Chungu 8
Association for the Development of Education in Africa (ADEA) 148, 212, 226
Association of African Universities 201
Association of Progressive Communications 188
Atieno Odhiambo, E. S. 123
AU 160. *See also* African Union
Author Solutions service 193

Bahan, Marlin 116
Baitwababo, Simon 108
Bakker, Anne 137
Banage, William 118
Baraza la Maendeleo ya Vitabu Tanzania- BAMVITA 151. *See also* National Book Development Council of Tanzania
Basic School Book Supply Scheme [Ghana] 81
Behrend, Heike 116
Beijing Treaty 257
Beijing Treaty for the Protection of Audio-visual Performances 257
Bellagio Centre 207
Bellagio Publishing Group 207
Bellagio Publishing Network 187, 191, 212, 225
Bellagio Publishing Network Newsletter 156, 225

Bellagio Studies in Publishing Series 225
Berne Convention 256, 262
Beyond Expectations: From Charcoal to Gold 9
Bgoya, Walter 193, 204, 215, 223
Bill and Melinda Gates Foundation 197, 230
p'Bitek, Prof. Okot 4, 29, 44, 60, 99, 109, 116
Black Aesthetics in East Africa 114
Black Sunlight 47
Blackwell Bookshop 207
Blundell, Michael 9
Boleswa Integrated Science project 83
Bonaya, T. W. 108
Book Aid International (BAI) 227, 239
BookData SAPnet 153
Book Development Centre (Nigeria) 151
Book Development Council [UK] 77
Bookmarks 153
BookPower 230
Book Publishers Association (GPBA) 245
'Book Publishing in Africa' group 154
Books Acceleration Programme [Nigeria] 79
Books and Learning Materials Working Group 212
Booksellers Association of Tanzania (BSAT) 229
Bookwise Publishers 117
Brooks, Jeremy 35
Bukenya, Austin 62, 63
Burt Award for African Literature 11, 244
Busara 115
Bushababy Books 103
Bw'Atebe, Onduko 6

Cabral, Amilcar 58
Caitaani Mũtharabainĩ 8, 15, 17, 21, 39
Cambridge University Press 72
Cameroon Book Commission 82
Canadian Organization for Development through Education (CODE) 11, 132, 230
Capital Shoppers 138
Carcase for Hounds 33
Cassava Republic Press 195
Catholic University in Luanda 166
Centre Africain de Formation à l'Édition et à la Diffusion (CAFED) 144
Centre for Ilorin Manuscripts and Culture 141
Centre for the Book (South Africa) 151
Chagula, Wilbert 118
Chakava, Dr Henry Miyinzi 1, 2, 3, 5, 6, 8, 9, 10, 26, 29, 30, 33, 42, 58, 180, 215
  ABC Council of Management 207
  academic publishing 123
  African Books Collective 184
  African language publishing 15
  as an academic 11
  children's books 37
  Department of Literature (UoN) 22
  founding of African Books Collective 204
  founding of East African Educational Publishers (EAEP) 40, 132
  future of publishing 252
  honours 12
  indigenous African publishing 188
  launch of *Mũrogi wa Kagogo* 21
  legacy 177
  oral culture publishing 32
  popular book market 36, 102
  post-independence publishing 202
  publisher and intellectual 42
  publishing Africa 158, 178
  publishing *Caitaani Mũtharabainĩ* 17
  publishing editor 28
  publishing *Matigari* 19
  publishing model 25

publishing Ngũgĩ 25, 52, 38
publishing orature 68
Spear Books Series 51
technological 'leap' 252
training opportunities 235
ZIBF Award for Life-Long Contribution to the African Book Industry 252
Chakava, Baba Joram 58
Chakava, Hillary 106
Chami, F. 113
Chembe cha Moyo 8
Children's Literature Association of Kenya (CLAK) 10
'China: Lost in Translation' 170
Chinelo [Achebe] 37
Churchill, Winston 59
Church Missionary Society (CMS) 71
ciopyright infringement 260
Clark, J.P. 38
CODE. *See* Canadian Organization for Development through Education
CODESRIA 158, 159, 162, 163, 164, 165, 169. *See also* Council for the Development of Social Science Research
CODESRIA Bulletin* 176
CODESRIA Documentation and Information Centre (CODICE) 164
CODESRIA publications 174
CODESRIA Publications Programme 168
CODESRIA's Publications and Dissemination Policy 175
CODESRIA Strategic Plan 2007 – 2011 167
Collective Management Organisation (CMO) 260
Colloquium of the Second Black World Festival of Arts and Culture 62
Committee for the Release of Political Prisoners in Kenya 26
Committee on Scholarly Publishing in South Africa 122
Commonwealth of Learning 241
Concepts of God in Africa 116
Contemplating the Fipa Ironworking 113
co-publishing 123
copyright 255, 256
Copyright Act Cap 130 Kenya 258, 261
Copyright Act of 2003 [Zanzibar] 258, 262
Copyright and Neighbouring Act of 1999 Tanzania 258
Copyright and Neighbouring Rights Act 2006 [Uganda] 258
Copyright Society of Tanzania (COSOTA) 262
Copyright Society of Zanzibar (COSOZA) 262
COSOTA 262, 263. *See also* Copyright Society of Tanzania (COSOTA)
COSOZA 262, 263. *See also* Copyright Society of Zanzibar (COSOZA)
Council for Promotion of Science Publications for Children in Africa (CHISCA) 10
Council for the Development of Social Science Research (CODESRIA) 158, 230
Cover2Cover Books 196
Cox, Justin 192
Crane Publishers 130, 132
CRASC 169
'Crisis of Science' 118
Critiques of Christianity in African Literature 116
Currey, Clare 40
Currey, James 8, 48, 55
Curriculum Development Unit (CDU)-Uganda 132

Custodians of the Land: Ecology and Culture in the History of Tanzania 112
Cybercrimes Act 2005 [Tanzania] 258

Dabashi, Hamid 172, 173
Dag Hammarskjöld Foundation 203, 211, 227
Daily Times 72
Dar es Salaam University 60, 113, 121, 126
Dar es Salaam University Press 113, 121, 126
Darko-Ampen, Kwasi 123, 125, 218, 219, 253
Darlite 115. See also Umma
Dawood, Yusuf 5
Decentralization and Devolution in Kenya: New Approaches 113
Decolonising the Mind 40, 115
Decolonization and Independence in Kenya, 1940-93 112
Delicious Bar 45
Denoon, Donald 111
Design of Appropriate Agroforestry Interventions in Uganda 118
Devil on the Cross 8, 17, 18, 55
DFID 85
Dhana 114, 115
Dialogue 120
Digital Rights Management System 104
Dlamini-Zuma, Dr Nkosazana 160
Dr Seuss 216

EAEP. See East African Educational Publishers 7, 8, 115, 116, 117, 121, 134
EAPH. See East African Publishing House
Early East African Writers and Publishers 97

Early Trade in Eastern Africa 111
'East Africa and Its Foreign Invaders' 109
East Africa Journal 108, 109, 115, 118
East African Book Development Association (EABDA) x, 10, 151, 239
East African Community (EAC) 112, 129, 138
East African Educational Publishers (EAEP) xv, 4, 20, 22, 24, 26, 40, 102, 112, 132, 158, 177, 203, 204
East African Expressions of Christianity 113
East African Institute of Social and Cultural Affairs 109
East African Journal of Peace and Human Rights 120
East African Literature Bureau (EALB) 73, 111, 112, 114, 128, 129, 202
East African Mathematics 129
East African Natural History Society 120
East African Publishing House (EAPH) 32, 46, 73, 108, 109, 110, 111
eBooks 190, 192, 193, 214
Echeruo, Michael 34
Editing Educational Materials 241
Eduardo Mondlane University 166
'Education in Revolutionary Africa' 110
Educational Research Network for West and Central Africa (ERNWACA) 164
Education Journal 120
Education Tax Fund (ETF)-Nigeria 80
Egimu-Okuda, N. 111
eKitabu 103, 104, 196, 197
electronic publishing 123
Emenanjo, Professor Emmanuel Nnolue 90
Emudong, C. P. 111
Enabling Writers, Bloom Software 244
ePub 89, 103, 195
Erapu, Laban 29, 30

Ethics: A Basic Course for Undergraduate Studies 117
Evans Brothers 72, 73, 129
EXTOP 240, 241
Eye of the Storm 5

Facebook 192
Facebook 'Publishing in Africa' group 154. *See also* Book Publishing in Africa' group
Falola 113, 124, 125
Fanon, Frantz 59
Farah, Nurrudin 3, 47, 48
Ferrel, Joseph P. 76
FESTAC 77 62
Festival of East African Writing 114
Florida Night Club 45
Fonlon, Bernard 159
Ford Foundation 206
For Home and Freedom 114
'Found in Translation' 172
Fountain Primary Science for Uganda 134
Fountain Publishers 112, 113, 116, 118, 121, 123, 127, 130, 131, 132, 134, 136
Fourth Dimension Publishing 190, 204
FP&M SETA 248. *See also* Media, Advertising, Publishing, Printing and Packaging Sector Education Training Authority
Franschoek 198
Freire, Paulo 66
FSS [Forum for Social Studies] 169
FunDza Literacy Trust 196

Gandhi Memorial Library 44

Geisel, Dr Theodor Seuss. *See* Dr Seuss
Ghala 115
Ghana Book Development Council (GBDC) 151
Ghana Publishing Corporation 73
Giblin, J. 113
Gikandi, Simon 29, 30
Girls at War 29
Going Down River Road 34
Goldsworthy, David 9
GoodReads 103, 199
Gopinathan, S. 76
Gordimer, Nadine 228
Gore, Michael 9
Governance and Transition Politics in Kenya 113
de Graft, Joe 38
Gray, Sir John 109
Griffiths, Prof. Gareth 101
la Guma, Alex 3
Gurr, Professor Andrew 2, 28
Guster, Josef 116
Gutenberg, John 72
Gwassa, Gilbert 110

Hadith series 109
Hans Zell Collection 240
Heinemann and Cassel 28, 129. *See also* Heinemann Publishers Kenya
Heinemann-Cassell 28
Heinemann East Africa 46, 48
Heinemann Educational Books (HEB) 2, 28, 42, 43, 45, 74, 92
Heinemann Publishers Kenya 15, 22, 23, 32, 96, 117, 121, 129, 132, 202, 203, 207

Heinemann UK 2, 3, 4, 6, 7, 10, 13, 14, 15, 16, 17, 22, 23, 27, 28, 29, 30, 31, 32, 33, 35, 36, 38, 40, 41, 42, 43, 45, 46, 47, 48, 50, 51, 55, 72, 73, 74, 83, 91, 92, 93, 94, 96, 102, 105, 117, 121, 129, 131, 132, 177, 202, 203, 207

Heinemann, William 47

Heyumann, Stephen P. 76

Higo, Aig 28, 30

Hill, Alan 3, 13, 27, 28, 30, 40, 47

Hill, David 28, 29, 33, 35

Hill, Enid 28

Historical Association of Kenya 108

Historical Association of Tanzania 110

History of the Abaluyia of Western Kenya 109

History of the Pare 109

History of the Southern Luo 108

History of the Swahili Speaking Peoples of the Kenya Coast 109

History of Uganda project 111

Hornby, Nick 95

Horn of My Love 32

Humanities and Social Sciences in East and Central Africa: Theory and Practice 113

Hyder, Mohammed 118

IBBY 244. *See also* International Board on Books for Young People

IBBY Canada 244

'Ideological Dogmatism and the Values of Democracy' 117

Ilesanmi [Publishers] 72

Ilieva, Emilia 106

Iliffe, John 110

'In African Publishing' 48

INASP. *See* International Network for the Availability of Scientific Publications

Independent Publishers' Association of South Africa (IPASA) 239

Indian Africa. Minorities of Indian-Pakistani Origin in Eastern Africa 112

Indiana University Press 117

Information and Communication Technologies (ICTs) 186

Ingham, Kenneth 109

Innovation and Discovery 118

In Pursuit of Publishing 13, 27

Instructional Materials Unit (IMU)-Uganda 134

Intellectual Property Policy [Rwanda] 258

intellectual property rights 255

International Board on Books for Young People 244

International Center for Writing and Translation (ICWT) 17, 19

International Literacy Association (ILA) 228

International Livestock Research Institute 121

International Network for the Availability of Scientific Publications (INASP) 212, 230

In Their Own Voices: African Women Writers Talk 115

Intra-African Book Support Scheme (IABSS) 182, 210

Introduction to African Religion 116

iPod 192

Irele, Abiola 21

Iribemwangi, P. 8

Iwe Irohin Yoruba 71

I Will Marry When I Want. *See Ngaahika Ndeenda*

James, Adeola 115
James Currey Publishers 40, 116
Janssens-Andrejew, Floris 137
Jay, Mary 193, 200
J. M. Kariuki. *See* Kariuki, J. M.
Joliso: East African Journal of Literature and Society 115
Jomo Kenyatta International Airport 18
Jomo Kenyatta Prize for Literature 10
de Jong, Daphne 104
Journal of African Religion and Philosophy 120
Journal of East African Natural History 120
Journal of Educational Research in Africa 164
Journal of Higher Education in Africa 176
Journal of the Language Association of East Africa 115
Junior Readers 6

Kabira, Wanjiku Mukabi 65
Kagumo High School 43
Kahiga, Samuel 4, 35
Kamĩrĩthũ Community Education and Cultural Centre 16, 17, 39
Kamĩtĩ Maximum Security Prison 15, 16
Kariara, Jonathan 44, 46
Kariuki, J. M. 44
Karugire, Samwiri Rubaraza 113
Karume, Njenga 9
Katoke, Israel K. 111
KECOBO. *See* Kenya Copyright Board
Kenway Publications 9
Kenwood House 46
Kenya Agricultural Research Institute 121

Kenya Air Force coup attempt 18
Kenya Copyright Board (KECOBO) 12, 261, 262, 263, 264
Kenya Historical Review 109
Kenya Institute of Administration (KIA) 12
Kenya Institute of Curriculum Development (KICD) 10, 85
Kenya Institute of Education (KIE) 134
Kenya Literature Bureau (KLB) 112, 114, 117, 129
Kenya Medical Research Institute 121
Kenya National Theatre 18
Kenya Publishers Association (KPA) 10
Kenyatta, President Jomo 16, 109
Kenya Vision 2030 120
Kerr, David 116
Kibaki, Mwai 20, 39
Kibua, Thomas 113
Kill Me Quick 10, 33, 34
Kimambo, Isaria 109, 110, 112, 113
Kimathi, Field Marshal Dedan 63
Kindle Direct Publishing and CreateSpace 193
Kiriamiti, John 5
Kisosonkole, Pumla 109
Kiwanuka, M.S.M. 109
KLB. *See* Kenya Literature Bureau
KNUST. *See* Kwame Nkrumah University of Science and Technology
Koinange Street 47
Kojwang, K. M. Okaro 108
Kokwaro, J. O. 118
Kumbukumbu za vita vya Maji Maji 1905-1907 110
Kwame Nkrumah University of Science and Technology (KNUST) 242, 245
Kwara State University 141, 240

Kwara State University Library 140, 141
wa Kĩbirũ, Mũgo 67

de Lanerolle, Ros 31, 33
Langaa Research and Publishing Common Initiative Group 158
Langat, S. C. 108
'Language Imperialism, Concepts and Civilization: China versus The West' 169
Law No. 31/2009 of 2009 on Protection of Intellectual Property [Rwanda] 258
Lessing, Doris 30
Lessons of the Tanganyika-Zanzibar Union 112
Lindfors, Prof. Bernth 96
Lister, Richard 36
Literamed Publications 73
Literature and Society in Modern Africa 114
lo Liyong, Taban 4, 28, 29, 32, 54
Lochcarron 140
Logos 11
Lomer, Cécile 236
London University Press 72
Longman 7, 35, 37, 54, 56, 72, 73, 129, 131, 132, 202
Longman Kenya 35, 54, 56
Ludeki, C. 113
Lweza Conference 133

Maathai, Wangari 65
Macgoye, Marjorie Oludhe 116
Macmillan 36, 72, 129
Maddox, G. 113
Mafeje, Archie 176

Maghreb Des Livres Book Fair 85
Magut, P. K. arap 108
Maillu, David G 5, 95, 100
'Maintaining and Expanding Research in East Africa' 118
Maitũ Njugĩra 17
Maji Maji research papers 111
Maji Maji uprising 110
Makerere History Department 111
Makerere Law Journal 120
Makerere Medical Journal 119
Makerere University 46, 60, 62, 63, 64, 111, 112, 117, 121
Makerere University Press 121
Makerere University Research Journal 120
Makila, F. E. 112
Makotsi, Ruth 220
Mama, Amina 122
Managing a Changing Climate in Africa: Local Level Vulnerabilities and Adaptation Experiences 118
Mapunda, Bertram 113
Mapunda, O. B. 111
Marechera, Dambudzo 3, 30, 47, 48
Markham, Bob 28, 36
Marrakesh Treaty to Facilitate Access to Published Works by Persons who are Blind, Visually Impaired or Print Disabled 257
Maseno University Journal 123
Masolo, D. A. 117, 123
Masomo ya Msingi 7, 8
Matigari 19, 21, 55
Matigari ma Njirũngi 18
Mawazo 120
Mawere, Munyaradzi 170
Mazrui, Alamin 8

Mazrui, Ali 109, 160, 176
Mazwi 197
Mbari conference 28
Mbele, Majola 114
Mbiru: Popular Protest in Colonial Tanzania 110
Mbiti, John S. 67, 116, 117
Mboya, Tom 109
Medicinal Plants of East Africa 118
Meja Mwangi 33, 37
Methodist Mission [Ghana] 72
Michigan State University Press (MSUP) 209
Microsoft 190
Mine Boy 3
wa Mĩriĩ, Ngũgĩ 39
Mission to Kala 47
Mkandawire, Thandika 176
Mkuki na Nyota Publishers 112, 118, 121, 204, 207
Mohamed, Said Ahmed 8
Moi, Daniel arap 16
Moi University 242
M-Pesa 197
Mpangara, G. P. 111
Mubaya, Chipo Plaxedes 118
Mude, Kenneth Ali 108
Mugambi, J.N.K. 116
Mũgo, Mĩcere Gĩthae 38, 44, 57, 114
Mugweru, Johnson 36, 39
Mũmbi [Ngũgĩ] 20
Mũrogi wa Kagogo 19, 20
Murua, James 198
Museveni, President 130, 132
Music Copyright Society of Kenya (MCSK) 263
Musimbi, Mama Lena 58
Mutahaba, G. R. 111

Mutahi, Wahome 46
Mutyaba, Mustapha 132
Mwabu, Germano 113
Mwagiru, Ciugu 46
Mwalimu Julius Nyerere International Conference Centre 229
Mwangi, Meja 4, 10, 29. *See also* Meja Mwangi
Mwangi Ruheni 29, 35
Mwangi, Wangethi 46
Mwanzi, Henry 112
My Life in Crime 5
My Life in Prison 5
My Life with a Criminal: Milly's Story 5

Nairobi City Hall 39
Nairobi International Book Fair 10
Nakumatt 138
Namboze, Dr Josephine 118
Namirembe, M. Bukenya 118
National Bank of Kenya (NBK) 12
National Book Development Council of Cameroon 151
National Book Development Council of Kenya (NBDCK) 10, 11, 151, 233
National Book Development Council of Tanzania 151
National Book Trust Uganda 151
National Curriculum Development Centre (NCDC)-Uganda 130, 134
National Educational Materials Procurement Programme [Nigeria] 79
National Institute for Medical Research (Tanzania) 121
National Integration in Uganda 1962-2013 113

National Library of South Africa 151
National Trust Adult Education Centre 111
Nature Kenya 120
Nazareth, Peter 114
NBDCK. *See* National Book Development Council of Kenya
Ndung'u, J. B. 108
Neill, Bishop Stephen 1
Neogy, Rajat 115
'New Perspectives on Medical Education' 118
New Dar School of Historiography 112
Newell, Stephanie 115
New Nigerian 72
New Partnership for Africa's Development (NEPAD) 222
New York University 19
Nexus 115. *See also* Busara
Ngaahika Ndeenda 8, 16, 17, 39
NGANO 108
Ngũgĩ wa Thiong'o. *See* wa Thiong'o, Ngũgĩ
Nielsen BookScan South Africa 153
Nigerian Book Foundation 151
Nigerian Educational Research and Development Council (NERDC) 79, 81, 151
Nigerian Film Institute 141
Nigerian Publishers Association (NPA) 72, 78
Njau, Rebeka 29, 34
Njeeri [Ngũgĩ] 20, 21
Noma Award for Publishing in Africa 156, 223
Noma, Shoichi 223
NORAD. *See* Norwegian Agency for Development Cooperation

Norwegian Agency for Development Cooperation (NORAD) 206
Nottingham, John 46
Not Yet Uhuru 9
Nouvelles Editions Africaines (NEAs) 82
Nsibambi, Apolo 113
Ntiru, Richard 46
Nwankwo, Chief Victor 190, 199, 204, 215
Nyambura, Gillian 189
Nyambura [wa Ngugi] 20
Nyamnjoh, Francis 5, 158, 247
Nyariki, Lily 216, 220
Nyerere, President Mwalimu Julius 109
Nyungu Ya Mawe 111
Nzeki, Jones 43

OAU. *See* Organisation of African Unity
Obama, President Barrack 231
Obanya, Pai 70
Obenga, Prof. Theophile 98
Obote II 130
Obote, Miria 109
Obote, President Milton 109
Observer 35
Ochieng', William 108, 112
Oculi, Okello 60
Odeon Cinema 45
Odhiambo, Douglas 118
Odhiambo, T. R. 118
Odinga, Oginga 9
Odoi, Frank 9
Ogot, Bethwell Allan 108, 109, 112
Ogot, Grace 4, 109
Ogunleye [Bisi] 74

Ohio University Press 116
Ojeniyi, Ayo 70
Ojiambo, Dr Hilary 118
Okalany, D. H. 111
Okot p'Bitek 4, 29, 32, 44, 60, 99, 109, 116
Okumu, John Sibi 46
Olembo, Reuben 118
Ominde, Simeon 110
Omosa, M. 113
Ongeti, Khaemba 8
Onibonoje [Publishers] 72
Onitsha Market Literature 72
On Safari in Kenya 9
Onyango-ku-Odongo, J. M. 111
Orange County, California 19
'Orature as a Skill and as a Tool for Africa's Development' 63
Organisation of African Unity 160. *See also* African Union (AU)
Oruka, Henry Odera 117
Ouma, Marisella 255
Owour-Anyumba, Henry 54, 68
Oxford Brookes University 12, 22, 143, 144, 242
Oxford English Course 129
Oxford International Centre for Publishing Studies 143, 242
Oxford University Press (OUP) 7, 38, 46, 72, 73, 129, 194, 202
Oyeyinka, Diekoye 5

Pacesetters 36
Pan African Booksellers Association (PABA) 229, 238
Pan-Africanism or Pragmatism 112
Pan African Reading conference 228

Pan African Writers Association (PAWA) 228, 238
Paris Act of 1971 256
Partners in African Publishing 156
Pattberg, Thorsten 169, 170
Peak Library Series 5
Penguin/Random House 193
Penpoint 115. *See also* Dhana
Petals of Blood 4, 16, 39, 52
Petroleum Trust Fund (PTF)-Nigeria 79, 80
Philosophy and Cultures 117
PIC News 120
piracy 261
Popular Culture of East Africa 54
Port Harcourt 198
Portrait of a Nationalist 111
Practical Philosophy: In Search of an Ethical Minimum 117
Primary and JSS Books Project [Nigeria] 81
Prince Clause Award 12
Print Industries Cluster Council (South Africa) 152
Print-on-Demand (POD) 11, 123, 190, 212, 241
'Priorities in Health Planning' 118
PTF. *See* Petroleum Trust Fund
Publishers Association of South Africa (PASA) 84, 239, 245
Publishers' Resource Pack project 239
Publishing, Books & Reading in Sub-Saharan Africa: A Critical Bibliography 12, 48, 154
Publishing, Books & Reading in Sub-Saharan Africa: An Annotated Bibliography 142
publishing in Africa 52
 academic presses 113
 academic publishing 106, 128

awards 223
book publishing 218
challenges 86
Civil Society Organisations (CSOs) 227
copyright infringement 255
data and statistics 145
desktop publishing 187
Digital Age 103, 186, 212
East Africa 106
eBooks 214
e-publishing 184
francophone West Africa 82
future 199
ICT developments 89
indigenous publishing 140
in Ghana 72, 81
in Kenya 73, 84
in Nigeria 71, 78
in South Africa 83
institutional framework 255
internationalisation 200
Internet selling 213
language problem 162, 211
legal framework 255, 256
Maghreb countries 85
'New Deal' 211
politics in publishing 216, 221
popular fiction 95, 103
post-independence publishing 202
professional organisations 216, 223
prospects 88
public-private collaboration 248
role of government 245
sponsored training programmes 243
textbook publishing 73, 86, 88
textbooks distribution 77
trade organisations 216, 223
trading in the US 208
'traditional' resources 198
training opportunities 235, 242
training resources 239
Wikipedia page 156

Publishing in Africa: One Man's Perspective 4, 12, 27, 51, 102

publishing in Uganda
 future 137
 'Golden Era' 134
 textbook publishing 134
Publishing Training Project (PTP) 239
Punishment and Terrorism in Africa 117
Pwiti, G. 113

Radimilahy, C. 113
Ranger, T. O. 111
Read, Anthony 77
reading CODE programmes 243
Readings in African Popular Fiction 115
Reading the African Novel 47
Recording East Africa's Past 110
Recording Industry Association of Kenya (RIAK) 264
Records of the Maji Maji Rising Part One 110
Regional Book Centre for Africa 227
Regional Centre for Book Promotion in Africa (CREPLA) 233
'Reintroducing the African Man into the World: Traditionalism and Socialism in African Politics' 108
Remarque, Eric Maria 19
Reprographic Rights Organisations of Kenya (KOPIKEN) 263
Reviving the Spirit 20
Revue africaine de la recherche en education 164. See also *Journal of Educational Research in Africa*
Rhodes University 188
Rights Management Information Systems (RMIS) 263
Ripples in the Pool 34
Roberts, Andrew 110, 111

Rockefeller Center 225
Rockefeller Foundation 206, 207
Rodney, Walter 59, 111
Rubadiri, David 4
Ruganda, John 44, 46
Ruheni, Mwangi 29
Rwanda Development Board 262
Rwanda Society of Authors (RSAU) 263

Sabatia Constituency 58
Sabre Foundation 230
Sachs, Jeffrey 176
Salim, Ahmed Idha 109
Sambrook, Keith 28, 30, 32, 38, 39, 40
Scholarly Publishing in Africa 235
'Science, Scientists and Society: Bridging the Development Gap through the Sciences' 118
Science Teachers Association of Nigeria (STAN) 78
Selected Works of Haroub Othman 112
Settlements, Economies and Technology in the African Past 113
Shakespeare, William 61
Shercliff, Emma 193, 194
Shivji, Issa 112
Shoprite 138
Shorter, Aylward 111
SIDA. *See* Swedish International Development Agency
SIL-LEAD 244
Simon Fraser University 144
SlideShare 103
Smith, Kelvin 142, 144
Song of Lawino 32, 99, 100, 105
Song of the Hearts Sublime 98

Son of Fate 5
South African Book Development Council 151
Sow, Mamadou Aliou 191
Soyinka, Wole 38, 63, 228
Sparrow Readers 6
Spear Books Series 5, 6, 36, 51, 96, 102
Spear, Thomas 113
Spectrum Books 73
Standard Media Group 12
Standing Conference of Eastern, Central and South African Librarians (SCECSAL) 229
Standing Conference on Library Materials on Africa (SCOLMA) 229
Stillborn 5
Stirling Centre for International Publishing and Communication 243
Storymoja 198
Stringer, Roger 186
Sunbird Readers 6
SUPER. *See* Support to Uganda Primary Education Reform
Support to Uganda Primary Education Reform 133
Sutton, J. E. G. 111
Swedish International Development Agency (SIDA) 164, 206, 239, 253
Sweet and Sour Milk 47

Tabansi [Publishers] 72
Tanzania Before 1900 110
Tanzania Publishing House (TPH) 129, 204
Tanzania Vision 2025 120
Tea Research Foundation of Kenya (TRFK) 12

Technological Protection Measures (TPM) 265
Temu, Arnold 110
Tertiary Book Acceleration Project [Nigeria] 79
Tertiary Books Reprint Programme [Nigeria] 79
Tertiary Education Tax Fund (TETFUND)- Nigeria 80
Text Book Centre 10
Textbook Development Policy [Ghana] 82
textbook publishing 70
'The Africa Book Conference' 229
The African Churches of Tanzania 111
The African Publishing Review 155
The Africans: A Triple Heritage 160
The African Writers Handbook 211
The Central Luo during the Aconya 111
The Companion for African Literatures 33
The Composition of Poetry and Creative Writing in Prose 116
"The Dead End of African Literature" 8
'The Development of Autonomous Publishing in Africa' 203
The East African Coast 111
The East African Slave Trade 111
The Future Leaders 35
'The German Intervention and African Resistance in Tanzania' 110
The Girl from Abroad 35
The House of Hunger 30
The Iteso during the Asonya 111
The Kings of Buganda 109
The Maji Maji War in Ungoni 111
The Making of the Karagwe Kingdom 111
The Meanings of Timbuktu 173
The Minister's Daughter 35

The Nile English Course 129
'The Psychology of Witchcraft' 118
The River Between 16
The Role of Religious and Traditional Beliefs during the Maji Maji War 110
'The Scientific Revolution in East Africa' 118
The Season of Harvest: A Literary Discussion 114
The Sinister Trophy 5
The Slums 34
'The State of African Publishing' 247
The Third World Writer: His Social Responsibility 114
The Trial of Dedan Kimathi 38, 63
The Verdict of Death 6
Things Fall Apart 3, 16, 47, 74
wa Thiong'o, Prof. Ngũgĩ 2, 3, 4, 8, 9, 11, 20, 28, 29, 32, 33, 38, 39, 44, 49, 52, 53, 55, 59, 115, 160
Third World books 203
Thomas, Akin 30, 34
Thomas Nelson 72, 73, 129
Thought and Practice: A Journal of the Philosophical Association of Kenya 123
Three Crowns series 38
Tiamiyu [Muta] 73
Tom Mboya Hall 47
Tom Mboya: The Man Kenya Wanted to Forget 9
Townsend, Reverend Henry 71
Trade Related Aspects of Intellectual Property (TRIPs) 256
TransAfrican Journal of History 109
TransAfrica Press 34, 46
Transition 115
Tumusiime, James 132
Tuskys 138

Twenty-sixth IPA congress 189
Twitter 192

Uganda Business Registration Bureau 263
Uganda Environmental and Natural Research Management Policy and Law 120
Uganda Journal 119
Uganda Ministry of Health 121
Uganda National Examinations Board (UNEB) 134
Uganda Publishers and Booksellers Association (UPABA) 132, 133, 134
Uganda Publishers Association (UPA) 135
Uganda Registration Services Bureau 262
Uganda Reprographic Rights Organisation (URRO) 263
Uganda Vision 2040 120
UIS. *See* UNESCO Institute of Statistics
Umma 115
UNESCO. *See* United Nations Educational and Scientific Organisation
UNESCO General History of Africa 112
UNESCO Institute of Statistics (UIS) 146, 147
UNESCO Science Report 120
UNESCO Statistical Yearbooks 146
United Nations Educational and Scientific Organisation (UNESCO) 94, 112, 120, 127, 146, 147, 148, 197, 201, 224, 227, 230, 233
United States Information Service (USIS) 79
Universal Basic Education Commission (UBEC)-Nigeria 80, 81
Universidade Pedagogica, Mozambique 170
University College of Nairobi 108. *See also* University of Nairobi
University of Buea (Cameroon) 242

University of California, Irvine 17, 20
University of Dar es Salaam 62, 110, 114
University of East Africa 54, 108, 113, 127
University of Ibadan 242
University of Ile-Ife 77
University of Nairobi 1, 4, 21, 39, 43, 44, 46, 48, 52, 54, 60, 61, 62, 114, 115, 117
University of Nairobi Press 113, 116, 117, 118
University of Nigeria 29
University of Pretoria 152, 242, 244
University of Southern Africa (UNISA) Press 169
University of Stirling 243
University of the Witwatersrand 243, 244
University of Zimbabwe 188
UPABA. See Uganda Publishers and Booksellers Association
USAID 85, 133, 134, 244
Uwalaka 73

Viewpoints: Essays on Literature and Drama 114
Visiki 8
Visions of Africa 114
Vokoli Village 68

Wafawarowa, Brian 190
Wahome Mutahi Literary Award 6, 10
Waiswa, D. 118
Wali, Obi 8
Wangari, Njeri 197
Wanjala, Chris 114
Wanjikũ [Thiong'o] 20

Wanyande, P. 113
War in Northern Uganda, 1985-97 116
Web 2.0 192
Webster, J. B. 111
Weep Not, Child 16, 24, 28
Were, G. S. 109
West Africa and the Atlantic Slave Trade 111
West African Examinations Council (WAEC) 83
West African Library Association (WALA) 229
WGBLM. *See* Working Group on Books and Learning Materials
What a Life! 35
Wikipedia 192
WIPO Copyright 256
WIPO Copyright Treaties 256
WIPO Copyright Treaty 257
WIPO Performances and Phonograms Treaty 256
Wizard of the Crow 19
Woman Question 110
Woodson, Carter 61
Wordreader 103, 197
Working Group on Books and Learning Materials (WGBLM) 226, 227
World Agroforestry Centre 121
World Bank 79, 85, 90, 92, 133, 181, 184, 187, 201, 240, 248, 251
World Bank Primary Education Project (PEP 1) 79
World Congress on Books 77
World Intellectual Property Organisation (WIPO) 74, 239, 256
Worldreader 197
World Trade Organisation (WTO) 256, 257
World Wide Web 188, 192, 251
Writers in East Africa: Papers from a Colloquium 114
Writivism 198

Yahya-Othman, Saida 112
Yanda, Pius Zebhe 118
Yes, In My Lifetime 112
YouTube 192

Zeleza, Paul Tiyambe 200
Zell, Hans M. 12, 48, 140, 181, 182, 199, 217, 219, 221, 236, 240
Zimbabwe International Book Fair (ZIBF) 6, 11, 187, 190, 208, 224
Zimbabwe International Book Fair (ZIBF) Award 12
Zirimu, Pio 62, 63, 114
Zuka: A Journal of East African Creative Writing 115
Zziwa, A. 118

www.ingramcontent.com/pod-product-compliance
Lightning Source LLC
Chambersburg PA
CBHW050528300426
44113CB00012B/2001